MIND AND
DEITY

MIND AND DEITY

*Being the Second Series of a
Course of Gifford Lectures
on the General Subject of*
METAPHYSICS AND THEISM
*given in the University of
Glasgow in 1940*

by

JOHN LAIRD

ARCHON BOOKS
1970

First published 1941
George Allen & Unwin, Ltd.
Reprinted 1970 with permission
in an unaltered and unabridged edition

ISBN: 0-208-00937-X
Library of Congress Catalog Card Number: 70-114424
[Reproduced from a copy in the Yale University Library]
Printed in the United States of America

Preface

THIS second series of lectures is meant to be the complement of the first, and indeed to be complement rather than sequel. True, I have made a few references to the first series in the present volume, and at the end of it I have said something about the mutual relations of the two series. Substantially, however, any reader of this book who had never heard of the first series would not be handicapped in any significant way. He might find the beginning of the second series indefensibly abrupt. That, I allow, would be due, in part at least, to the fact that there *was* a first series, which series, indeed, began in appropriately leisured fashion. But, in my judgement, awkward little things like that are incidental and not substantial. If I have failed in some such way, the cause is my own artlessness and is not interknit with my theme.

I should like, once again, to thank my friends in Glasgow, and among them my patient and very faithful audience, for all the encouragement they have so generously given me. I could not be more grateful had I deserved their kindness. If I helped some of them to forget the war for a brief space, I should permit myself to feel a certain tempered satisfaction.

J. L.

KING'S COLLEGE
OLD ABERDEEN
November, 1940

Contents

LECTURE		PAGE
	Preface	7
	Synopsis of the Discussions	11
I.	*The Ontological Argument*	29
II.	*The Nature of Mind*	57
III.	*The Implications of Idealism*	86
IV.	*Omniscience*	114
V.	*Divine Personality*	143
VI.	*Providence*	173
VII.	*Value and Existence*	202
VIII.	*The Moral Proofs of Theism*	229
	Appendix to Lecture VIII: "Ut puto, deus fio"	257
IX.	*Pantheism*	266
X.	*Concluding Reflections*	294
	Index of Proper Names	321

SYNOPSIS OF THE DISCUSSIONS

I. *The Ontological Argument*

THE earlier lectures in this second course attempt to reconsider the provisional realism of the cosmological first course, and so may help to remove preconceptions that might hinder an equitable discussion of such themes as God's providence and "personality". The celebrated Ontological Argument is a natural bridge between the first course and the second. It was regarded, from Anselm to Descartes and Leibniz, as a straightforward piece of realistic logic. After Kant had refuted the realistic argument, Hegel transformed it into an idealistic assertion, and Hegel's assertion is still accepted in principle by several eminent contemporary or near-contemporary philosophers.

The realistic Argument (to the general effect that perfection would be imperfect if non-existent) had a chequered career between the eleventh and the eighteenth centuries. Even at its zenith (with Descartes and Leibniz in the seventeenth century) it is doubtful whether, e.g., Spinoza and Malebranche relied very strongly upon it, Malebranche preferring the simple assertion of the priority of the infinite to the finite.

In Kant's refutation of the realistic form of the Argument what was most original and most effective was his perception that the predicate "exists" in the statement "God exists" has a status altogether different from the status of such a predicate as, say, "omnipotent" in the statement "God is omnipotent". The second can be denied in two ways, either because there is no God or because there is a God who is not omnipotent. The first can be denied in one way only, i.e. by the denial that there is a God. In short, Kant perceived not only that there was *something* wrong with the (realistic) Ontological Argument but also *what* was wrong with it. On the other hand Kant's further assertion that all good evidence for existence must be derived from *sensation*, need not be accepted (although most modern philosophers would accept it).

Hegel himself was prepared to admit that the traditional or realistic

Ontological Argument was a "rotten prop" of theism, but he held that the Argument authenticated itself triumphantly upon a higher plane since it was in substance the cardinal (idealistic) assertion of all genuine philosophy, viz. the literal identity of Thought with Being. "The standpoint of religion," he said, "is this, that the true to which all consciousness relates itself has all content in itself."

That is similar to Malebranche's assertion of the priority of the infinite to the finite, and may be called the Grand Ontological Assertion of Absolute Idealism. It is not a "proof" or an "argument" but is said to be the prius of all proof and argument.

I conclude that the Ontological *Argument* is a sham. It remains possible, however, that the Grand Ontological Assertion is the last word in metaphysical insight. On the other hand, some of the glosses that some eminent idealists seem to put upon the Assertion, do not seem to tell us very much, e.g. that all thought claims to investigate reality, that error and fancy and all hypotheses are in some sense reality-bred; and the like.

The Grand Ontological Assertion of Absolute Idealism seems to be the professedly non-mythical counterpart of the Christian redemption-myth. According to Christianity the world exists to be redeemed, yet it is redeemed already and always has been. Similarly according to Absolute Idealism the obscurities and recalcitrancies of nature and of sensible appearances exist to be surmounted by victorious Thought, but are surmounted already and always have been. If the clue be the "identity" of thought with being, it seems to be a brittle thread. In any case the "God" who is presupposed in such an alleged "identity" would not be the "God" of the Christian or of any other of the major religions.

II. *The Nature of Mind*

Despite the protests of certain idealists it is permissible and not unimportant to begin by asking what we mean by *a* mind, yours or mine. We may make a start by asking what we mean by being awake, and how the waking state differs from sleep or coma.

When we are wide awake we are always conscious, that is, our lives have the conscious quality. This quality may be too simple or too hard to describe with accuracy, but we may note that certain authors ascribe to it (*a*) pure phenomenalism and (*b*) reflexiveness. The former would mean that consciousness is a pure apparition, all show and surface, exhausting its entirety by the mere fact of appearing. That may be true, say, of pleasure-pain but scarcely of all that we call consciousness. Reflexiveness, again, is not all that we mean by self-acquaintance and waking "presence of mind". But the conscious quality *is* reflexive. We are, quite literally, self-aware as well as aware of other things.

Making a fresh start, let us consider attention. The term includes in its signification a certain alertness in our conative attitude *towards* something and connotes a certain promptness, e.g. in the recall of what is or seems to be relevant. Various modern authors have tried to show that such attention is only a function of the "objects" attended to, and so that "mind" drops out of the analysis. Mind, however, cannot be dropped because the analysis presupposes it all the time. An "object" means, not a thing *simpliciter*, but a thing-in-a-certain-status, a thing-that-is-minded. It is folly to attempt to eliminate the "minding" by a theory of "objects" without a mind.

If pure phenomenalism were the truth regarding the conscious quality there would be no appearance *of* anything *to* anything, since the appearance *ex hypothesi* would exhaust its properties by appearing. Most of our cognitions, however, claim to be transcendent, to be apprehensions of what is not themselves. Even the claim would be absurd if pure phenomenalism were true. (In memory, for instance, we profess to transcend the present and refer to the past.) When we attend we normally attend to something not ourselves. We need not attend to ourselves *only*, whether or not we are capable sometimes of attending to ourselves (in introspection).

Can we say that *all* cognition is transcendent?

Many philosophers, assuming that all cognition is transcendent, have denied the possibility of reflexive (and of introspective) cognition. This denial seems to be opposed to experience, and is quite unnecessary. For even if all cognition were transcendent there would be nothing to prevent the possibility that it was *also* reflexive. If such reflexiveness were itself transcendent in its own peculiar way (as some suppose introspection is when, as they think, one constituent in a mind refers to another constituent in the same mind) the thing might be just conceivable. And it is clear that much in what we call self-acquaintance *is* transcendent, e.g. the memory process involved in the recognition of what we call "personal identity". Self-acquaintance, however, is something much wider than the mere reflexiveness of the conscious quality, and this basic reflexiveness does not look like anything transcendent. The solution, I suggest, is that attention (and, in general, all cognitive awareness) is *both* transcendent *and* reflexive but that these two "ways of knowing" are quite different from one another although conjoined in all cognition. In the transcendent way there is always aloofness, non-identity, "psychic distance" between mind and "object". In the reflexive way there is *no* aloofness or psychic distance between knower and known and there *is* literal identity.

If so we should avoid two mistakes, (1) the mistake of supposing that there is anything suspicious or "imperfect" about the knowledge of an object that is not identical with the apprehending mind or any absurdity in supposing non-mental things to exist, (2) the mistake of trying to get rid of minds and still present an adequate theory of knowledge. In the result we should emancipate our metaphysics.

III. *The Implications of Idealism*

Philosophical idealism is either epistemological or ontological, the ontological variety being the more important for theists. It is sometimes held, however, that epistemological idealism either compels or facilitates the acceptance of ontological. So we may begin with the epistemological type. It has two principal subdivisions, pan-idea-ism and pan-ideatism, that is, when "ideas" are distinguished, as they should be, from "ideals".

Pan-idea-ism is the doctrine that nothing but ideas exist. It is pure phenomenalism, not necessarily sensory. By denying all transcendence of ideas it deprives many ideas of their very lives and so is untenable. Sometimes it attempts a rescue by introducing a theory of contextual quasi-transcendence. Then it holds that ideas signify other ideas by redintegration of context. This subterfuge is inadequate. We cannot prove in this way that all that exists is a "mentity".

Pan-ideatism is the doctrine that all that is known to exist or that can be imagined to exist must be *ideated* although it may not consist exclusively of ideas. An extreme form of the theory (to which it might be driven by logic) is that we may know *that* there is a reality beyond our ideas but not *what* such a reality is. All such views come to ruin when they are worked out in detail, e.g. they would reach an alleged "reality" that neither changed nor didn't change if the "ideas" of change and of permanence were explored in this way.

Ontological idealism may be called pan-psychism. It is the doctrine that nothing exists except mind (or minds).

This theory is defended (*a*) by the argument from universal interiority. It is held that we know ourselves in the interior way and other things by external observation. Generalizing, we are asked to infer that everything has its inner content as well as its exterior aspect and should be presumed in some sense to "know" its inner content. We have seen, however (in the last lecture), that there is no sufficient reason for believing that everything that exists must be knowledgeable, i.e. capable of being aware either of itself or of anything else.

The theory is defended (*b*) by the argument from the general continuity of existence. This would show that all that exists is material or is alive as readily as that all that exists is mental. The argument dogmatizes without warrant if it rests on the causal statement that like must come from like.

The theory is defended (*c*) by the argument from indefeasible thinghood, i.e. that only substances exist and that minds are the only possible substances. In Leibnizian pan-psychism God was credited with powers over the other substances that, in terms of the theory, *no* substance could have over any other substance. A more general argument would be that a substance must have a high degree of unity and integrity, and that mentality and it alone can supply the requisite *vinculum substantiale*. Here the empirical evidence is very disturbing. Minds seem to vanish in sleep and trances; so the alleged substantial bond seems to be peculiarly weak in their case.

To what extent should ontological idealism transform our conceptions of nature, man and God?

Leibnizian pan-psychism tells us that only spirits exist; but a spirit as stupid and as low-grade as an electron, say, would not seem to differ appreciably from an unspiritual electron. Berkeleyan pan-psychism would tell us that stars and sand and sea are the representations of animal (?) human and divine spirits, which select company of representing spirits constitute all reality. To a Berkeleyan, nature would look the same as it does to others but would not be the same. Nevertheless, although Berkeleyan water could not drown us, the experience of suffocation would not be changed, and would be followed by the extinction of the drowning spirit.

The arguments applying to nature and to human nature are broadly similar.

As regards theism we should have either a monistic or a pluralistic ontological idealism. In the latter a Leibnizian might say that, since all was spirit, creaturely beings were liker the image of God than they would be if they were, say, material. The main theistic difficulty, however, is why a perfect being should create *anything* imperfect. Berkeley's form of theism was full of serious special difficulties. In the main it attempted to simplify by abolishing the "useless" intermediary of "matter", but such a simplification of God's supposed *modus operandi* need not make any other difference of major importance.

IV. *Omniscience*

We have to discuss two questions, whether we *must* believe in the esistence of an omniscient being (or college of beings) and whether the existence of such an omniscient being (or college of beings) is so much as credible.

I

Here the question is whether we can be intimidated into this belief by the threat that nobody could know anything unless somebody knows everything. The traditional "proofs" are the Proof from the Sovereign Essences and the Proof from the Eternal Verities.

The first of these "proofs" is Platonic and is to the effect that there must be a sovereign essence of all essences, an Idea of the Good. Plato's Idea of the Good, however, could not be God, and Plato denied that *any* essence owed its reality to being known (or that it required to be known). It may also be complained that the existence of an essence of all essences is very disputable even if the existence of essences is not.

The argument from the eternal verities has usually been accompanied by the explanation that all truths are propositions and that all propositions are either mental or part-mental. That may be substantially true, although there may be certain senses of truth in which truth is not propositional and although we seem to have acquaintance (say, in tasting bacon) with what is not a proposition. Keeping to propositional knowledge, however, we should be dreaming if we held that no true proposition can be known unless it has always been known. If such a "truth" were remembered, what about our first acquaintance with it? If it is told us, who told the teller?

The reference to *eternal* verities raises the whole distinction between "eternal" truths and contingent or merely factual ones, the differences between Cartesian and Leibnizian philosophy on this matter, and the sense in which these authors were disposed to allow that an atheist could have any knowledge at all.

II

We have to consider two senses of omniscience corresponding to the distinction between omnificence and omnipotence, viz. (*a*) as meaning the knowledge of everything that *is* known, (*b*) as meaning the knowledge of everything that *could* be known.

Regarding (*a*) we should distinguish between (α) reflexive and (β) transcendent knowledge.

If reflexive knowledge is immitigably private, a point that requires detailed discussion, God could not have the reflexive knowledge that *we* have of ourselves, although he might know us in some other way and have reflexive acquaintance with himself. The point would have extensive applications if, e.g., all our pain and all our sensations were wholly or predominantly a matter of reflexive knowledge.

While there are difficulties regarding God's transcendent knowledge, these would not seem to be insuperable. But God's transcendent knowledge would not literally include *all* transcendent knowledge, say ours, if the personal and individual selectiveness of our transcendent knowledge indelibly stamped that knowledge.

Regarding (*b*) we may profitably enlarge the question by asking whether much that is real may not be unknowable, i.e. could not be known by a being who knew all that could be known. Thus it may be held that the absence of visible connection in physical laws is a metaphysical absence and therefore invisible to God as well as to physicists. The future, infinity and the "alogical" may be in the same metaphysical plight. In short, we should not glibly identify reality with knowable reality. Even if God knew everything in *some* way (intellectually, say, or super-intellectually) his "knowledge" need not be exhaustive acquaintance with all that is or will be.

V. *Divine Personality*

Orthodox Christianity asserts personality *in* God, not the personality *of* God, in its doctrine of the Holy Trinity; and the third "person" in the Trinity may well appear to be impersonal.

In the present lecture we may ask (i) whether it is credible that God is a person and (ii) whether the denial of God's personality is necessarily a kind of atheism.

(i) Personality (or, in the abstract, "personeity" to use Coleridge's term) has its primary empirical reference to a certain type or level of existence. This is shown in what we call responsible manhood and appears to be never sub-human. In its ordinary sense such personality applies to the whole responsible body-mind that we call a man. Such a conception, however, does not of itself imply insuperable difficulties regarding God's personeity; for God may be embodied although it is unlikely that his body resembles a man's at all closely. The objections that personality implies an environment, and that responsibility, being forensic, implies a plurality of litigants seem also to be inconclusive. The need for a foreign environment for personality does not seem to be demonstrable, and God, if he were personal, need not be a litigant among other litigants or their separate judge. Even if, strictly speaking, God had no moral obligations, he might still be righteous.

If God were the All and were also personal his personality would have to include all finite personalities. Is that impossible? Can a personality be compounded of or disintegrated into personalities?

The empirical evidence (from so-called "dissociated personality") does not tell us much. There is little good evidence, although there is just a little, in favour of the view that a personality may be disintegrated into personalities or that several personalities in the same human body may be united into another personality. Less radical hypotheses suffice although we may have doubts about the empirical principle "One mind, one body". Again, a group of minds need not form *a* group-mind. A society of persons may be nobler or more ignoble than a single person but we need not hold that any society ever has personeity in the strict sense.

Synopsis of the Discussions

McTaggart asserted, principally on non-empirical grounds, that selves could not share experiences or coalesce into different selves, either on the human or on any other level. But even if McTaggart had proved (which seems doubtful) that each of his experiences could be shown to belong to *his* ego, he did not prove that such an experience might not *also* belong to some other ego. Others might say (though McTaggart didn't) that our self-acquaintance is always primarily reflexive and that reflexive unities are always immitigably private, but it would not seem to be certain (although it may be very highly probable) that a reflexive unity of experiences could not contain clusters that were also reflexive unities; and these might conceivably be selves of a sort.

(ii) Those who welcome instead of repudiating the "drift towards the impersonal" in theistic theory argue in general that the *order* of reality is divine, but does not require the hypothesis of divine personeity to account for itself. This question has been discussed in earlier lectures so far as deism and cosmology is concerned. We may now begin the examination of the moral order of reality and its relations to theism.

The alleged "ethical neutrality" of physical nature need not be opposed to cosmic morality, and if physical nature is peculiarly propitious to man, such *de facto* beneficence need not imply benevolent will. If, again, it be said that what theism disputes is the *episodic* character of man's place in the cosmos, the reply is that it is a metaphysical question whether human life *is* thus episodic and that the answer to this question may well be independent of God's personality or impersonality.

Let us turn from beneficence to justice. It is sometimes said that an undiscriminating justice would evince a low moral level and that discriminating justice must be the justice of a personal being. Here there seems to be a play upon the word "discriminating", a confusion between nicety and personal surveillance. The impersonal conceptions of Nemesis and of Karma need not surely be contemned simply on account of the accuracy or inevitability of the justice they assert. Again, if human justice is the better on account of the judge's discretionary power, the reason is the inaccuracy of the best human rules. Accordingly neither the bounty of nature to man (if it exists) nor the distributive justice of the cosmic order (if that be the truth) is necessarily inconsistent with an impersonal type of theism.

19

Mind and Deity

VI. *Providence*

A distinction may be drawn between God's general and his special Providence, or, in the language of Herbert of Cherbury, between his common and his special grace.

The discussion of God's common grace may be conveniently restricted to an examination of his common grace towards mankind in respect of happiness and of moral opportunity. Regarding the former we are told in the theodicies that human suffering is not purposeless evil, if it is evil at all. Actually, however, it *is* evil and much of it seems to be purposeless. To ask, however, whether the favourable balance of happiness over misery (which on the whole seems to occur) is so great as to need an over-worldly providence to account for it, is to ask a question to which the answer must be indeterminate.

Sin is clearly an evil, and the Christian view that the Founder of Christianity was sinless shows how empty it is to say that freedom to sin is essential to the development of a higher type of moral character than would be possible if there were no sin. No determinate answer can be given to the question whether the preponderance of decency over wickedness in the world demands an over-worldly cause.

It may be argued that morality is "conformable to human nature" and therefore an instance of God's common grace. But secular moralists have accepted that premiss as the secular utilitarians did when they opposed the earlier theological utilitarians. Again, moralists of quite a different stamp could consistently maintain that man's (partial) independence of bodily ills and of fortune and of interfering gods was itself "natural" to man.

Expressed in general terms, the doctrine of Providence is a special form of the Argument to Design. It moves in the region of purpose, means and ends, holding that God provides for his creatures in a purposive way.

In certain respects the argument to a providential designer is stronger than the deistic argument to a mere skilful world-carpenter. The deist's Designer might only be clever and not wise. He would contrive for no purpose that was clearly shown. In comparison the plans of a bountiful, compassionate and righteous providence might seem to be reasonable and intelligible.

Synopsis of the Discussions

In other respects, however, the theistic notion of a designing providence seems to contain even greater difficulties than the deistic notion of a mere designer. There is no point in purposive action except in the overcoming of difficulties. *Ex hypothesi* therefore a designing providence would have to overcome obstacles either in himself or in some foreign substance, and moral obstacles in this kind seem to be more formidable than any others. Why should a "perfect" being create an inferior world and proceed slowly to improve it? Why should such a being have to contend with moral obstacles within himself?

There should not be a special logic for God's "special" providence; but there are quite special difficulties. Is miracle and prophecy the field of special providence? If so the conception smacks of magic. There may be more force in the argument contained in Blake's lines:

> Then every man of every clime
> Who prays in his distress,
> Prays to the human form divine
> Love, Mercy, Pity, Peace.

But Blake's argument leads us back to the topic of the last lecture, viz. whether moral discrimination implies a personal discriminator. It seems plain in any case that if the moral order were nicely adjusted to human action and forbearance, such adjustment would necessarily be highly specialized. More generally the doctrine of *gratia sanans* seems to be a sort of spiritual pharmacology, and the distinction between "natural" and "non-natural" on which it may rely evinces the same sort of looseness of thought as is found in most vulgar arguments about the sort of drug-taking that is legitimate and the sort that is illegitimate. In any case *gratia sanans*, if it existed, might be a property of the cosmic moral order; it need not be *put* into the cosmos by a hypercosmic designer.

VII. *Value and Existence*

We have to examine the general abstract statement that value and existence are inseparable.

Any such theory should try to avoid the trap into which the Ontological Argument fell, since "existence" can never be connected with

Mind and Deity

any property in the way in which one property of existence may be connected with another property of existence. Again, it is never legitimate to say that "to be" *means* "to be so and so"; for "to be" means quite simply "to be". It might be true, however, that "whatever is must be good", although it could not be important to say truistically that whatever exists has *some* connection, perhaps remote, with *something* that is intrinsically good.

Some people hold that "ideals" must be "real"; but in the ordinary sense of language, ideals may be quite impracticable. Moreover, there is often an ambiguity in "ideal"-ism. Idealists have a way of passing surreptitiously from the assertion that everything must be either-good-or-bad to the quite different assertion that everything must be good and not bad.

"Values" are either maintenance-values or axiological values. The two types seem to be ultimately different. For the rest of this lecture axiological values and these only will be meant when "value" is discussed. Indeed we shall be concerned with the familiar triad of the true, the beautiful and the (morally) good.

Should we hold that "whatever is, is true" and consequently a value? If this means that "whatever is, is a proposition" it would seem to be false, and the statement would be tepid and sterile if all that was meant was that "whatever is, is apprehensible in some true proposition". While many believe that insight and candour are great intrinsic values, it is not plain that "truth" in any other sense is a value at all, and many existents are incapable either of insight or of candour.

Should we hold that "whatever is, is fair"? It is not at all obvious that everything that exists must be beautiful-or-ugly, and there are strong grounds for thinking that beauty-or-ugliness is relative to minds, i.e. to beings with a privileged status. Again, even if everything were in some sense beautiful-or-ugly, the *value* of its aesthetic properties might be confined to the beholder's mind.

Should we hold that "whatever is, must have moral worth"? This would seem to be false if the meaning be that whatever exists is a moral being, although it might be true that all existence is, say, designed for a moral purpose.

Certain philosophers maintain that "value" properly means "validity" and that validity is prior to existence itself. In that case logical aesthetic or moral value would *make* nature and all else that there is.

But only minds are capable of inferring logically and we need not believe that whatever exists is a mind. The same would be true of aesthetic and of moral validity. In any case existence could not be generated from non-existent validity.

It is sometimes held that validity of inference and validity of taste are really a sort of moral duty, and consequently that all validity is ethical in the end.

Such a view may be congruent with an analysis like Brentano's, viz. that there is a right way of loving and of desiring as well as a right way of thinking and inferring; and it would seem to be only a dogma (though true perhaps) that emotion and desire are incapable of such a logic-like relation. If so a "right" satisfaction would easily be distinguishable from mere satisfaction and from mere human satisfaction. But even if everything that existed were in some sense desirable or detestable, we could not prove that all ideals must be actualized or that every existent must be capable of desiring validly.

In general, it is always illegitimate to try to discover a reason for existence itself. There are valid inferences and there are right moral decisions. Validity, however, appears to be *sui generis*, incomparable with anything else. It could not devour all other properties, because these other properties are simply *different* from it in an ultimate way.

VIII. *The Moral Proofs of Theism*

I

A traditional argument, not infrequently revived at the present day, is based upon the supposed implications of moral law. A moral law is said to be an imperative, that is, a command, and so to imply a commander. But although morality is principled it need not be commanded except in the metaphorical sense in which a principle is said to "govern" its instances.

II

A more considerable argument rests on the reputed primacy of the practical reason. Here the contention is that reason energizes all reality and that the active is the moral reason.

Out of caution it should first be noted that morality is not identical with mere reason and that the application of reason to practice need not be exclusively moral.

Mind and Deity

The most famous argument of this order is Kant's in whose pages the primacy of the practical reason meant the metaphysical primacy of rational freedom. If men are free such a metaphysics need not be over-bold.

According to Kant there would be a contradiction at the very heart of reality if the free rationality of man and the determinism of "nature" had both to be understood realistically. Kant's solution was that the former may be the reality and the latter appearance. The rational (noümenal) order might be the reality and "nature" only a name for the necessitation of sensory representations which themselves were but shadows.

If "freedom" meant sense-emancipated rational determination we should be "free" only when we acted rightly (i.e. rationally). This could not be identical (as Kant seemed to think) with elective freedom, which includes the freedom to sin and to be foolish. More generally, if there be an order of validity as well as an order of patterned causal consecution, the order of validity could not itself be a cause or capable, say, of taking sides in a moral struggle. Our recognition of rightness might be such a cause, but not rightness itself. Kant oscillated unintelligibly between elective and purely rational freedom.

It also seems to be wholly impossible that *anything* could be wholly compounded of "reason". Since noümena could not exist they could not energize all that exists.

All theories of this kind, including Kant's, are wont to generalize from the supposed primacy of the practical reason *in us*. The above criticisms apply to *our* reason. Human beings are capable of recognizing the rightness of duty and of acting in accordance with duty. But the rightness itself is not an operative agent. Compare the matter to a green light. The driver of a motor car proceeds when he recognizes the green signal; but the mere greenness of the green signal does not affect either his car or him. Validity is undeniable; but it never acts.

These matters have theological implications; for the supersensible is the rationalist's substitute for the God of Christian theology.

III

Some remarks are appended upon the relation between theology and religion of the one part, and ethics, of the other part.

Synopsis of the Discussions

Theology cannot determine the essential meaning of good or of right; for morality is either self-justifying or unjustified. It does not follow that religion and theology are irrelevant to ethics. Nevertheless, the precariousness of the boundaries between "natural" and "non-natural" offers quite peculiar difficulties to an ethics that takes pride in repudiating all that is "non-natural".

Theologians often claim that man needs God to show him what is good, to enable him to do what is right, and to assure him that his morality will not ultimately be in vain. The first of these claims seems to be arbitrary, even allowing that duty may be almost as hard to see as to do. The second also is arbitrary since morality may be fired with very deep emotion (supposing that these emotional fires are indispensable to action). The third is of greater consequence. It is man's duty to adapt himself to his circumstances, and the cosmic status of morality is highly relevant to such adaptation.

IX. Pantheism

Most theological criticisms of pantheism are apt to be hurried and partial. That is regrettable because every theist who denies the theory of a limited deity must necessarily be a pantheist. If such theologians go on to say that they are not *mere* pantheists they should be invited to explain themselves more precisely.

The main types of pantheism are the distributive and the totalitarian. These are not necessarily irreconcilable.

Distributive pantheists hold that everything that exists is divine, and (strictly) is wholly divine. Here the Hegelian criticism that, if it were so, everything would be mere empty being is quite unwarranted. So is the criticism that such a pantheism must reduce everything to the lowest naturalistic rank. There might be one glory of the sun and another glory of the moon, even if both sun and moon were divine. Still if "all that there is" included all ordinary things interpreted in the ordinary way there would not be much point in calling tables and suns and electrons "divine". But other accounts might be given of what the things are that comprise "all that there is". It might be held, for instance, that the apparent bodies of men and of animals evidenced souls that were very different from the relevant external appearances and that apparent physical nature evidenced troops of angels and the high gods. If all the *ultimate* beings so evidenced were divine and together were the All, we should have distributive pantheism. Many have held that the human soul is divine; and the super-human constituents of reality (in terms of some such theory as the above) might well be divine even if they could not be selves or spirits like the human soul.

The most interesting form of totalitarian pantheism is that which asserts that the Whole is God although the parts are not.

Certain philosophers deny that we are entitled to believe that "the whole" exists, and metaphysical pluralists would deny that the Whole is a single highly integrated entity. Some of these pluralists base their denial upon the supposed certainty that selves are indiscerptible unities that always resist the omnivorous appetite of monism; but even if it is unlikely that selves could form part of a totalitarian *Self* it would not follow that they could not be parts of a Whole that is not a self. Pluralists may also maintain that moral responsibility implies freedom to rebel against the alleged Whole, and indeed that volition refutes monism; but this talk about "rebellion" seems to be metaphorical, and the restriction to volition seems to be indefensible. In general, however, it seems to be improbable that the Whole could be morally healthy although the parts were morally sick, and there would seem to be a similar improbability in many spheres outside morality. Indeed the only plausible analogy of this kind would seem to be aesthetic. In that genre the blemishes in the parts may have fine dramatic effect.

Certain theists are monarchical pantheists because they hold both that God is All and that he is Lord of All. This would seem to imply that the Whole could be ruling part of itself, which seems impossible. A relative distinction might perhaps be drawn between participating and dissociable parts, but such a distinction could not avail, and, in any case, nothing can be dissociated from the All. Hence monarchical pantheism is untenable. The All or the Absolute must be beyond God as it must be beyond good and evil.

It is not unusual to believe in what with some imprecision may be called a mitigated pantheism, i.e. to believe that everything is divine though not completely so, a species of limited theism.

Such a theory might find it difficult to divinize anything unless that thing had at least the axiological values that pertain to some human minds, and, so far as we know, to nothing sub-human. If such values are always personal, an impersonal pantheism might seem to be quite shut off from divinity. To this it may be replied, in conformity with former lectures, that impersonal value-patterns, even moral ones, are not impossible, indeed that an impersonal cosmic axiology, perhaps pantheistic, is a conceivable metaphysics.

X. *Concluding Reflections*

This lecture attempts (i) to sketch the course of the discussion in the second series, (ii) to examine the relations between the first series and the second, (iii) to offer some general comments.

I

The first three lectures of the second series discussed the philosophy of idealism with a view to discovering, if possible, whether all reality must either be mind or mind-constituted. Our conclusion was adverse to the sufficiency of such proofs. The Ontological Proof is invalid. Pan-idea-ism and pan-ideatism are untenable. Pan-psychism is indemonstrable. It would seem, indeed, that minds, although genuine, are not the whole of reality.

The next three lectures dealt principally with divine personality. This part of the subject was introduced by an examination of the conception of an All-knowing being and ended with a debate concerning divine Providence. The discussion tended to favour an impersonal interpretation of deity in respect of moral as well as of other axiological attributes.

The third triad of lectures began with a more abstract examination of axiology and existence, and debated the logic of a cosmic moralism and of an immanentist and even of a pantheistic theology, largely axiological. It was held that the attempt to connect value with existence by an abstract metaphysical argument failed for the same reason as the Ontological Proof; and the argument, in general, tended to be favourable towards immanentism in theology.

II

Theism dare not neglect and should not belittle cosmology and we must allow that the path to theism is not made easier if it cannot be shown that all reality is spiritual. Axiology as well as cosmology is requisite for an adequate theism, and in axiology the natural trend of the argument is human or social, not cosmological. There may indeed be high values that are super-human or, more generally, non-human, but none is discernible below the human level, and all are conjectural above that level.

The paradox of the Incarnation in Christian theology illustrates this matter. The Jesus of the Scriptures did not look like a "cosmic Christ". Theism accordingly has to try to steer a course between the Scylla of a cosmology that may seem to be godless and the Charybdis of an escape-theology, escape to an "other world". To say that there could be no solution is to go beyond the evidence. It may seem simplest to believe in the existence of a personal deity of the highest excellence despite the apparent intractability of much in astronomy. On the other hand, theism of an impersonal type may be less perturbed by cosmological evidence and is not anti- or ap-axiological. Its potentialities should therefore be explored. Impersonality, that mere negative, to be sure, would not help very much. If the supposed impersonal axiology, for instance, meant only the substitution of a society, say a church or a nation, for a single personal deity, it could not plausibly be said that either a church or a nation is an appreciable dia-cosmic force. But cosmic axiological philosophies of an impersonal type are not excluded by the evidence. They may imply something that cannot be proved, an inevitable affinity between mind and astronomy. But what is indemonstrable need not be incredible, and there may be rational evidence on its side.

III

These lectures may have interpreted their subject matter rather austerely, for there may be sources of evidence, e.g. "religious experience", that they have not tapped. The lecturer would have used the evidence of such experience if he had had it; but even without it an important field for enquiry remains. The chief penalty of neglecting natural theology of the straiter sort is the revival of weaker forms of the old arguments, produced with a flourish, and received with an eagerness disproportioned to their force. That is a grave penalty and it need not be incurred. Theism will always be one of the major theories of speculative metaphysics. It is part of the business of all philosophers to treat it in a calm and speculative spirit.

I

The Ontological Argument

THE first series of these lectures was concerned with cosmology. Its theme was such questions as the following: whether the world had its source in God, whether God as well as the world was in the making, whether God pervaded the world in every part, whether the world was teleologically patterned and, if so, whether that pattern was deiform. This enquiry, in its intention at least, was regarded, quite simply, as a philosophical investigation into the intelligibility or unintelligibility of a godless world debated in terms of cosmological requirements and of these only. The enquiry was provisionally realistic and was occupied, in the main, with the deistic aspects of theism in the sense of "deism" in which God's grace and bounty and tender mercy, in other words, his providential care, were regarded as more human than cosmological, more "intimate" than the stars.

In the second series of these lectures I shall reconsider the provisional realism of the first series, and, partly as a consequence, shall enlarge the scope of the discussion.

Plainly a philosopher who is not pressed for time—and I have a generous allowance in these lectures—cannot be satisfied with a merely provisional realism. He should examine with all due assiduity whether his *prima facie* realistic beliefs concerning nature, man and God should not be radically transformed, and, among other things, whether some form of anti-realism (perhaps some form of idealism) should not be required of him. If required, it might transfigure all his previous provisional conclusions.

That is the first question I want to examine now. Many believe that unless a very thorough-going affinity can be shown to subsist between minds and physical nature, a spiritual meta-physics of reality cannot be sustained, and, further, that a spiritual metaphysics of reality is essential to theism although it may not suffice for a theist. God, we are told, may be super-spiritual, but he cannot be sub- or non-mental. What is best in our minds cannot be peripheral or episodic in reality if theism be true. It must be central and stable in the very heart of things or, at the least, give sure and solid testimony to what is central and firm. So idealists say; and some others who are not idealists say so too. Idealists further tell us that they can prove the point, but that others cannot. Cosmology indeed remains. As we have seen, God, if he exists, must at least be dia-cosmic. But, we are told, he is much more than cosmological. And that is the problem that is now before us.

Again, the distinction between an arid deism and a generous theism is relevant here in several ways. For the present I shall be brief about it. According to most of its exponents, theism is able to transfigure the world, and to show that the higher attributes of the human spirit—transhumanized, indeed, but not trans-essentiated beyond all recognition—are what is dominant in reality itself. God's bounty and grace and tenderness, in a word, his providence, is the visible effluence, they say, of the invisible quality of his deity. So is cosmic righteousness. The union of cosmology with axiology, that is to say, the union of natural fact with all that is best, most just and most precious, shines through the visible world. That, they tell us, is the context in which God's providence and the arguments that favour a cosmic moralism should be investigated.

So I propose to begin this second course by discussing philo-sophical idealism; and, first of all, I shall examine the celebrated Ontological Argument.

In doing so I allow that I am throwing art to the winds, and that I am not being very kind. The Ontological Argument is very abstract, very austere. If I were artful, I would try to introduce it very gradually, asking my audience to ascend a gentle slope instead of transporting them, without their leave, in

The Ontological Argument

a rapid funicular journey. It is hard to breathe in the rarefied atmosphere of the Ontological Argument, and cruel to make tourists inhale it abruptly, even if the tourists are rather tough. Nevertheless, I mean to do that inartistic and cruel thing. The Ontological Argument is the natural vehicle for passing from the first course of lectures to the second. Both historically and in many other ways it began with realism and abandoned realism. Anselm, its chief mediaeval exponent, interpreted it realistically. Descartes reconstructed it in what he declared was a realistic spirit. Leibniz, in the same realistic spirit, accepted it with emendations, and Kant understood it realistically when he set about to smash the idol. That is one side of the affair. The reverse side appeared when Hegel, opposing Kant, transformed the Proof into the boldest possible idealistic claim. It is in the latter sense that we are now most familiar with the Proof in this country. Bosanquet, in 1912, held that the truth of the argument should be "conceded in principle".[1] "It is the only proof of God", said W. E. Hocking in the same year[2]. In the next year Pringle Pattison told another Scottish audience that he accepted what "the ontological argument had been labouring to express"[3] and regretted earlier utterances in which he had thought himself (but had not really been) "a child of the light". Dr. Oman, a zetetic theologian, has recently said much the same although with rather less emphasis,[4] and it appears to me, despite certain of his disclaimers, that what Bowman calls "transcendental realism",[5] i.e. his doctrine that existence itself is conditioned by certain prior principles, is essentially an instalment, and not a very modest instalment, of this traditional Proof. Very recently indeed, Mr. Collingwood, with the evident intention and the justified expectation of casting a tempting fly upon waters that seemed too placid, remarked that after Hegel had worsted Kant

---

[1] *The Principle of Individuality and Value*, p. 80 n.
[2] *The Meaning of God in Human Experience*, p. 307.
[3] *The Idea of God*, p. 240.   [4] *The Natural and the Supernatural*, p. 103.
[5] *Studies in the Philosophy of Religion*, I, p. 89.

"the Ontological Proof took its place once more among the accepted principles of modern philosophy, and it has never again been seriously criticized".[1]

Mr. Collingwood's statement is engagingly outrageous. It would be easy to compile a long list of serious and very competent philosophers who know their Hegel and reject the Ontological Proof. There is at least as much scepticism regarding the Proof today as there was when the monk Gaunilo or the Angelic Doctor Aquinas criticized Anselm, or as there was in the seventeenth century when Cudworth and Locke said what they had to say about Descartes. It may suffice here if I quote a solitary instance, that of the late Professor Alexander who told his Glasgow hearers, some years ago, that "the famous ontological argument proves nothing more than that the totality of things is real; which is a bare tautology".[2] Indeed I mentioned the views of Mr. Collingwood and of some others largely with the purpose of forestalling the specious objection that discussion of the Ontological Proof in the twentieth century was a mere anachronism, an instance of the dead exhuming their dead.

'Anselm's form of the argument[3] was that the conception of God was the conception of that than which nothing greater could be conceived. The *insipiens*, the fool who saith in his heart "There is no God" had, like everyone else, to admit that there was such a conception. He forgot that what is conceived as existing is greater than what is merely conceived. Therefore the *insipiens* did not notice that the definition of God implies his existence; and Anselm added the explanation that other things "existed less truly and therefore had less of existence" than God had.[4]

The *insipiens*, we may say, deserved his unflattering name if he conceded Anselm's addendum. It is not folly to find the doctrine of "degrees of existence" nonsensical. Neglecting the addendum, however, we may ask two questions, viz. (1) whether there is any difference at all between "conceiving X" and "con-

---

[1] *Philosophical Method*, p. 126.   [2] *Space, Time and Deity*, II, p. 343.
[3] *Proslogion*, chap. ii.   [4] *Ibid.*, chap. iii.

ceiving X to exist", and (2) whether the idea of "maximum greatness of being" is in fact an intelligible idea.

(1) The first of these questions is the crux of Kant's criticism of the Ontological Proof, and may conveniently be postponed. I may here quote a well-known statement of Hume's: "To reflect on anything simply, and to reflect on it as existent, are nothing different from each other. That idea, when conjoined with the idea of any object, makes no addition to it. Whatever we conceive, we conceive to be existent. Any idea we please to form is the idea of a being; and the idea of a being is any idea we please to form."[1]

(2) The second question seems to have escaped Anselm's notice, but is very prominent to a modern eye. There is no natural integer than which no greater integer can be conceived.[2] Why should there be a maximum of conceivable existence?

It may be replied that the "God" of this argument is simply "All that there is", the *omnitudo realitatis*. In its innocent sense (that is, when no attempt is made to declare the sort of omnitude that is real) this argument (we may be told) is surely valid. We cannot, without contradicting ourselves, even imagine legitimately either that more exists or that less exists than actually does exist.

This reply, I think, is correct. Indeed it is a tautology; but it need not perturb the *insipiens*. It would hold if "all that there is" were chaos, or gross matter, or devilish, or worthless; and a "God" in any of these senses was not what the *insipiens* was denying in his foolish heart.

Descartes himself said that Anselm's form of the argument had been refuted by St. Thomas.[3] It was therefore an altered Proof that Descartes made so famous in the seventeenth century and afterwards, but this altered Proof was the centre of his metaphysical theism. In a letter to Mersenne, dated November 25, 1630, Descartes wrote: "As for me, I really dare to boast

---

[1] *Treatise*, Selby Bigge's ed., pp. 65 f.

[2] For a fuller discussion of the senses in which "the most perfect being" may be mere verbiage see Broad, *Journal of Theological Studies*, Jan. 1939, pp. 16 ff.

[3] *Works* (Adam et Tannery), IX, 91.

that I have discovered a proof of God's existence which I find entirely satisfactory and by means of which I know that God exists more certainly than I know the truth of any geometrical proposition." Descartes, it is true, offered several proofs of divine existence, but he gave the Ontological Proof the place of honour in his fifth meditation; and in the *Principles of Philosophy*, the most mature expression of his thought, he was at pains to show that the argument was demonstrative. There his thesis was (Part I, xiv) "that we may validly infer the existence of God from necessary existence being comprised in the concept we have of him." He added in article xv "that necessary existence is not in the same way comprised in the notions we have of other things, but merely contingent existence".

As I have said, Descartes developed the Proof realistically. In the fifth meditation he says: "Not that this is brought about by my thought or that it imposes any necessity upon things, but, on the contrary, the necessity which lies in the thing itself . . . determines me." The demonstration, he said, in the same meditation, was as good as any in mathematics and would hold even if all the other proofs in the meditation fell. We cannot object (he remarked) that although a mountain implies a valley, there might be neither mountain nor valley; for the crux of the argument is that existence is inseparable from deity. We cannot regard existence as an arbitrary addendum to deity like fancying a horse with wings; for there is no choice in the matter. We cannot, like some scholastics, say that the Proof is hypothetical —"if there were a perfect being, he would exist"—for it is not a case of supposing.

The reception of Descartes's argument in the seventeenth century has considerable historical interest. There was a pretty general opinion in Scotland, in Holland, in England and among the Jesuits that Descartes's proofs of theism were an impudently transparent fleece on a grimly lupine back. A rather unusual example of embarrassed candour is to be found in Cudworth's *Intellectual System*,[1] where the author, being indisposed (as he

[1] Harrison's ed., III, 37 ff.

said) to quarrel with any argument *pro Deo*, but being also highly suspicious of the Ontological Proof, made a manly effort to state both sides of the case.

Cudworth's objections were in substance that nothing more solid than *possible* existence follows from the non-contradictory character of a perfect being, that a hypothetical premiss cannot prove a categorical conclusion, that the argument, if valid, would establish all the other attributes of God by the same too comprehensive logic, and that since God, being ultimate, cannot have a prior ground, any *a priori* proof of his existence must be defective.

In favour of the argument Cudworth reasoned as follows: We say of things "contradictious" that they cannot exist, and of things "imperfect" but not "contradictious" that they might or might not exist. Why then should we deny that things perfect *must* exist? How could there be "ifs and ands" about the existence of a being which, by definition, is a necessary existence? If God, by definition, must exist, how could it happen that, peradventure, he might not exist? The necessity, again, would be inherent in God's nature, and would therefore be immune from the objection that divine existence could not be grounded *a priori* in something logically anterior to God.

Having said these things, Cudworth concluded with some relief: "And now we shall leave the intelligent and impartial reader to make his own judgement concerning the fore-mentioned Cartesian argument . . . whether it be merely sophistical or hath something of solidity and reality in it. However, it is not very probable that many atheists will be convinced thereby, but they will rather be ready to say that this is no probation at all of a deity, but only an affirmation of the thing in dispute and a mere begging of the question."

Leibniz dissented. In the *Nouveaux Essais* he said that the scholastics were wrong when they called the argument fallacious. There Descartes was right, but Descartes (Leibniz said) overlooked an important point when he said that the argument had mathematical certainty. In Descartes's statement of it it had only a *moral* certainty.[1] Leibniz held, however, that the formal defect in the Cartesian argument was relatively easy to correct. A proof that he said he had shown Spinoza "when I was at the Hague"[2] contends that all perfections are compatible *inter se* and may apply to the same being. The lacuna in the Cartesian proof was its neglect to show that God's existence was "possible" and not chimerical like the idea of perpetual motion. The Leibnizian addendum secured God's possibility and rescued the Ontological Proof. Leibniz defined a "perfection" as "a simple quality which is positive and absolute and expresses without any limits whatever it does express". In the world of things, so complex and so nicely graded, much that might seem to be *possible* in the abstract turns out not to be *compossible* in the concrete, but there is no such difficulty (Leibniz held) regarding the union of "perfect" attributes.

In all these discussions the Ontological Proof was developed as a straightforward piece of realistic demonstration depending upon the nature of the facts that were in debate. That *is* the Ontological Proof. It has to be confessed, however, that although Descartes, in his *Meditations*, clearly asserted the independence and the sufficiency of the proof, he also combined it with other proofs in such a way that its self-sufficiency was not always apparent. In the result the Ontological Argument tended to lose some clarity of outline.

Thus in what may be called the official proofs of God's existence in Prop. xi of the first book of Spinoza's *Ethics* it requires the greatest nicety to distinguish what is the cosmological and what is the ontological argument. Yet the two are quite distinct since the cosmological argument argues from existence to the perfection of existence while the Ontological Argument professes to derive or generate existence from the implications of the concept of perfection in the sense of absolute fulness. A similar difficulty, I think, confronts a commentator when he investigates some of the things that Leibniz said. Take,

---

[1] In the comments on Locke's *Essay*, IV, x, 7.
[2] Russell, *The Philosophy of Leibniz*, p. 287.

for instance, the following argument. "Since the ultimate root of all must be in something which has metaphysical necessity, and since the reason for an existing thing is to be found only in an existing thing, it follows that there must exist one Being who has metaphysical necessity, one Being of whose essence it is to exist."[1] In that argument the statement "since the reason for an existing thing is to be found only in an existing thing" appears to deny that existence can be derived argumentatively from anything except existence, whereas the rest of the argument declares that God's essence generates all existence.[2]

Similarly while it is plain that Malebranche consistently maintained that the infinite (i.e. God in his utter fulness or perfection) was prior to the finite in every significant way it is much more doubtful whether he set much store by the Ontological Proof strictly interpreted.

Oddly enough Malebranche seems to have thought that the Ontological Proof was peculiarly effective for propagandist purposes. In his *Dialogue between a Christian and a Chinese Philosopher*, a late work in which Malebranche, with some reluctance, undertook the delicate task of helping the missionaries in China to conquer the Chinese in argument, he began with the Ontological Argument. "God", says the Christian collocutor, "is, as the prophet said, *He who is*; that is, the Being who contains in his essence whatever there is of reality or perfection in all beings, the infinite Being in every sense, in a word, Being

---

[1] As translated by Russell, *The Philosophy of Leibniz*, p. 285.

[2] If the (unique) necessary being necessitated its own being (or existence), the cosmological argument from contingent existence to *the* necessary being would be only a sham, and the ontological argument would be the only genuine argument in the case. So Kant said (*Critique of Pure Reason*, Trans. Dialectic, II, chap. iii, sect. v) when he discussed the Leibnizian form of the cosmological argument. Logically, however, the argument *a contingentia mundi* is quite distinct from the ontological. The former argues from existence to a complement or, more generally, to implications that may be wrung from an admitted piece of existence. The Ontological Argument falls (if, as I shall argue, following Kant, it does fall) precisely because it does not distinguish as it should between "existence" and a characterizing predicate. The cosmological argument should and may decline to regard existence as a characterizing predicate.

itself"; and he proceeded to impress the Chinese with pretty technical arguments of the traditional ontological sort. God's reality, he told them, was without limitation or imperfection. Hence he was different from the material God of Chinese philosophy; for matter was very limited indeed. He also said that from the realistic premiss: "To think of nothing is the same thing as not to think", the simplest demonstration of God's existence might be drawn. The reality inseparable from an idea is to be drawn from the content of the idea, and surely the idea of the infinite is the most opulent idea that there is.

Nevertheless in Malebranche's greatest book, the *Recherche de la vérité*, the crucial chapter (III, Part II, 6) in which it is proved that we see all things in God luxuriates in so many converging arguments that close analysis is baffled. Malebranche did make it clear, however, that the strongest of all his reasons was the way in which awareness of the whole precedes awareness of detail in all human experience. Thus he paved the way for what he called "the most beautiful, the highest and the most solid of the proofs of theism, and the one that has fewer presuppositions than any other, viz. the proof from the idea of the infinite".

In a subsequent chapter (iv, 11) Malebranche accepted the Ontological Proof in Descartes's statement of it, and offered it in illustration of what could be proved by clear ideas, adding that the Proof applied only to infinite deity with his unlimited perfections and not to anything finite or limited. In a later section of the same chapter, however, he went on to say that, in his opinion, something had to be added to the Cartesian proof, namely an explanation of the relation between essence and existence. We do not, Malebranche said, perceive any *creature* as it is in itself. We are aware of creatures by participating in the divine ideas that represent them. That is how we can see their archetypes in God even when there are no corresponding existent things. The infinite being, however, cannot be represented by any idea. We are aware of it non-representatively, that is to say, as it actually is.

This argument seems to be definitely opposed to the Ontological Proof for that proof does proceed from "ideas" and undertakes to show that the *conception* of "perfection" implies existence.

But it is time to pass to the immensely important things that Kant had to say.

Kant's celebrated refutation[1] of what he called "the ontological or Cartesian argument" was directed against the Leibnizian orthodoxy of his day, that is to say, against the Cartesian argument as amended by Leibniz. The shortest way of describing his main contentions is to say that he held, negatively, that existence was not a "real" predicate, and positively that human beings were entitled to assert existence on one basis only, namely the basis of sensory evidence. We may supplement these brevities by a fuller account of what he said.

(1) Kant maintained that the conception of a necessary being was a sham. Necessity, he said, pertained to judgements and not to things. It is a relation which holds of propositions, and consequently cannot be applied directly to any subject. Again, (2) the Leibnizian addendum that Leibniz showed to Spinoza "when he was at the Hague" is also a sham. There is no health in the idea that all unlimited predicates are consistent *inter se*. Finally (3) "existence" was not a real predicate since it added nothing to the conception of its subject. A hundred real dollars contain no more than a hundred possible dollars. In logic the word "is" signifies the copula of a judgement, never its subject or its predicate. Therefore the difference between existence and non-existence is not an affair of conceptions or of predicates but concerns our title to posit or to affirm. The title to affirm existence is derived, in the case of sensuous objects, from sensation itself, either immediately or at several inferential removes. Although Kant, in other places, was prepared to admit the abstract possibility of a mode of intuition adequate to deity— though never for men—he here affirmed bluntly that all our knowledge of existence is based upon sense-experience. Our title to affirm existence depends upon the *given* in sense. In the

[1] *Critique of Pure Reason*, Transcendental Dialectic, chap. iii, sect. iv.

absence of sensory givenness all conceptions are empty including the conception of "the most real being".

Kant remarked, not without pride, that these logical questions "resisted nearly every attempt to explain and illustrate". In other words he believed that it was easy to suspect a fallacy in the Ontological Proof, but a very arduous task to refute the fallacy with precision. There, I think, he was unquestionably right. The fallacy, if there is one, is very hard to detect. That is why so many philosophers today are inclined to say "You are a sophist because you are committing the fallacy of the Ontological Argument"—in other words, they are content to name the alleged fallacy instead of dissecting it. I shall try to show that Kant did dissect the fallacy, although, in doing so, he committed himself to certain views that seem to be in excess of what his refutation required.

Let us take these points *seriatim.*

(1) Kant's contention that necessity pertains to judgements and not to things seems to me to be plainly true. As I said in a former lecture,[1] necessity is a modal predicate. Therefore there is a fallacy of amphiboly if anything "S" is said to be "necessary". The only legitimate subject for such a predicate is the *proposition* "S is P". Accordingly it is a mistake to say "God is *a* necessary being" or "*the* necessary being" for there can be no such thing as a "necessary being". The neglect to notice that the adjective "necessary" is a modal predicate, and not a first-order characterizing predicate of a *subject*, is a serious flaw in all the arguments that speak so glibly about "necessary" or "unconditioned" being.

(2) It is equally plain that the addendum to the Cartesian argument that Leibniz showed to Spinoza "when he was at the Hague" is unsound. The addendum is that all unlimited attributes are compatible, and so that God, who has them all, being the *ens realissimum* just because he is the bearer of all perfections, must be a *possible* being, exempt from internal inconsistency.

That is an attempt to prove that incompatibility of properties

[1] Lecture III of the First Series.

pertains to finite things and only to finite things. A given area, if it be square, cannot also be round; if it be uniformly blue it cannot also be uniformly pink; but such facts as these are said to depend upon the finitude of the area.

There may be a sense in which "space" is the home of all figures. If so, the abolition of all limits to any figure, say squareness, is the abolition of figure. What should be said about unlimited colours I do not know; but it can hardly be said to be evident that a universe that was all pink could also be all black.

In general the argument is that the abolition of all limitations is the abolition of negation itself. In the unlimited, all would be pure positivity. If so there could be no difference or distinction between the divine perfections. We could not say that eternity, say, meant anything different from unlimited wisdom. In other words, we could not say anything at all. Wherever there is difference there may (for all we know to the contrary in the abstract) be incompatible difference, that is to say, negation. If different attributes are compatible, we must have some positive reason for saying so. We know that beings who have bodies in space and in time may be strong and wise and good. Therefore an eternal and ubiquitous deity, who is omnificent, omniscient and wholly righteous is at least conceivable. If, however, we had no evidence regarding the possible consilience of these properties we could have no means of judging whether the absence of human limitations in these attributes could or could not allow their coalescence in a deity.

(3) The root of the matter, however, is to be found in Kant's contention that existence is not a "real" predicate. This phrase may not be very illuminating, especially as it is plain (as Kant would not deny) that existence, in some sense, *is* a predicate, since it is significant to say that God exists, and also significant to say, on the contrary, that God does not exist. I shall try, however, to discuss Kant's argument in a freer way than would be appropriate to a strict commentary upon his *ipsissima verba*.

Substantially, I think, Kant's assertion is the same as Hume's in the passage I quoted from that author. There is no added idea or conception in a hundred "real" dollars when compared with a hundred "possible" dollars, and the fact has nothing to do with the finitude of the dollars. The statement "I have a hundred dollars" is certainly different from the statement "I imagine I have a hundred dollars". In the former it is stated that I have them. From the latter, i.e. that I fancy I have them, it cannot be inferred that I do have them. None the less the meaning of "having a hundred dollars" is precisely identical in both cases.

Putting the matter in another way, we might say that the statement "This unicorn has a single horn" could not be true if there were no unicorns, whereas the statement "This elephant has two tusks" might very well be true if there were the elephant, and would certainly be true (I opine) if there were the elephant and if it were not disfigured. In other words, the statement "X has so and so" may be challenged in two ways, either by denying that there is an X, or by denying that, if there were one, it would be such and such. But X's existence is not a "such-and-such". Thus there is an ocean of difference between saying "God exists" and saying, for example, "God is omnipotent". The latter statement tells us something about God, and would be false *either* if there were no God, *or* if there were one who was not omnipotent. The former statement tells us nothing about God, and could be proved false in one way only, namely by showing that there was no God. This argument is quite general and has nothing to do with the special meaning of the term "God". Kant seems to me to have been wholly right in saying that the Cartesian Ontological Argument ignored this vital distinction, and consequently that it was fallacious.

If it be replied that since the statement "God exists" is significant, it cannot be true to say, in all senses, that it "tells us nothing about God", I should reply that what it tells us about God is simply that, existing, he has a certain epistemological status. The statement "God exists" asserts that we have the right to refer to him as a trans-presentational entity. The statement "I conceive deity" may be allowed to imply that if he existed he would have a trans-presentational status, but is also consistent with the possibility that all that the statement describes is intra-presentational. Hume's contention that there is no difference between "conceiving X" and "conceiving X as existent" is another way of putting the same matter.

This contention has been challenged by Meinong and others, who say in effect that all our thought is trans-presentational, therefore that if you think of anything there must *be* something to think of, therefore that if you think of round squares there must *be* round squares, and in general that we should rid ourselves of our "prejudice in favour of the actual". It seems sufficient to reply that, if it were so, the "God" of the Ontological Proof need not have any being except in the sense in which a round square has being. That concession would not satisfy any theist. There is no need, however, to agree with Meinong that intra-presentational differences and characteristics necessarily imply the existence of trans-presentational entities having corresponding differences and characteristics.

To maintain, as I have maintained, that Kant detected the fallacy in the Ontological Proof does not necessarily imply that he was right in certain further important comments that he made. If it is a fallacy to infer God's existence in the Ontological way, nothing follows regarding the sort of evidence that would entitle us to conclude truly "There is a so and so". Kant's own philosophical view was that we are never entitled to assert existence, unless existence is somehow *given*, and that, for us, the "given" must be the sensory. In rejecting the Ontological Proof we need not accept this further positive assertion, and I propose to discuss it now at the risk of a certain deceleration of the pace of the argument in the present lecture. The importance of the matter seems to me to compel that course.

It has been a favourite opinion in modern philosophy that evidence of existence must be sense-evidence. According to Hume, reality, or at any rate, reality *quoad nos* consisted of sense-impressions or of what, for one baddish reason or another, felt like a sense-impression. According to Kant (but only *quoad nos*) it consisted of the permanent necessitation of our sensations.

According to F. H. Bradley, "We perceive on reflection that to be real, or even barely to exist, must be to fall within sentience".[1] According to Mr. Ayer, voicing the sentiments of the modern logistical positivists, "no statement which refers to a 'reality' transcending the limits of all possible sense-experience can possibly have any literal significance".[2] So there is a cloud of very independent witnesses.

I may therefore be accused of rashness, vacuity, obstinacy and other forms of wrongheadedness when I try to dispute this view, as I am now going to do.

In the first place, I do not believe that there are any *absolute data*, sensory or non-sensory. If it be said that there must be some sense in which sense-data (so-called) are metaphysically adamantine and cannot deceive, I should reply that, by parity of conception, there must similarly be some sense in which all appearances, imaginative, memorial, intellectual, passionate or mystical are just what they are, and metaphysically irrefragable. In all such instances we have still to ask "What precisely is *given* in this indubitable sense? What is it that can abide all our probing and be irrefragable?" In the alternative I should ask "If sensations are *given* in this absolute way, and so are unchallengeable witnesses, how do you know that you have a sensation when you have one?" For it is plain that many apparent sensations can be challenged.

I may be told in reply that this objection only shows that sensations need not be infallibly given and need not be impeccable witnesses to trans-presentational reality. It could not so much as begin to show that there could be any other credible witnesses in this matter.

Accepting this rebuke, I should ask, secondly, whether it is really so difficult to conceive that evidence of existence could be given in a non-sensory way. Suppose, for instance, that John Thomson of Paisley has what he believes to be a telepathic communication from a dead friend. His belief, I concede, may be false; but it may also be true that his experience was due to a

[1] *Appearance and Reality*, p. 144.　　[2] *Language, Truth and Logic*, p. 17.

super-normal source. I further concede that the dead friend might have a "psychic" body (although such bodies usually resemble muslin very closely when spirit-photographs are taken). All these things may be true; but it is not inconceivable that the dead friend might exist although he had no attributes that could be sensed in any known human or animal way. Metaphysics is not entitled to put an absolute embargo upon such suppositions, and neither is the anti-metaphysics of logistical positivism.

In the third place, I should like to challenge what I may call the metaphysical sensory positivism of Kant and of so many others. We should all, I allow, agree with Kant in objecting to arm-chair natural philosophy. Mere thinking, without observation and without experiment, yields little light and less fruit. It does not follow, however, that thinking, even "mere" thinking, is never entitled to make any existential assertions whatever. However general these assertions may be, they might still be existential. If it be said, as Mr. Ryle has recently said[1] in his criticism of Mr. Collingwood's defence of the Ontological Proof, that "one of the biggest advances in logic that has been made since Aristotle [is] Hume's and Kant's discovery that particular matters of fact cannot be the implicates of general propositions, and so cannot be demonstrated from *a priori* premisses", I should like to ask why general propositions cannot be existential simply because they are general, or why such a general phrase as Wittgenstein's "the world is everything that is the case"[2] does not refer generally to existence?

It is not impossible in fact that a particular might be uniquely specified by general terms, e.g. "the oldest rabbit that ever was", and although we might not be able to tell without sensory evidence that there ever had been such an animal as a rabbit, it would not follow that all particulars are in like case. In any case the truth would remain that general accounts of the existent *are* accounts of the existent. It is at least conceivable that *all* thought refers to the existent unless it is false—in short, that the gener-

[1] *Mind*, N.S., No. 174, p. 142.   [2] *Tractatus Logico-philosophicus*, I.

ality of intellectual thought is not a barrier to its existential reference. Even if it be true in fact that all our existential statements do refer to sense-evidenced existence, the thing should not be declared to be a metaphysical certainty.

With this discussion of Kant I have completed what I wanted to say about the traditional realistic Ontological Proof of God's existence. We have now to ask whether the proof can be transmuted in an idealistic way. That brings us to Hegel.

According to McTaggart "what Hegel calls the Ontological Argument is not what was previously called so, and is not what Kant intended to disprove",[1] and McTaggart's views about Hegel carry great authority. It seems to me, however, that this particular statement of McTaggart's should not be accepted without some reserve. What I think that Hegel held was that Anselm and all the other philosophers he mentions—Descartes, Leibniz, Wolff, Mendelssohn and Spinoza—had the better of the exchanges, but that both they and Kant missed the true significance of the situation.

This may be shown by recalling what Hegel said about Anselm, whom he called "a thoroughly learned theologian".[2] "Anselm's proof", Hegel maintained, "as well as the form given to it in the Ontological Proof, contains the thought that God is the substance of all reality, and consequently contains Being as well. This is perfectly correct. Being is such a poor characteristic that it attaches directly to the Notion."[3] Hegel went on to say, however, that there was a "defect" in the traditional Ontological Proof, for it presupposed the unity of the Notion with Reality, yet also argued from the former to the latter. Therefore, it could not satisfy reason. Indeed, from this standpoint, Hegel was prepared to include the Ontological Argument among the "rotten props that passed for proofs".[4]

In these statements the essential point that Kant disputed is expressly affirmed. According to Kant *no* conception could

[1] *Some Dogmas of Religion*, p. 190.
[2] *Philosophy of Religion*, Eng. trans., II, 389.
[3] *Ibid.*, II, 354.
[4] *Ibid.*, III, 156.

generate existence. According to Hegel the Notion really did so, for it could and did contain the "characteristic or quality" of Being. He derided this alleged characteristic as "utterly poor",[1] "mere dry being",[2] "a wretched form of existence".[3] That was refutation by invective. It ignored Kant's careful argument that existence could not be a "real predicate", and it could not deny the possibility that the boasted opulence of the Notion might not consist only of "possible" dollars, and their like.

Hegel believed that the triumph of the Ontological Proof was assured if the cardinal difference between "understanding" and "reason" were fully understood. The "understanding", for him, was only the clumsy understudy of the "reason". It worked with "either-or" methods, that is it say, it mistook provisional distinctions for ultimate differences. It was also prepared to accept something Other than thought as a thing metaphysically final, to regard the finite as bedrock in philosophy, to accept mere sensuous immediacy without passing it through the crucible of thought. In another metaphor, it was prepared to accept bran in place of bread. Kant had held, it is true, that "reason" in this sense was more than a dream. It was the vision without which the sciences perished. But it never became attested truth. According to Hegel this was dangerous pusillanimity, pusillanimous because "reason" in fact *has* the power that Kant denied it, dangerous because philosophical poltroonery is philosophical treachery.

What "reason" affirmed, according to Hegel, was the literal identity of thought with being. That was the verity that the traditional Ontological Proof had missed in its creditable but inadequate attempt to condense a great truth into a short demonstration. "We", said Hegel, "shall accept as a simple statement of fact the assertion that the result of philosophy is that God is the absolutely true, a Universal in and for itself, the All-comprehending, All-containing, that from which everything derives subsistence."[4] "Thought alone is the substratum of this con-

---

[1] *Philosophy of Religion*, Eng. trans., II, 350.
[2] *Ibid.*, III, 203.   [3] *Ibid.*, III, 363.   [4] *Ibid.*, I, 90.

tent."[1] "To think of God is to rise above what is sensuous, external and individual. It means to rise up to what is pure, to that which is in unity with itself."[2] "The standpoint of religion is this, that the true to which all consciousness relates itself has all content in itself."[3]

I have been rather sparing with these quotations, but have cited enough of them to show what Hegel claimed. He was maintaining, like Malebranche, that what is really *given* to us is the infinitude of all being, and *not* the piecemeal revelations of sensation, and that this Absolute Whole which is given is thought-laden throughout. It is dianoetic. That is Hegel's Grand Ontological Assertion, and he took it to mean that truth, reality and thought are one and the same, that fulness of being cannot be distinguished from fulness of *conceived* being, that is to say, cannot be distinguished from the "God" of Anselm and of Descartes. It can be distinguished, indeed, from a merely abstract conception of such a "God"; for God is not abstract. It can also be distinguished from men's private fancies about the Truth and from their sense-pictures and their private imagery. For God is not exhausted in these. But it cannot be distinguished from *the* Truth, which is Reality, which is self-completed thought.

That is the Grand Ontological Assertion of Absolute Idealism, but it differs *toto coelo*, despite Hegel and despite Malebranche, from the Ontological Proof that (I submit) Kant definitely refuted. The difference is perfectly clear. The Ontological Proof attempts to deduce existence or actuality from the concept of "fulness of existence or of actuality". The Grand Ontological Assertion, as with Malebranche, states that the infinite fulness of the whole is *given* and not deduced, explorable but not inferable. There could not be a plainer difference in all philosophy. Hegel's opposition to Kant is an opposition concerning what, in ultimate analysis, is *given*; and that was the reason, among others, why I took pains to dissociate Kant's refutation of the logic of the traditional Ontological Proof from

---

[1] *Philosophy of Religion*, Eng. trans., I, 94.
[2] *Ibid.*, I, 94.
[3] *Ibid.*, I, 204.

his further assertion that, for us at least, only the sensory was given. I have not, so far, attempted either to dispute or to examine the Grand Ontological *Assertion*, I have been dealing with something quite different, namely the Ontological *Proof*.

When philosophers talk about the "given" they are apt to find themselves in a very sticky mess; but, if we mean by the "given", "that with which we have to do" or "that which puts all our questions" instead of regarding it as something that is handed out to us upon a plate, we can see, readily enough, that a thought-laden Whole *might* so be "given". We might even be able to see that the *quaesitum* of all philosophy *may* be what is truly "given" rather than the so-called "data" of sense, or other (superficial and provisional?) starting-points for philosophical operations. Such a view may or may not be true; but it is quite intelligible.

The general plan of Hegel's own philosophy, that is to say, of his Dialectic, seems to me to confirm these statements. The Dialectic began with an existential assertion, and continued to make existential assertions up to its majestic end. It professed to make an absolute start with the category of mere being, declared to be an idea undeniably and universally applicable although hopelessly impoverished, the least that could hold of reality. It ended with Absolute Spirit when the Absolute Idea had gone forth into nature and had returned to its spiritual home. Thus the beginning and the end were both adamantine. There was no Alpha logically antecedent to Being, no Omega subsequent to Absolute Spirit. Nevertheless the ethos and animating motive of the Dialectic was the Grand Ontological Assertion. Short of Omega there was always frustration, intellectual and spiritual dissatisfaction, in brief, philosophical failure. The moving force in the entire Dialectic was the concealed presence of the End declining to be cheated (although it was always half-instructed) by lesser conceptions until its revelation was accomplished.

That seems certainly to have been Hegel's view, however we may interpret him in detail. Did he mix logic with history, like his Marxist followers today, treating the stages of his logical

Dialectic as epochs or phases of cosmic change? Can we seriously believe, or believe that he meant, that nature, even in its sensible guise, is *simply* a thought-manifestation resoluble into the pure ether of the Notion? Is *that* what cosmology means to an absolute idealist? And what did Hegel mean by God?

We know something of what he meant. God, philosophically understood, he said, was the Absolute; the Absolute was Spirit and was the All. It was infinite both in the negative sense that it could be limited by nothing outside it, and also in the positive sense that it was perfect, full and self-completing. Hegel further believed that the religious conception of God shadowed forth this truth with a profundity and with an insight that no other human activity—not science, not poetry, not art—could approach, philosophy always excepted (since it was philosophy's business to transfigure the misty images of religion and obtain the clarities of the truth). But did Hegel mean that God was the spiritual community, or that the Father of All Spirits was supreme in the spiritual community? And was the spiritual community the Church or the Prussian State? In either case could nature be regarded as the body of the ecclesia or as the body of the Hohenzollern dynasty? It is small wonder that modern exponents of Hegelianism in mufti, such as Professor Jaspers in his *Existenz-philosophie*, prefer to renounce such cosmological implications, and to treat God culturally as a Folk, an art-form, a tradition, a spiritual unity far grander and greater than the temporary runners who carry the baton in humanity's relay race, but very much smaller than the *moles et machina mundi*. It is small wonder if the Marxists supplant "God" with the proletariat dialectically contradicting the bourgeois.

For the remainder of this lecture I shall abandon the Ontological Proof. I have tried to show that it is not a proof but a sham, and that Kant did refute it; but I shall make some further remarks about the Grand Ontological Assertion of Absolute Idealism.

The Grand Ontological Assertion has been the acropolis of

certain philosophies and a rock of offence to others; but assertion and counter-assertion are not philosophy. What the friends of the Absolute maintain is that this assertion, so far from being merely an assertion, is a piece, and indeed, *the* piece, of ultimate metaphysical insight. It cannot, they say, be established on any firmer basis, but its denial brings all our philosophy to ruin. If there be any insight it is here. If there be any truth or any reality it is summed up in the Grand Ontological Assertion.

Let us examine this ultimate matter.

A part of what is meant seems to be, in Mr. Collingwood's words, that "thought cannot be a mere thought, but must be a thought of something"[1]—as Malebranche also said. If this statement means that one of the claims of every thought is to have transcendent or trans-presentational reference, then there is such a claim. All thoughts make this claim, and the claim is made good if the thought is true. The thought, however, may be false. If I think of the present First Consul of Scotland, or of the present First Consul of Utopia, there is no such being. Nobody disputed that Anselm *claimed* to have discovered God's existence. The question was whether he had really done so.

It may be replied that even the most absurd and fantastic idea has a certain foothold in reality. There is no First Consul in Scotland, and there never was; but there were consuls in ancient Rome. There is no such place as Utopia, but all Utopiasts borrow freely from their knowledge of the actual world. When they try to fly clean away from our planet, they find that their wings are clipped.

That seems to be true. The truth in it is wrongly stated, however, if its contention is that we begin with reality, and, on that assured basis, permit ourselves the luxury of fancy and of conjecture. Such a view would apply neither to our own childhood nor to the poetry and mythology of an infant race. It would apply only to deliberate make-believe. If we have now gone some way in discriminating between reality and fancy, the process has been both ruminating and critical. Let us admit,

[1] *Philosophical Method*, p. 124.

however, that fancy feeds on fact, and also that, when we distinguish between reality and fancy, we never leave home although we may only be beginning to appreciate (with luck) what home really is. Why, on these grounds alone, is the Grand Ontological Assertion so widely believed to be heartening, and inspiring, and obviously a major philosophical issue? Let it be granted that illusions are drenched with reality. The admission cannot inform us how far we have gone in sifting reality from illusion. All that we learn is that if there is chaff there must somewhere be wheat, unless we learn the still smaller lesson that chaff is the husk of wheat and so is not quite un-wheat-like. Such admissions cannot assure us that God is not a myth, or that our favourite philosophy of reality may not be mythological too. It would tell us only that *if* God (or *if* our philosophy) were a myth, the myth must somehow have drawn its nourishment from reality.

Mr. Collingwood, like some others, uses a more technical argument when he says that philosophical thought (or in other words idealistic philosophy) is "categorical" and is never merely "hypothetical". This may be generalized by saying that possibility, conjecture and hypothesis are never logically anterior to an assertion about what is real, but, on the contrary, are begotten of insight into fact. In substance, this is the criticism that Brentano, among others, made of Meinong's attempt to surmount the "prejudice in favour of the actual". Such critics hold that there is no "subsistence" of pseudo-existents or of unrealities. There is just the actual, the existent.

I have no quarrel with such statements, and I hope they may be true. Indeed, if, as I have maintained in earlier lectures, the whole conception of "epistemological objects" is mistaken, it would seem that Brentano, Bosanquet and Collingwood—very different authors—must here be near the truth. I submit, however, that this particular contention does not tell us very much. It is invoked by radical empiricists when they ask for a manifest of the commodities on which any conceptual currency is based. It is asserted by many realists at every turn, as well as by absolute idealists. I do not even see how it could be shown, on such very general grounds, that the hypothetical method is not the most promising course that any philosophy or any system of philosophical theism should pursue. Even the catchword "This or nothing" suggests a hypothetical method. All that would follow would be that serious hypotheses cannot be wholly empty.

What I think idealists have to assert when they make the Grand Ontological Assertion is neither the relatively tepid statement that thought, if it be true, must refer to reality, nor the slightly bolder statement that reality must be thinkable, but something much more ambitious. They mean to assert that what is central in thought must be central in reality, and that thought's ideal is also reality's goal. This type of argument (if they try to argue the point instead of merely asserting it) used to be called "immediate inference by added determinants" in the logic books, and these sensible manuals carefully pointed out that caution had to be exercised. They remarked, for instance, that from the premiss "cricketers are men" it was hazardous to infer that "poor cricketers are poor men". They might have said the same about Hegel's criticism of Kant, and so have refused to admit that because thought referred to reality, therefore Kant's poor thoughts referred to Kant's poor reality while the rich thoughts of the absolute idealists referred to the rich reality of absolute idealism.

Let us accept the premiss that thought refers to reality, and, if the matter be deemed important, that it does so "categorically". We need not, on that account, accept the conclusion that false thought refers to false reality, or that there is a special brand of reality called "true reality" to which true thought refers. Similarly we should be circumspect regarding other reputed inferences of the same order. If it were maintained, for instance, that the ideal of thought is integration, that the best thought therefore refers to the most integrated reality, and that perfectly integrated thought, for the same reason, refers to perfectly integrated reality, a fallacy, to say the least, is not impossible. If, again, it were maintained that the ideal of thought

Mind and Deity

is intellectual clarity, and so that, since thought refers to reality, the clearest thought refers to the clearest reality, a certain diffidence regarding this conclusion would seem to be justified.

As it seems to me, that is precisely what Hegel did argue. What he called the "pure ether" and "transparent" texture of the triumphant Notion were assertions of the necessary reality, the inconcussible certainty of fact that had become pellucid. He proclaimed a certain ideal of "thought", of "reason" and of philosophical "logic". Since, in appearance at least, this ideal has never been reached in the apparent thoughts of any apparent thinker, Hegel proclaimed the paradoxes, firstly, that the ideal always is attained, secondly that it is forced to reveal itself in the debilitated and partly erroneous form of sensuous immediacy, finitude or "nature", thirdly that this necessary obfuscation is also necessarily overcome, and fourthly that the process of overcoming *is* the reality that, in principle, is always overcome. That is his philosophical interpretation of the redemption myth of Christianity. Earth's crammed with heaven, for nature is the Incarnation. There must be this Incarnation, but it must also be redeemed and its redemption is assured because it is always accomplished. If anyone denies these things he is still, philosophically speaking, in his sins. He has made the Great Refusal. It is This or Nothing.

I shall permit myself two reflections.

The first refers to the alleged identity between thought and being. Let us grant that thoughts exist, that they are *of* something, and that, if they are true, they are of something real. The further assertion of Absolute Idealism would seem to be that so long as the word "of" remains there is a certain aloofness, or, as we might say, a certain psychic distance between the thought and its goal, with the consequence that genuine unity is impossible. Therefore, in the end, thought and being must coincide and must do so absolutely. The Absolute Idea must be incorporated into the psychical body of Absolute Spirit.

A familiar reply is that any such ideal is misconceived. Without psychic distance, thought could not be transcendent or trans-presentational. If it loses its trans-presentational reference it cannot be the thought "of" anything, and it cannot be true. Support for the criticism may be obtained from the obvious reflection that thought and being need not be identical. I do not become my friend or my enemy by knowing him, and I do not necessarily know myself by becoming myself, for, despite all my self-deceptions and self-ignorance, I have always been myself. Even if it were granted, in the extreme case, not only that reality's properties are always properties that thought can grasp, but also that its properties are always integrated in the way that gives our thought its greatest sense of mastery, it would not be conceivable that thought and its object could ever be literally identical.

I think now, although I did not use to think, that this reply is not quite the last word upon the matter. It is true, and finally so (as I now think) for all that pertains to thought except thought's self-reflexiveness, but I shall try to show in the next lecture that all conscious thinking has a reflexive as well as a transcendent dimension. I shall also maintain, however, that the reflexive and the transcendent dimensions of conscious thinking are quite distinct, although neither can be absent. If so, it is false to hold that all thought must become wholly reflexive and shed its transcendent properties. In other words, one possible meaning of the Grand Ontological Assertion of Absolute Idealism, namely the view that reality is ultimately the *reflexive* mind of deity and is nothing else, cannot be sustained.

My second observation concerns the sense in which the Grand Ontological Assertion can be said to be an assertion of "God's" existence.

It is clear that such a "God" need have no close resemblance to the "God" of many other arguments in natural theology. A Great Designer, for instance, could not be the "God" of the Grand Ontological Assertion, for even if design did not itself imply an imperfection, namely the need for an ultimate distinction between means and end, a Designer, *ex hypothesi*, would not be the limitless and self-contained being whose existence is affirmed in the Grand Ontological Assertion. Similarly there does not seem to be any intelligible way of uniting the Cosmological Argument with the Ontological Assertion. The Cosmological Argument would prove the existence of an extramundane complement to the self-insufficiency of the world. Such a complement could not be the All; but the *ens realissimum* must be the All. I know that both Descartes and Leibniz said the contrary. The Cartesian deity was transcendent,[1] *l'être souverainement parfait*, and Leibniz, as we saw, argued to the existence of "the ultimate *extramundane* reason of things". I conceive, however, that the Ontological Assertion is inconsistent with the Cosmological Proof in respect of the "God" whose existence each proclaims.

It is abundantly plain that the *ens realissimum* need not be, say, the Jewish or the Christian or the Persian "God", though it might come nearer to the Mohammedan. It would consequently be difficult to reconcile the *ens realissimum* with much that the faithful in these religions believe about "God". I do not think that this reflection need dismay Christian theists; indeed, Dean Inge,[2] following Eckhart, is quite willing to say that the "God" of high (or, more precisely, of the highest) theology should be distinguished from the "God" of popular homiletics. I allow, however, that unsympathetic persons might translate such views into the more provocative statement that the "God" of the Christian pulpit is only a surrogate of the (true or philosophical) "Godhead", adapted to the readier apprehension of churchgoing and church-fearing humankind.

[1] *Deuxièmes réponses*, Adam et Tannery ed., IX, 109.
[2] See e.g. *God and the Astronomers*, p. 255.

II

The Nature of Mind

ANYONE who makes the Grand Ontological Assertion, holding either that knowing and being, mind and reality, are one, or, more quietly, that what is central in mind is central in existence, must be prepared to explain what he means by "mind". The same is required of anyone who, as I am at present, is anxious to reconsider the *prima facie* realism of man's common outlook.

To avoid misapprehension, I should like to say that although I do not see how to escape the frequent use of the terms "realism" and "idealism" I am not enamoured of the names. Each has a shifting connotation. Each may be a label for very miscellaneous contents. They are not ideal designations. They serve, however, to call attention to problems that cannot be ignored.

Although many idealists dissociate their philosophy very vigorously from what they call "mentalism" or "psychologism", and although certain idealists—those, namely, who call themselves "objective idealists"—often speak as if they had no concern at all with anyone's particular mind, it can hardly be doubted that your mind or mine, the vulgar minds of vulgar thought, somehow come into this matter, and indicate something that is highly pertinent to the enquiry. Particular minds, I allow, are not philosophical Untouchables, but if they are not the end of the story, they are a very suitable beginning for it. Consequently I make no apology for making a start with the question "What does anyone mean by a 'mind' when he speaks about his own mind or about someone else's mind?"

In an essay "On my real world" F. H. Bradley[1] argued that the *terminus a quo* for each of us when he asks this question must

[1] *Essays on Truth and Reality.*

be what Bradley variously described as our waking life, our waking self or our waking body, here and now. The emphasis was upon the state of being awake, and it seems clear that if we could describe with some precision what we mean by being awake, we should be in a favourable position for attempting further excursions.

I suppose there are various physiological differences between sleep or coma or anaesthesia, on the one hand, and the alert or waking state, on the other hand. There may even be a sense in which the oak or the ash may be said to be awake in the spring, and asleep during the winter. At present, however, I am not talking about the oak or about the ash, but about mankind. What do *we* mean by being awake?

The first thing we should say, I think, is that when we are awake we are conscious and are taking notice. It is also apparent, both from vulgar experience and from the disputes, formerly very heated although now rather languid, about pre-, sub- and un-consciousness that some delicacy may be needed for explaining the apparently innocent statement that when a man wakes he gains or recovers "consciousness". I shall assume, however, that this phrase has a definite empirical meaning, despite the difficulty of analysing its meaning with precision, and that, in some important sense, every reasonable person admits that there is such a meaning.

By employing the methods of ostensive definition, it is easy to put the point into plain relief. What happens to a man when, of a sudden, he "comes to" after concussion or after an anaesthetic, or when he suddenly wakes up in the morning? Clearly, from his own point of view, he becomes conscious. He consciously resumes his personal identity, roughly speaking, from the point at which it had broken off. He "comes to" himself, and, as some philosophers say, is "for" and "to" himself with the sort of psychical continuity that allows for, but does not include, gaps of unconsciousness. No one can have missed such an experience, and no one can reasonably suppose that it is irrelevant.

The Nature of Mind

For the purposes of illustration and of ostensive definition, I have chosen the marked and striking instance of suddenly becoming wide awake, and I have mentioned anaesthesia and concussion because of certain vivid recollections of my own. There is, however, another column in the account. We also speak of the waking state as a thing of degrees, distinguishing between being wide awake, being awake *sans phrase*, and being half-awake. We know that persons who "come round" after an anaesthetic or who wake drowsily after their normal slumbers, may "come round" slowly and gradually, not suddenly. We know that persons recovering from concussion may suffer from retrograde amnesia, so that, in their case, there seems to be a blank where formerly there was genuine consciousness. We know that in sleep there may perchance be dreams, that dream and waking may sometimes be almost if not altogether indistinguishable; and we suspect that all of us have many dreams that we do not remember at all when we wake up. Therefore it is possible to argue that where there is life there is always consciousness, however dreamy, leaden and dull. The sudden experience of waking up may be treacherous ground after all.

When such surmises are mooted it is well to remember certain things. The first is that we *are* conscious in the waking state. In that state the presence of consciousness is assured, whatever doubts there may be about the boundaries that should mark its total absence. The second is that any faculty that can show the presence of anything should also be credited with the power of giving *some* evidence about the total absence of that thing. If you see a thing, you have evidence that the thing is there. If you don't see it when you look, you have some evidence that it isn't there at all. Certainly there are relevant differences in these matters. A clear memory is very good evidence of some actual occurrence in the past. The absence of such a memory is poorish evidence that there was no such occurrence. If, however, a man had been present when some disputed event is alleged to have occurred, but has no recollection of the incident, there is *some* evidence that the incident did not occur.

Mind and Deity

To return: The waking state, we say, is clearly a conscious state. To express this fact, and for want of a better term, I shall say that the waking state possesses the conscious quality. Is it possible, then, to describe what the "conscious quality" is?

Some would say that no explanation is necessary. Anyone who is conscious knows what the conscious quality is. It would be just as reasonable to ask what pain feels like. Everybody knows from his own experience. If he didn't, it would be futile to try to instruct him. If this sort of water chokes you, what in the world do you expect to drink?

I have a great deal of sympathy with this exasperated reply, but even if its truth is conceded in substance (as I think it ought to be) it would be desirable, if it were possible, to say something more about the conscious quality. It would also be prudent to do so in view of the volume of comparatively recent discussion about "consciousness".

Our language is apt to be highly metaphorical when we speak about consciousness, and is often associated with pyrotechnics. We speak of the "fulgurations" of consciousness, of its "light", of its "self-luminosity". We talk about the consciousness of day-to-day waking life as if it were a set of Lucretian suns, a day-to-day series of incandescent perishing existences. Such metaphors, perhaps, are the best we can choose, but it would be pleasant if we could describe the conscious quality with as little metaphor as plain English permits.

When such an attempt is made, emphasis, I think, is usually put (1) upon the pure phenomenalism of the conscious quality and, again, (2), upon its reflexiveness. These technical terms, I allow, may not sound very like plain English; but they can at least be examined. I believe that the first of them covertly implies what the second in strictness entails, and that the second is apt to be described too loosely and too generally to be accurate in its services. I also believe that the first of them describes something very much less than consciousness truly is, and is therefore misleading if it is supposed to be exhaustive. These, however, are questions for the sequel of this lecture. I am mentioning them now with the intention of giving notice of what I am about to discuss. I have first to examine what the terms, in the common way, are supposed to describe.

(1) A "pure phenomenon" should mean an apparition whose entire nature and existence are exhausted in the fact of its appearing. This definition tallies very closely indeed with certain familiar philosophical views about the conscious quality. What is a pain? It is quite precisely what it is felt to be, no more and no less. Unfelt it is nothing—a mere contradiction. To feel it is to feel the whole of it.

Berkeley said the same about colours and sounds. A colour, for him, was just the hue that was seen. Unseen, it was nothing. Seen, it was all that a colour could be. Similarly of sounds, and smells, and tastes. Their *esse* was their *percipi*, and their *percipi* was their *esse*. He said the same, indeed, about everything thinkable except what he called "notions" and what he called "spirits". If he had reflected longer about "notions" he might have found the rest of his philosophy less convincing. Nevertheless, his statement about sensory apparitions conveys a very clear meaning, and is often thought to say something true and very important about the conscious quality. If true, it would explain the general opinion that a man, by being conscious, must know quite precisely what consciousness is. Most things, we believe, are inexhaustible in their nature. The revelation of them comes slowly and has no end, but an apparition whose self-revelation is the whole of it would be altogether on a different footing. It would be known exhaustively by the mere fact of being known at all. Its *esse* would be just its *aperiri*.

I shall later try to show that pure phenomenalism gives an utterly inadequate account of the waking life, and I am not asking anyone to accept the above account of sensory and of other apparitions. On the other hand, I am not asking anyone to reject the view in the case of sensory apparitions, or to believe that an argument of Berkeley's kind may not offer a true description of pleasure-pain and perhaps of much else. Berkeley's description certainly seems to be relevant to many instances of the presence of the conscious quality, and it has affinities with the reflexiveness to which I now proceed.

(2) The reflexiveness of the waking state is sometimes described as its *self*-consciousness. Awake, I am aware of my situation and of its surroundings, but I am aware of them *mecum*. I have self-acquaintance as well as other-acquaintance, and, if I choose, I can pay explicit attention to this aspect of the affair. It seems clear that these statements describe a genuine characteristic of the waking state. They may, however, be challenged in what may seem to be a very damaging way. We are often, it may be said, quite un-self-conscious when we are very wide awake. In nearly any engrossing occupation, self-consciousness tends to diminish if not to vanish altogether. To be self-conscious (some say) is to be introspective, and the introspective attitude, so far from being inevitable in the waking state, is a rarity hard to acquire and impossible to sustain for very long. It occurs when people search their hearts, self-righteously or un-self-righteously, when they indulge in self-pity, when the oracular injunction *Nosce teipsum* is sedulously obeyed, perhaps when a golfer analyses the technique of his swing, not to the advantage of his game. In short, introspection is difficult and is (perhaps fortunately) rather unusual. Besides, many philosophers go further, and assure us that there is, and can be, no such thing. The alleged introspection that is either vaunted or deplored, they say, cannot literally be the "inward looking" that it is supposed to be.

These are important matters, and I shall return to them. For the present it seems sufficient to repeat what has already been said, namely that when we are awake we do have some form of self-acquaintance. Such self-acquaintance is not, in the usual case, deliberately introspective, that is to say, intentionally self-observant; but there would seem to be what Mr. Broad calls "undiscriminating self-acquaintance" even when a man is said to be "quite un-self-conscious". When we try to be deliberately self-observant, we are, in the main, attempting to turn undiscriminating self-acquaintance into discriminating self-acquaintance. In observant self-retrospection we want to clarify that which begins by seeming blurred. In introspection we want to notice what, if we did not look for it, might remain dim. Self-acquaintance, in some sense, does attend the conscious quality.

I shall contend that the reflexiveness of the conscious quality is an essential part of the basis of our self-acquaintance, but that it is not the same thing as self-acquaintance, which, indeed, is very much broader. The distinction in point of breadth may be illustrated by the type of reflexiveness that would go along with pure phenomenalism, if there were such a condition.

In pure phenomenalism the reflexiveness would be, so to say, automatic and self-contained. The apparition whose *esse* is *percipi* would be, by definition, self-luminous. That would hold of any pain or of any pleasure, however simple and isolated. The self-acquaintance of the waking state, on the other hand, would seem to be much more intricate. The waking self looks before and after on interior as well as on exterior lines. That is its *presence of mind*, and the "mind" thus present is highly complicated, being compact, at the very least, of emotions and volitions and attentive activities.

Again, in the case of a pure apparition whose *esse* was *percipi* there would seem to be no room for error, but it is hard to believe that self-acquaintance, in its general sense, is infallible, and the tangled philosophy of this subject, together with the apparently well-grounded belief in the extreme difficulty of reliable introspection (and retrospection), seem to make the claim to infallibility peculiarly hard to sustain. It is possible, indeed, to hold that self-acquaintance is infallible when it is freed from all impurities. But how could we be certain that this catharsis had taken place?

In self-acquaintance, the complexity and continuity of that with which we are acquainted seem quite undeniable. That is the first thing a man notices when he examines his personal identity, and it seems expedient to linger over this matter in view both of recent and of earlier controversies.

In the earlier literature one of the most consistent of would-be pure phenomenalists was David Hume, and Hume was also what his critics call a "psychical atomist", for he held that each "perception" (to use his own term) was "complete in itself". In that case, each "perception" would separately exhaust its own reflexive self-luminosity, and the natural inference would be Hume's inference, namely that the self or the mind was only a "heap" or "bundle" of self-reflexive "perceptions" each of which might exist separately. According to neo-Humians each "perception" might be a constituent in all sorts of other bundles that need have no resemblance to personal unity or continuity.

Similar views are sometimes held by those among the moderns who believe in the sub- or un-conscious. They may hold, it is true, that the conscious quality of wishes, ideas and the like is of negligible importance. A wish, some of them say, is a perfectly good wish whether it has the conscious quality or not. Its relation to what we call "consciousness" is not important. On the other hand, they may hold that the sub-, fore- and unconscious are always and necessarily states of *consciousness*, although they may not form part of waking self-consciousness. Each, they say, has the characteristics of a pure phenomenon, and may be associated or dissociated into various strata or bundles other than the personal unity that we usually designate when we talk about self-acquaintance. It is of primary importance that each should be admitted to some kind of *consciousness*.

Dreams, "twilight sleep" and the rambling mentality of extreme fatigue may be cited in favour of such views, and it is fair to remark that our speculations about the evidence may be heavily biassed by prepossessions regarding the waking state. The evidence from dreams is from the memory of dreams *recalled in the waking state*. The evidence from delirious ramblings is derived from the memory of delirious ramblings, unless it comes from the testimony of others about these ramblings. And so forth. Perhaps, therefore, it is highly significant that we do have sufficient waking memories to understand fairly well what a moment-to-moment consciousness induced by a drug like scopolamin would be like. Again, so far as I can tell from my own recollections, it is very plausible indeed to say that a man's state of mind, just before he falls asleep, may approximate to a condition of pure phenomenalism or of mere seeming. There are successive fulgurations of consciousness each very nearly "complete in itself", and each very brief. I think, however, that if all the evidence in favour of theories of this type were derived from what, waking, we could remember of dreams and delirium and tired ramblings of our minds it would be most highly conjectural.

It is generally held, of course, that the evidence for hidden consciousness is not derived from such faint and ambiguous waking memories, but from quite different sources. It is derived, we are told, from *results*, that is to say, from facts that seem to have the stamp of mind on them although we are not acquainted with them in the waking state. Such contentions, if they were sound, would emancipate mind pretty thoroughly from the conscious quality of waking experience, and the possibility of such emancipation is one of the bigger problems we have to discuss. I propose, therefore, to make a fresh start with my argument, although I shall not abandon the older discussion for ever.

It is useful to remember the venerable tripartite division of mental powers into the cognitive, the conative and the affective. The first of these seems to be the chief. It enters into the constitution of every volition and of every conation that is not wholly blind; and it is unlikely that mental striving ever is wholly blind. *Ignoti nulla cupido.* An entirely blind emotion is also, in all probability, a mere chimera. Therefore we are principally concerned with problems about cognition.

"Attending" and "being aware" are commonly used as synonyms or near-synonyms for cognition. Each, however, raises problems. To say that we are aware is to assert the presence of the conscious quality, and some would hold that the conscious quality is not at all essential to entirely genuine cognition. "Attending", in strictness, is a still narrower term. It has a nuance of volition, of setting oneself to notice as well as merely of taking notice. In this sense it is possible, and indeed quite usual, to be aware without being attentively aware, and even to have clear and vivid apprehension of an inattentive kind. That may happen in dreams, especially in exciting dreams. It may happen when bright ideas turn up, as we say, out of the blue. In the more usual way, a man may be said to be aware without being attentive when he is slack and listless, giving his mind to nothing although it is not a complete blank.

None the less, it seems reasonable to give an account of "attending" and of "being aware". In pursuing this plan I do not think I shall run any serious risk of deluding myself or other people. I shall try, however, to use these terms in as neutral a sense as I can, and, regarding "attention" in particular, I shall include dispersed as well as concentrated attention, and "attention" in which there is little evidence of serious volition.

We should note the wide range of attention as well as the relevance and the promptness that attach to the attentive state.

The width of its possible range is obvious. We may attend, conceptually, to principles and to general notions. We may attend, imaginatively, to fancies and to images. We may attend, conjecturally, to what we anticipate in the future. We may attend to the past, conjecturally if we do not remember it, non-conjecturally if we do. In the present (or in what we take to be the present) we may attend to internal organic sensations like rheumatic pains or to what appear to be shapes and colours outside our own apparent bodies. We may also attend, introspectively or retrospectively, to the conscious quality of our waking personality—at any rate if, as I shall try to show, introspection and retrospection are not delusions. The range of "being aware" is, of course, at least as wide as the range of attending.

In describing such facts we invariably speak of attending *to* something or of being aware *of* something, and it is usual to call that *to* which we attend or that *of* which we are aware, the "object" of attending or of being aware. As we have frequently seen, there is a snare in this use of the word "object". It should indicate an epistemological status and nothing more, but it is often illicitly reified into a special kind of *thing*. The term, however, is convenient in many contexts, and is unavoidable in the present context if pedantic verbosity is to be avoided. I shall therefore employ it despite the risks.

In attending and in being aware we are usually concerned with what *seems* to be relevant. In saying this I am using the term "relevance" rather widely. Relevance is a logical notion. It designates what is to the point, and it is clear that we are very apt to miss the point, largely on account of our own logical debility. We are often associative rather than strictly logical in what Scotsmen call the "uptak". Indeed, in speaking of "relevance" in connection with the process of attending, I shall refer as much to the semblance of this logical virtue as to its real presence. When we are attentive we *think* we are keeping to the point, we think our associations[1] have something to do with the matter, we are organizing our "objects" into apparent cohesion, or, in the alternative, appearing to refine them analytically. Association apes logical relevance even when it does not attain it. We are often the dupes of this semblance but it would be pessimistic to conclude that all the semblance is mere empty show.

As well as relevance, there is celerity. In speaking of the promptness of attention I am recalling a very trite piece of knowledge. "Thought is quick", said Hobbes very concisely,[2] referring to the association of a Roman penny with the betrayal of Charles I through the "skipped intermediaries" of Judas Iscariot and his pieces of silver. Thales, according to Diogenes Laertius, said the same thing; and Lucretius wrote:

> Nil adeo fieri celeri ratione videtur
> Quam sibi mens fieri proponit et inchoat ipsa;
> Ocius ergo animus quam res se perciet ulla,
> Ant' oculi quorum in promptu natura videtur.[3]

---

[1] Unless we explicitly recognize them as irrelevant associations. That also happens.   [2] *Leviathan*, chap. iii.   [3] *De Rerum Natura*, III, 182 ff.

In attending we are in a state of readiness, ready to adapt ourselves to the cognitive situation, ready to recall what may be of use. The *esse* of attention is very largely its *posse*. That is one of the implications, perhaps the chief implication, of the phrase "presence of mind", and it is one of the respects, perhaps the only effective respect, in which we distinguish attention from simple awareness.

So far, since I made a fresh start with my exposition, I have said nothing about "attending" or about "being aware" that did not march in step with what I said, in the earlier part of the present lecture, when I talked about the waking state and its conscious quality. That is as it should be, for "attending" and "being aware" are terms to which we naturally (and I think correctly) attribute the conscious quality. As we have seen, however, attention is attention *to* something, and to be aware is to be aware *of* something. I made a fresh start with my exposition in order (I hoped) to be able to deal the more effectively with this all-important circumstance. For here we reach the point where discussion of the nature of mind, the general subject of the present lecture, frequently takes a surprising turn. Many philosophers profess to be unable to discover any entity at all that can be said to be attentive or to be aware. There is no such discernible being, they say. Attending and being aware are names for some of the properties of "objects". These names signify certain changes that are changes in the "objects". It is the "objects" that are associated so promptly, the "objects" that are logically relevant or that seem to be so. The range of attending is just the range of the "objects", and there is nothing else to describe.

The consequences are momentous. According to the "neutral monists" in the earlier philosophy of the present century the very matter-of-fact that is mental in *one* set of relations may be physical in another set of relations. It is mental in memorial and in biographical relations, but it may also be physical without any intrinsic change. This view is usually elaborated on the basis of sensory phenomenalism. Sensations are said to be the stuff of minds and of physical things. Being sensations, they are phenomena, that is, they must *appear*; but they need not appear *to* anything. Whatever, *prima facie*, is not sensation may somehow, with pains, be reduced to sensation—or so it is ardently hoped and vehemently asserted.

This particular form of neutral monism, however, is not the only doctrine that may be set out on these lines. Mgr Olgiati,[1] for instance, has recently maintained, with great force and acuteness, that the essence of Descartes's philosophy was a *fenomenismo razionalistico*, a noëtic phenomenalism in which thought's clarities *were* the real and were *all* that is real. Hegel's "pure ether" of thought into which sensuous immediacy (while not denied) was said to be transmuted seems to have been similarly conceived.

The doctrine, in short, is a doctrine of mentality without a mind, and also without the conscious quality. The thesis is that there is mentality where there is association, significance, implication and the like. According to much philosophy in earlier centuries, these "mental" properties were due to the operation of some mind. That is part of the problem involved in interpreting the famous (and provocative) *Cogito* of René Descartes; but we are often informed today that one of Kant's many services to philosophy was the complete destruction of this battered idol. According to some of Kant's statements the work of the mind takes place behind the scenes. The basis of it, he said, is synthesis, "a blind but indispensable function of the soul, without which we should have no cognition whatever, but of the working of which we are seldom even conscious".[2] The operative activity of the synthesis, according to Kant, is beyond any man's observation. What confronts a man is synthetic connectedness itself, the product and not the productive process. That is the whole proscenium. What occurs off-stage is utterly secret, a *mens abscondita*. Kant, indeed, called the operation of synthesis "indispensable". He was fond of leaving "indispen-

---

[1] *Cartesio* (1934) and *La Filosophia di Descartes* (1937).
[2] *Critique of Pure Reason*, Transcendental Analytic, chap. i, sect. 3.

sable" ghosts to haunt the wreckage of the armada he had vanquished. But ghosts, in fact, are never indispensable, and the out-Kanting of Kant is such a simple game that, after Kant, any pigmy in philosophy can play it.

The *Ich denke*, the "I think" that according to Kant "must be able to accompany all my representations",[1] is not a psychological phenomenon. In it there is no *Cogito ergo sum*, no residue of what Mgr Olgiati considers the unregenerate part of Descartes, the part of him that conflicted with his pure noëtic phenomenalism. Instead there is a pale logical result, the property of being connected. To say "I judge" is to say "This proposition holds". Kant held, it is true, that all logical connection was wrapped up in what appeared to be the simple garb of mere propositional assertion, and he was sometimes prepared to offer a "subjective" or semi-psychological vindication of his views. The "manifold" had to be run through and held together in what is commonly called a single mind. We may paraphrase Kant's argument by saying that if Jones knows only that Smith was on board the *Girl Pat*, and if Robinson knows only that the *Girl Pat* sailed in ways that were not authorized, neither Jones nor Robinson could infer that Smith might be in danger of jail.

In such arguments the ghost of a personal mind and of its conscious quality almost comes to light; but in the main they are Kant's concessions to human weakness. The substance of his theory concerns not your thought or mine but the function of consciousness-in-general—of *Bewusstsein überhaupt*. It is impersonal, schematic, timeless, formal, a linking of implications in which logical hooks slip into logical eyes. In Hegel's development of the theory, and in many other idealisms, "reason" ousts "understanding" and the *Ich denke* becomes the monarch and not merely the inevitable attendant of sensory "representations". Nevertheless, personal minds and their conscious quality are left in exile. According to such theories, one may speak of "subjectivity", using the term to name an imperfect thought-connection. If so, the thing would be a mystery, not always understood to

[1] *Critique of Pure Reason*, Transcendental Analytic, chap. ii, sect. 12.

be one. But the reality would be an impersonal logical con-
nexiveness, a whole of implication.

Accordingly, a most peculiar situation arises. The putative
"objects" of the mind have devoured their putative parent with
such industrious voracity that they come to be regarded as born
orphans. An "object", we used to believe, was always an "object-
of-consciousness", that of which someone was aware. We are
now informed, for example in the very clear statements of Mr.
Woodbridge, that "we know what our objects are and what we
may expect from them, not at all by considering their relation to
consciousness but to one another",[1] that "there is no reason to
conclude that consciousness is in any way a determining factor
in the contents or limitations of knowledge",[2] and that all that
is present is a set of "manifold and irresistible meaning-connec-
tions".[3] In place of the conscious quality we have "mental"
connections, formerly imputed to a mind, now denied that
ancestry. There is said to be no visible connection between
"mental connections" and the conscious quality. Therefore,
since mental connections are the important matter, the conscious
quality may be dismissed. There is still talk about "awareness",
"appearing" and "the conscious situation"; but that is only for
convenience' sake, and not for edification.

In view of this, arguments about sub- or un-consciousness
and about the legitimacy of such conceptions acquire a flavour
of antiquation. The old-fashioned question was whether if a
man seemed to reach a conclusion without consciously inferring,
if he acted as if he remembered when he didn't consciously
remember, if he seemed to act for an end without consciously
having any end in view, it was then legitimate to say that he
was sub- or un-consciously inferring, remembering or willing.
If, however, consciousness be given its *congé*, it is a matter of
indifference what happens to its retinue. The whole staff is
dismissed. All that is said to matter is "mental" connection. It is
irrelevant whether there be a mind, or sub-mind or un-mind.

We have now reached the metropolitan area of our present

[1] *Nature and Mind*, p. 311.   [2] *Ibid.*, p. 312.   [3] *Ibid.*, p. 340.

topic. Are mental properties independent of the conscious quality? Could reality be thought-laden, that is, suffused with mental properties, if there were nothing that had the conscious quality? In the alternative, if there are beings that do possess the conscious quality, may it still be maintained that the existence of such beings is irrelevant to the "mental" constitution of reality? I have drawn illustrations from America, and particularly from Mr. Woodbridge who, in his turn, was commenting upon William James's celebrated essay *Does Consciousness Exist?* But I might have referred to our own country with equal ease, and to philosophers in it of a very different bent. "The objects of finite mind", Mr. Bosanquet said just before the First Great War, "are, according to the view to which our argument has led us, neither minds nor products of minds, nor states of mind."[1] His argument depended upon things "being mind-component, that is, possessing a logical nature or implicit unity".[2] More than a quarter of a century has passed, and some of the catchwords have gone out of fashion; but there is nothing dead about the contention.

I shall now try to show that nothing should be said to have mental properties except in its connection with an entity that has the conscious quality, or in other words, with what we commonly call a "mind". Such a connection may be covert rather than overt, but it must exist. It is covert, for example, when we speak of "truth" or of "certainty". We say that it is "true" and that it is "certain" that one and one make two without implying that integers are mental things. Nevertheless, the statement "P is true" means, in the long run, that if anyone apprehended it, his apprehension would be true. Similarly the statement "P is certain" means, in the long run, that if anyone apprehended P he could have no doubts about it, or, on another interpretation, that if anyone apprehended P he would see that it was certified by irrefragable evidence. I do not of course deny that we may discover the nature of things by the exercise of our

[1] *The Distinction between Mind and its Objects* (1913), p. 43.
[2] *Ibid.*, p. 42.

mental powers, and that what we discover in this way is present in the things themselves. If *mentally discoverable* properties are said to be "mental," then things do have "mental" properties and might have them, to use Bosanquet's phrase, in "an anaesthetized universe".[1] In the same way we might say that plums would be edible if there were no eaters. But the remark would be pointless unless there were potential eaters.

Let me begin by pointing out that "things" and "objects" are not identical terms. An "object" is a "thing-cognized", and its properties are "cognized-properties". Grant that the "cognized-properties" are the thing's properties. You still have cognition on your hands. When you speak about "objects" you are imputing an epistemological status, and you have no right to assume that the imputation is an empty formality. The same would be true about the plums. Their edible properties are *their* properties, but we say something more about them when we say that they are edible than when we say, quite simply, that they are they. We assert a relation to actual or potential eaters.

There are, no doubt, many important differences between the edibility of plums and the cognoscibility of things. One of the differences (I believe) is that plums are constitutionally altered when they are eaten and that things are not constitutionally altered when they are known; but it does not follow that nothing happens, or that nothing happens *to them*, when they are known. In this respect, common language may often have to be rectified. We say, sometimes, that the clouds "mean" rain, but we easily perceive, on reflection, that the clouds cannot *mean* at all. They do not signify, or suggest, or indicate (unless to a mind) any more than a tombstone at the bottom of the sea. The tombstone has significance for those who can read its inscription; but if we say that "objects" signify although mere "things" do not, it is surely clear that something is true of "objects" that is not true of things *simpliciter*.

It may be replied that these statements merely describe the puzzle and do not attempt to solve it. Very well then. I submit

[1] *The Distinction between Mind and its Objects* (1913), p. 41.

that what happens to a thing when it becomes an "object" is that it *appears*, which is another way of saying that someone, or at any rate that *something*, is aware of it. I further submit that in this apparently simple fact of *appearing* the marriage between mental properties and the conscious quality is indissoluble. I should like, however, to call attention to something that I am *not* saying. I am not saying either that things "present appearances", or that "objects" are things which have become "apparitions". If that were the truth I should be harder pressed than I need be. It would be plausible to hold, in that case, that the so-called "things" were only apparitions, perhaps in the way described by sensory phenomenalism, perhaps in the way described by *fenomenismo razionalistico*. But what I am actually saying is that things appear, and that, directly or indirectly, we include this property when we call them "objects".

At this point, the second division of the present lecture, the part of it at which I made a fresh start, becomes interknit with the first division. For the future there should be a united fabric.

If pure phenomenalism were an adequate philosophy, I allow that there would be nothing distinctive about being aware. The "objects" or phenomena would *be* the reality, and pure phenomena, as we have seen, would be pure apparitions that must seem what they are and be what they seem.

I have therefore to show that pure phenomenalism is an utterly inadequate theory of the entire range of cognition. It may be plausible, I hold, in certain instances of cognition, but only in these and not in all.

The theory is plausible in respect of pleasure-pain and, more generally, in respect of pure emotion. The reality of a pain may be just what is felt. The same may perhaps be said about certain forms of imagination. In their case it may be true that we have (or are?) mere apparitions, that we have (or are?) presentations that have no trans-presentational reference, and so cannot be false, or unconscious, or anything at all except just what they seem to be. It may also be maintained, although in this case with less verisimilitude, that pure sensations are, in the same way, pure apparitions, quite non-transcendent, quite immune from error and quite immune from truth. I think, however, that there are no other cases in which pure phenomenalism is so much as plausible.

In all other instances, it is abundantly plain that our cognitions claim to have transcendent reference, and are hopelessly mis-described unless there is room for such reference. Consider memory, and, more generally retrocognition. I remember *now*, but, in doing so, I mean to refer to something that I experienced in the past. A self-enclosed present apparition could not conceivably be a memory. Again, if I refer to the capture of Constantinople by the Turks in 1453, I am referring *ncw* to an event five centuries old. Without such reference I could neither be nor seem to be retrocognitive. Similarly, when I perceive the typescript I am at present producing, I believe myself to refer to something that, in some important sense, endures and is legible for quite a long time. Its existence could not be exhausted, like a shooting pain, in a momentary apparition.

Cognitive experience, for the most part if not invariably, is transcendent. No doubt, in casting its transcendent net, it does not infallibly make its catch, but without such transcendence there could be no errors of memory, of intellection or of other such processes, and the risk of error is not its certainty. If transcendence be denied in such instances the possibility of truth is also denied. Most phenomenalists conceal this denial from themselves and from others by surreptitiously assuming that the intra-presentational complexity of pure phenomena may generate trans-presentational reference. That is the theory of contextual phenomenalism, but it cannot be sustained. An apparition or pure phenomenon, something that is all seeming and show, exhausts its being by appearing. It has nothing to contribute to anything else, no matter how complex it may be. If a pain is just what it is felt to be, that would be true of the most complex as well as of the simplest pain.

Pure phenomenalism, therefore, is an untenable theory of cognition, and if pure phenomenalism be denied, it follows that to be and to appear are *not* the same. Things may exist without appearing, that is, without being mental "objects". When they appear they must appear *to* something. Something must be aware *of* them. I have not denied that there are beings, namely minds, that appear *to* themselves and are aware *of* themselves. I am about to examine that question more closely. But there is not the least reason to believe that *everything* that exists has this capacity. The mere fact that we are aware of this or of that yields no particle of evidence that the things of which we are aware are aware of themselves. They have what some idealists call the "privilege" of appearing to us. Dirt has the privilege of appearing to be dirty, and lice have the privilege of appearing to be lousy. It does not follow that dirt appears dirty to itself or (although this may be true) that lice appear to be lousy to themselves.

Let us consider (or re-consider) this matter of appearing to oneself or (which is the same thing) of being aware of oneself.

When Hume averred that he could notice "perceptions" but never a self,[1] when Earl Russell says that mental "acts" are "mythical and are not to be found by observation",[2] they were both assuming, I think, that all knowledge is transcendent knowledge (however difficult it may be to reconcile such transcendence with their phenomenalism). On that ground they denied the presence of any vestiges of mental self-acquaintance. For a long time I also was disposed to assume the transcendence of all knowledge. It is very hard to avoid. I tried, nevertheless, to convince myself that there might be transcendent self-acquaintance, and so I differed from Hume or Russell.

I am still of opinion (indeed, I think it can be proved) that much that we call self-acquaintance *is* transcendent, and I still believe that the arguments that attempt to show that *transcendent* self-cognition is demonstrably mythical are, for the most part, either baddish or thoroughly bad. I have come to see, however, that it is false to believe that in our waking consciousness we are aware *only* in the transcendent way. I allow that we *are* so

[1] *Treatise*, Book I, Part IV, sect. vi.   [2] *The Analysis of Mind*, p. 21.

aware. Indeed I believe that we are never aware without being aware *of* something. But I hold that we are *also* reflexively self-aware. Indeed I believe that if we sedulously refuse to treat the reflexive dimension of our consciousness as either itself transcendent knowledge or as analogous to transcendent knowledge there is no difficulty at all, no lack of empirical evidence, but, on the contrary, a superabundance of such evidence. When Hume stumbled[1] (transcendently) upon "objects" he was *always* aware (reflexively) of himself.

If all cognition were transcendent, the principal objections to the possibility of self-cognition would be the following: There is, firstly (1) the argument from non-observation. We can notice red or blue, but cannot (according to the objectors) notice our noticing of red or blue (assuming that sensations of ocular adjustment and the like are not really what we mean by such "noticing" but are "objects" like red or blue). There is, secondly, (2) the metaphysical argument that since "subject" and "object" are eternally distinct, a subject that objectified itself would be an impossibility. There is thirdly (3) Comte's well-known argument to the general effect that "the organ observed and the organ observing being identical . . . observation could not take place".[2]

(1) The argument from non-observation is disputed. The unregenerate who believe that self-cognition is possible although all cognition is transcendent have only to say, as they do say with conviction, that they *can* see what their critics have missed. Even the most careful observers may be looking for their spectacles when they have them on.

(2) The second objection should not, I think, deceive anyone. To consider anything simply and to consider it "as an object" are nothing different from one another. To call the thing an "object" is merely to assert that it is considered. Therefore if we could consider our selves at all we would be bound to "consider them as objects", and would be deceiving ourselves in the

---

[1] *Treatise, loc. cit.*

[2] *Cours de philosophie positive*, I, 34 ff. Quoted by James, *Principles*, I, 188.

woolliest way if we supposed that we altered ourselves by "objectifying" ourselves. As it stands, therefore, this metaphysical objection is unavailing.[1]

(3) The third or Comtian objection may be put in various forms. The complaint might be that a cognate accusative is not a genuine accusative. You cannot catch a catching although you can catch a football, or measles. Substantially, however, the complaint is that cognition implies a relation, and that identity is not a relation but denies all relation.

If all cognition were transcendent it would obviously imply a relation, and what is more, a relation between the cognitive process involved and something else, the "object" of that process. We may therefore ask whether transcendent self-acquaintance is downright impossible.

Plainly it is not. As we have seen, all memory is transcendent and Comte's objection has no relevance at all to our being aware of our *past* selves. Most people believe that they can remember their own past experiences and conscious attitudes just as easily and just as clearly as they can remember foreign events that they have formerly observed. Nothing that Comte says contradicts such a belief; and that was one of J. S. Mill's answers to Comte. "We reflect", he said, "on what we have been doing, when the act is past, but when its impression in the memory is still fresh."[2] In so far as self-cognition and so-called introspection are really retrospection, occurring "the moment after" in the most expeditious of all *post mortems*, there is a transcendent relation of the mind to its former condition.

Mill also said, however, that "we know of our observings and our reasonings either at the very time or by memory the moment after; in either case by direct knowledge and not (like things done by us in a state of somnambulism) merely by results".[3] We generally believe the first part of this statement as well as the second, and we should suppose our plain experience to be flouted if we were told that our self-acquaintance is always and

---

[1] See my paper to the IXth International Congress of Philosophy (Vol. VIII, 189 ff.). [2] *Auguste Comte and Positivism*, 5th ed., p. 61. [3] *Loc. cit.*

merely retrospective, and that we can have no acquaintance with ourselves "at the very time". Clearly, however, an act cannot be transcendently related to *itself*. If, therefore, transcendent introspection "at the very time" is possible, there must be two acts simultaneously present in the same mind at the same time, one that observes, and the other that permits itself to be observed.

Such a state of affairs is logically possible. The primary fact would be the observing (x) of an "object" (y)—let us say $x\,R\,y$. The more complicated hierarchical fact would be *another* piece of observing—the observing of the primary observing-of-the-"object". Let us symbolize it as $[x'\,R\,(x\,R\,y)]$. Even an infinite hierarchy of this type would be logically virtuous; for $x\,R\,y$ does not depend upon $[x'\,R\,(x\,R\,y)]$ but contrariwise. Our minds, on that hypothesis, would contain a box-within-box arrangement like a Chinese puzzle, but there is no great difficulty in believing that they might be internally hierarchical in some such fashion.

I believe that the first complexity of this kind—the complex I have symbolized by $[x'\,R\,(x\,R\,y)]$—actually occurs in deliberate introspection, although I doubt whether more elaborate instances of this internal hierarchical arrangement ever have occurred. In any case, since x' is a different act from x, there is, as I have said, no logical impossibility in the theory. I do not think, however, that this kind of complication occurs very often, or that it describes our normal self-acquaintance when we are not intentionally dividing our minds in a strenuously introspective way. Some other account must therefore be given of our normal un-introspective self-acquaintance "at the very time".

In my opinion, it is here that we reach the crux of the matter. The arguments of Comte and of others do not prove to demonstration that if all knowledge and acquaintance were transcendent, self-knowledge and self-acquaintance must be sheer impossibilities. I do not believe that any such "proof" can stand up to criticism, and it seems to me to be plain that much that we call "self-acquaintance" and that much that we call "introspection" does assume and rest upon knowledge and acquaintance of the transcendent kind. I am also of opinion, however, that much in our self-acquaintance, especially "at the very time", is not transcendent *at all* but is strictly reflexive. So I believe that reflexive non-transcendent self-knowledge and self-acquaintance occur as well as and in conjunction with knowledge of the transcendent kind.

Let me proceed to develop the main implications of this solution—for I believe that it is a solution.

In transcendent cognition there must be a certain aloofness or psychic distance between our mental process and their objects. This aloofness and psychic distance do not prevent us from apprehending the objects. We do apprehend them. On the other hand, it does emphatically imply that there cannot be literal identity between the cognitive processes and their objects in any instance in which the cognition is transcendent.

Everything is quite different, diametrically different, in the reflexive non-transcendent dimension of the conscious quality. In reflexive cognition there is no aloofness, no psychic interval or psychic distance, and there *is* existential identity. That would be impossible if the two dimensions of the conscious quality, the transcendent and the reflexive, were not *toto genere* distinct. If, however, they are quite different and not even analogous to one another, the reflexive dimension of the conscious quality may evince just what we commonly believe to be true of our normal waking life, namely that we can literally have self-acquaintance "at the very time" without any psychic interval and without any psychic fission.

That, I submit, is what actually occurs. When we are aware, we are always aware *of* something in a transcendent way. But we are also self-aware in the reflexive way, and there is no occasion for confusion unless we confuse the transcendent dimension of our waking experience with its reflexive dimension.

Thus we may learn to avoid two serious errors. The first is the mistake of those who, assuming that all cognition is *merely* transcendent, declare that we can notice "objects" but never our noticing. They neglect the reflexive dimension of the mental process of noticing. The second is precisely the opposite error. It results from the belief that *any* psychic distance between cognition and its object, any relation of transcendence, is a mark of imperfection. In perfect knowledge, according to this belief, there would have to be literal identity between cognition and its object. We would *be* what we know. Reality must either be ultimately unknowable or else be something that, in the end, we may literally become. That is to deny the ultimacy of the transcendent dimension of our consciousness, to declare in set terms that the reflexive dimension of our consciousness ought to be able to swallow and digest the transcendent dimension. My submission is that this idea is just as extravagant and just as unnecessary as the other.

If by "self-cognition" we mean the knowledge that a man may have of his own continuing ego, it is plain that self-cognition, in that sense, is very much ampler than the reflexive self-awareness "at the very moment" that I have attempted to describe. The ego thus known is known partly by inference, partly by what is sometimes called "intellectual construction" and very largely by retrospection. Retrospection, *ex vi termini*, is transcendent. What is sometimes called our "undiscriminating self-acquaintance" with ourselves as continuants is also very largely retrospective, and therefore very largely transcendent. Deliberate introspection may also be transcendent in the complicated hierarchical fashion of which I have spoken. On the other hand, the primary basis of all such knowledge and acquaintance is the reflexive dimension of the conscious quality of our waking minds "at the very moment". Such reflexiveness would attach to pure phenomena if there are such apparitions. But it is not confined to "pure phenomena". There is no reason to doubt that it is a dimension of the conscious quality of an entire complicated waking self at every moment of its waking existence.

To sum up: A mind cannot be just a certain connectedness of "objects", for an "object" means that of which some mind is aware in the transcendent way. In the waking state our minds are always cognitive in the transcendent way, but they are also self-aware in the reflexive way "at the very moment", and that is the primary basis of their self-acquaintance and self-cognition. The conscious quality of waking experience contains both a transcendent and a reflexive dimension. Waking experience may not wholly exhaust the life of any mind, but it gives the only clear evidence of the nature of mind that we have, and there is no sufficient reason for believing that the boundaries of mentality are very much wider than the waking experience of conscious beings.

I may be told that I have only approached and have not even begun to attack the really interesting problems in this field. Are our minds separate entities, or can they be pooled in some wider mind, perhaps God's mind, perhaps the soul of the world? And what of our bodies? Do we not speak about our waking "lives" or about our waking "bodies" as well as about our waking "minds" or "selves"? Am I trying to defend the conception of possibly discarnate minds? Am I trying—horrible thought!— to animate the spectre of metaphysical dualism, holding that we refer transcendently to physical bodies but reflexively to our own immaterial selves? If I have no such ulterior motives, have I not wasted a lecture? If I have them, is not this lecture a sinister enterprise?

Many of these problems will meet us in subsequent lectures and I am anxious to avoid shock tactics. The present lecture has been a preliminary piece of analysis, and it has covered quite a lot of ground. In the short remainder of the lecture, however, I shall try to give some indication, tentative, brief and hazardous, of the sort of bearing its enquiries may have upon more ambitious metaphysical and theological themes.

(1) I am unable, in my own case, to detect anything besides attention, volition and emotion that possesses the conscious quality, and I find these occurring in a unity that is always cognitive in the transcendent way. (In this statement, all the relevant terms are given the widest interpretation that they can reasonably bear.)

(2) A great many things may exist without possessing the conscious quality, that is to say, there may be non-mental existents. I believe there is a host of them. We apprehend them transcendently and not reflexively unless we are the victims of illusion.

(3) Much discussion is possible regarding the status of sensations and of images. According to many philosophers, sensations and images are apparitions, i.e. are pure phenomena which *ex vi termini* possess the conscious quality of appearing, and are said to be among the "contents" of our minds. I can see no sufficient reason for believing that this account of the status of sensations and of images is true. As it seems to me, sense-data (so-called) are selections from matter of fact of which we are transcendently aware. This statement, if it is defensible, must hold for all sense-data, that is to say, for sense-data that, like colours, appear to be outside our apparent bodies, and also for sense-data that like joint-muscle-tendon sensations appear to be inside our apparent bodies. I should say the same about images. In the case both of sensations and of images, however, the defence of the views I am here expressing so summarily would be a protracted affair. It is not a necessary consequence of the general contention I have put forward in this lecture. I am only remarking parenthetically that it is my opinion.

(4) From the fact that dreams, unless they are very recent, are so very hard to remember, it may perhaps be inferred that the conscious quality may exist when it is not effectively present in waking self-consciousness. The same argument applies to the conscious quality in a fever or in great fatigue, and it may be supplemented by indirect evidence of the presence of some mind-like process that might have been subsequently forgotten in the waking state. In these matters I hold that it is rash to attempt to advance very far beyond our base, that is to say, very far from waking self-acquaintance. There may perhaps be floating experiences, "little thoughts of q", to use William James's phrase, which are aware of "q" and are also reflexively self-aware. There may also be clusters of such experiences, sometimes

ephemeral, sometimes stubborn and dark. This would not seem to be impossible, although the clinical and other evidence adduced in support of it may be interpreted in very various and in very conflicting ways. It is easy, however, to slip into fairyland in these journeys, and I think we should leave the fairies and the ghouls alone. In any case it seems to me that there is very insufficient evidence for the existence of *sub-minds* or of *un-minds* additional to the "minds" of waking experience.

(5) Nothing that I have said implies either that waking minds could exist discarnately, or that, when they exist, there is a union of two substances, the mind and the body. All I have said is consistent with the view that it is our bodies that are awake when, as we say, *we* are awake. It is also consistent with very different theories, including the theory of metaphysical dualism.

(6) If it be said that there must be something wrong with any account of these matters that so much as admits the possibility of a metaphysical dualism I should reply that such metaphysical dualism is a two-substance theory and that, in the concrete sense of "substance", it is largely a matter of definition whether there be such a logical possibility or not. If all that be meant by a concrete "substance" is some distinctive type of unity of events, then our waking selves may be "substances" in that sense—for they do form a unity, perhaps of the type in question. If, on the other hand, it is held that a concrete substance must at least have uninterrupted continuity in time, then, although Peter wakes up Peter, and Paul wakes up Paul, there is no convincing evidence that the sleeping "Peter" has any Petrine "self" or that the sleeping "Paul" has any Pauline "self". In this sense of "substance", the substantiality of Peter's self or of Paul's is suspect every night.

(7) If it be said that our minds have certain properties that no physical body can have (e.g. the property of being logical or the property of being loyal) I should reply that a question of this kind is also, very largely, a matter of definition. I allow that logic and loyalty seem to be properties wholly inexplicable in

terms, say, of nervous transmission. On the other hand, I cannot allow that wherever a special property can be shown to exist, a special "substance" may legitimately be inferred *ad hoc*. If it were held that we are "minding" bodies, and that psychologists, logicians and moralists are concerned with the "minding" aspects of our existence although physiologists are not, I can see no adequate reason for believing that such a view is just nonsense.

(8) If the problem is supposed to concern, not concrete empirical "substances" but substance in some recondite metaphysical sense, I should like to be told in detail what that recondite metaphysical sense is supposed to be. In general I should deny that we are bound to believe that a metaphysically vital substance is necessary in order to hold empirical life together, or that a metaphysically fiery substance keeps empirical flames going. I should similarly deny that we must suppose that a metaphysically egoistic substance keeps empirical egos together.

III

The Implications of Idealism

THE question I want to consider, in the next place, is not so much whether philosophical idealism be true—though I would not avoid that topic—as whether, if it were true, it should transfigure cosmology, anthropology and theology. How and to what extent do the world, man and God look very different to the eyes of a philosophical idealist from the way they look to other men, including other philosophical men? The first impact of philosophical idealism upon any of our minds, I think, is full of mystery and of delight. It is a marvellous dawn that seems to spring, not from dreams and fancies, but from hard thinking and from rigorous argument. Should it fade into a light not dissimilar from the light of common day or does it retain its magic when the rapture of its first enchantment has to yield to inevitable familiarity?

Part of the reason for the enchantment, I think, is that the term idealism suggests ideals, especially ideals of beauty and of righteousness. That, however, is largely a trick of words. Ideals may always be made out of ideas, but plenty of ideas are not ideals, and, quite obviously, are not aesthetic or moral ideals. Yet in most forms of philosophical idealism the gravamen of the argument is an affair of *ideas*. That is my present theme. The rest will come a good deal later.

This being understood, we may say that philosophical idealism has two principal species, the epistemological and the ontological. The epistemological species of it has two main varieties. I shall call them pan-idea-ism and pan-ideatism. According to pan-idea-ism, things *are* ideas and ideas *are* things. According to pan-ideatism, although ideas may refer to things without

86

being these things, they, nevertheless, must ideate the things to which they refer. Therefore, according to this theory, we have always to do with ideated things, with things *sub specie idearum* and never with things *per se*. In the ontological species of philosophical idealism the contention is that nothing except spirit can exist. I propose to call this doctrine pan-psychism, although that term is sometimes interpreted rather more narrowly. Pan-psychism is monistic if it maintains that there is only one great spirit, a single spiritual whole of experience, or the like. It is pluralistic in those philosophies which declare that reality consists of a society of spirits, or of a mob of spirits.

The ontological species of philosophical idealism has the livelier interest for us in these lectures; for natural theology is metaphysical, that is, ontological. Nevertheless, it seems best to begin by discussing idealisms of the epistemological kind. There are two reasons for this preference. The first of them is that modern philosophy has tended to be busier about epistemological idealism than about pan-psychism. Indeed, many philosophers of repute appear to believe that although the epistemological highway has no exit, all that a genuine philosopher can do, and all that he should want to do, is to trudge along it. Any other design, they seem to think, is a mark of philosophical frailty. If that were true, philosophical theism would have to fall into step, perhaps in the van, perhaps somewhere else. The second, if true, would supply a much stronger reason. It is the argument that epistemological idealism *entails* ontological idealism, and is the best if not the only way of proving that conclusion. The highway (it is believed) *has* an exit, and it leads to the spiritual city which is our home.

Pan-idea-ism is a form of pure phenomenalism. On its showing, ideas are what they mean, mean what they are, and there is nothing else. It need not, however, be a sensory phenomenalism. Indeed it could not be that, unless all ideas were sensations. To speak accurately, it extends its hospitality to all ideas, that is to say, to sensa, percepts, images, memory-ideas and concepts together with various complexes of these.

On this theory there is no room for illusion or error, and no possibility of any transcendent reference on the part of any idea. Hence I should say that the theory was non-suited from the start, and I gave some reasons in support of that judgement in the last lecture. Here I shall add some more. Let us consider Berkeley's example of the trees in the park. According to pan-idea-ism, strictly interpreted, this phrase "the trees in the park" shelters a multitude of different ideas. If the trees are perceived they are arboreal percepts. If they are remembered they are arboreal memories. If they are imaged they are arboreal images. If they are only conceived they are arboreal concepts. The same is true of the park. That pleasance is shredded into a mass of "epistemological objects". It is a name for pleasance-percepts, pleasance-images and the rest. "Trees" and "park" are collections of *mentities*, if I may be allowed to invent, for convenience, a portmanteau-word that I admit to be a barbarism, without classical or (so far as I know) even mediaeval warrant.

Such a theory, I submit, overlooks the very first requisite in any adequate account of what we mean by "the trees in the park". It forgets the trees. Therefore I do not think I need solemnly discuss its bearing upon nature, man and God. If the theory could be believed, "God" would either be a name for all the mentities there are (supposing that the theory could give an intelligible meaning to the word "all", and was not self-condemned by having to maintain that the word "all" is also a mentity), or would be a name for a deiform concept, a deiform retrospect and so on. In the latter case God's status need not be different from that of a devil-concept or a diabolical memory, from a conceived- or from a remembered-Jabberwock; and so forth—in short, from a puerility.

We should notice, however, that pan-idea-ism should not necessarily be reproached with solipsism (if solipsism be a reproach) and I shall linger over this matter for a little space. I think it is informative for our present theme.

The reproach of solipsism might be justified if all these mentities had to be *someone's* mentities, your ideas or mine. I believe it to be true in fact that all mentities are someone's mentities. *Quoad nos*, is more precisely, *quoad quemque*, and I have argued that what are called "epistemological objects" expressly or covertly imply the presence of a mind whose nature is most clearly exhibited in its conscious quality. Phenomenalism, however, could have no place for the sort of *ipse* that the theory of solipsism implies, and therefore could not be solipsistic. According to phenomenalism the ego, if there were one, would be just an idea like any other mentity. It could not be what Berkeley, for example, thought it was, something that had ideas without itself being an idea.

A certain type of solipsism would indeed be consistent with pan-idea-ism. If ideas never "float" in a detached way but are always clustered into the sort of company that is usually described as a private mind, and if these private companies never unite to form a regiment, the result would be a form of solipsism. These additional assumptions, however, need not be made by any pan-idea-ist. Thus, although it is difficult to deny that concepts, in some relevant sense, are privately entertained, occurring only when someone's conception occurs, it may be stoutly asserted, none the less, that conceptual mentities are not private in the sense in which sensory mentities are private. We are sometimes informed, for example, that conceptual mentities are universal while sensory mentities are particular, and are further informed, in authoritative quarters, that one of the relevant distinctions in this instance is that universal mentities are not "subjective" but are "inter-subjective" and therefore, in a special sense, more public than private. In these genial breezes the mentities may shiver a little less visibly. In any case solipsism is an imputation that pan-idea-ists can effectively repel.

But let us leave this by-path.

I have said that I did not intend to enquire further into what pan-idea-ism had to say about the trees in the park. The reason was that it had forgotten the trees. In other words the theory, being wholly non-transcendent in its account of ideas, cannot be a witness to nature, to man or to God. For these are *not* mere ideas. It may be replied, however, as we hinted in our last lecture, that ideas, consistently with the theory of pan-idea-ism, might be held to be capable of generating a certain type of quasi-transcendence, by means of their context, although only to other ideas. A contextual quasi-transcendence of this kind (it is suggested) would meet the objection.

I think it is clear that the quasi-transcendence thus supposed to be generable is not transcendence proper, and consequently that the reply is quite inadequate. I shall try to show this very briefly.

The theory of contextual quasi-transcendence is similar to the historical philosophy of associationism, with the very important difference that the connection of the associated ideas, instead of being capricious and unreasonable, is said to be steady and logical. As F. H. Bradley picturesquely said: "Association marries only universals."

The difference between such a marriage of universals, and the less hallowed and more promiscuous union of associated ideas as described by the Mills and by some other well-known British philosophers, is certainly very considerable. In the main, however, the objection to both forms of the contextual theory is the same. This insuperable objection is that union in a context, although it is sometimes described as "meaning", is not the sort of meaning that is involved in the transcendence of ideas. Ideas that cling together do not refer to one another, do not indicate one another, any more than a barnacle indicates a ship. Most of us would say that only minds can "mean" or "refer" in this sense; but if "floating ideas" or other mentities that are not minds in the ordinary sense have such a power of meaning, indicating or referring, the power is not derived from any context but is presupposed in the ideas themselves. The contextual theory seems to be derived from the correct observation that association is or involves some sort of redintegration. Ideas that have belonged to a certain context tend to "revive" the rest of the context. That they tend to do so seems to be a fact of human psychology, pretty well attested. But it is clear, on reflection, that any such contextual "revival" is not the transcendent reference of any idea whatever.

Consider, for instance (as we considered in the last lecture), the sort of transcendence that is involved in memory. In memory some present event B is the memory of some past event A. If the present event B does not refer to the past event A, there is no memory. What does the theory of contextual or associative redintegration tell us? It says that the present idea B calls up another idea A which either coalesces with it in the present or immediately succeeds it. Let it be allowed that this occurs. It is still clear that what is said to be "revived" and is in fact either simultaneous with B or successive to it cannot be the past event A. The dates of the various ideas prohibit that interpretation. In other words the new B–A context could not conceivably be a reference to the past event A.

The argument is quite general and is not restricted to memory transcendence, although it is peculiarly easy to grasp in that instance. I do not need to pursue it further. I have discussed contextual idea-ism, partly because of the frequency with which it appears in the literature of this subject, and partly because, if it were true, it would be one of the very few arguments that would build a bridge between pan-idea-ism and pan-psychism. For then it would be true that in so far as any idea or other mentity transcended itself it would necessarily refer to the remainder of a context of the same order as itself, that is to say to other ideas or to other mentities.

Let us turn now to pan-ideatism.

According to this theory ideas may and do have transcendent reference. The theory further asserts, however, that nothing is apprehended except through ideas, and that this circumstance inevitably affects everything that we apprehend. Whatever is not apprehended (we are told) is, in relation to us, nothing. Whatever is apprehended, even if it be not an idea or a context of ideas, is inevitably ideated. Whatever is ideated must be stamped with an idead component.

That is the general contention. In examining it we may conveniently make a start with an extreme but very usual form of the theory, namely that our ideas inform us *that* things-in-themselves exist, although they can never tell us *what* these things (or this Thing) are (or is).

That, according to many of his interpreters, is what Kant maintained; and Mr. Paton, in the admirable commentary to which I have referred in a former lecture,[1] puts the point as follows: "An appearance is nothing in itself; it must be an appearance *to* something, and an appearance *of* something. . . . The very word appearance implies a reference to 'something' in itself."[2] That is part of the contention. Of another part of it Mr. Paton says: "Things as they are in themselves are the very same things that appear to us, although they appear to us, and because of our powers of knowing must appear to us, as different from what they are in themselves."[3]

One is tempted to ask "Must they indeed?" There is no logical contradiction whatever in supposing that a thing which appears to us may reveal its nature as well as its bare existence, and the alternative view, namely that it reveals its existence but never its nature, seems to me to encounter intolerable difficulties. How do we know, except by interpreting our knowledge of the natures of things, that there are things in the plural and not just one great Thing-in-itself in the singular? What, in general, can be meant by knowing that something exists if we do not have the faintest inkling of its nature and properties?

Regarding such questions Mr. Paton says: "We might indeed object that differences and likenesses in appearances must imply some sort of differences or likenesses in the thing, or things, that appear; but we have no means of knowing the respect in which things-in-themselves, or their qualities, differ from or resemble one another. We do not even know that there is a plurality of such things, or that things-in-themselves can have qualities, although we must think of them, by analogy, as a plurality and as having qualities. In such circumstances a state-

[1] Lecture V of the First Series.
[2] *Kant's Metaphysics of Experience*, II, 445.   [3] *Ibid.*, I, 61.

ment of their differences and likenesses is too vague to convey positive meaning".[1] It would seem, however, that according to Mr. Paton the situation is not too vague for the very explicit negative statement I have just quoted from his pages, viz. that the things must appear to us "as different from what they are in themselves".

In another passage Mr. Paton says: "An appearance is always the appearance of a thing wholly independent of our mind and existing in its own right. Even the spatial and temporal characteristics which it possesses are appearances of real characteristics of the thing as it is in itself. Because of the nature of our minds, things must appear to us as spatial and temporal; but it is because of the character of the thing in itself that we see one object as round and another as square. We do not know what this character is, but we cannot regard it as roundness or squareness, because we cannot regard it as spatial at all. Indeed, we know the thing only as it appears to us, or as it is in relation to our minds: and consequently we do not know whether we can rightly speak of it as 'existing' or 'possessing characteristics', since for us these terms must imply a reference to time and space."[2]

I do not think that the statements in the last passage are consistent with one another, and I cannot think that all of them are consistent with all the others that I have cited from Mr. Paton's pages. That, I believe, is Kant's fault and not his commentator's. The real trouble, I submit, is that Kant's position in this matter is untenable.

Consider, once again, what Mr. Paton says about time. Temporal appearances, he says, are appearances of real characteristics in the thing; but the thing's real characteristics are not temporal. How could that happen? If the thing-in-itself changed would there not be concomitant variation *ex hypothesi* between the temporal appearances of its changing characteristics and the real changes in the real thing? How could such correspondence be other than temporal? If the thing-in-itself didn't change, how could the changes in the temporal appearances be appear-

---

[1] *Kant's Metaphysics of Experience*, I, 168 n.   [2] *Ibid.*, II, 417.

ances of real characteristics in the thing? To suppose so would be to infer correspondence from *non-concomitant* variations, to hold that there *is* some specific kind of correspondence because there is *no* correspondence. Are we then to say that the thing-in-itself neither changes nor doesn't? That I submit is downright impossible even in God.

Not even Mr. Paton's silvery tones (I believe) can mitigate the harsh sentence that must be passed upon this aspect of Kantianism. Certainty regarding a thing's existence cannot be intelligibly combined with total ignorance of its nature and properties. On the other hand, the extreme form of the theory of pan-ideatism that I have just been considering seems to be the theory's compulsory terminus. The theory is that the ideation of anything affects that thing's reality in a way that can never be absent but remains unknown in its manner, range and type. If, in any instance, we could subduct the mind's contribution with accuracy we should be acquainted in that instance with the thing as it is in itself; but that is contrary to the hypothesis.

In other words, pan-ideatism results in complete agnosticism, and it is useless to consider what it could tell us about nature, man and God, if it were true. If the theory were true there would be nothing to know *in* these things, not even if they were the same or different.

There is therefore a complete estoppel of the theory. Consequently its initial assumptions must be revised. Plainly, when we examine the matter, we perceive that it does not *follow* that because I am aware of X, X itself becomes either me or mine, or, more generally, that X must suffer an ideational change because it is ideated. If this does not follow, we need not believe that it happens, and we are at liberty to believe that what our ideas tell us about nature, man and God is just what nature, man and God really are.

That is the main point, but I shall append certain observations.

Pan-ideatism might avoid solipsism just as pan-idea-ism can

avoid that conclusion. To be sure if it is the ego that transforms everything that is known, the shadow that it casts would be the shadow of the ego; and that must mean the shadow of any ego that knows. *Quoad nos*, as I have said, must mean *quoad quemque*. In that case, both in pan-ideatism and in pan-idea-ism, Peter would be petrine to himself, his friends would all be petrine to him and so would his countryside and his God. If it were held, however, that ideas and appearances need not be anybody's ideas and appearances, that we can dive beneath the surface of egoity and reach something deeper, or muddier or at any rate *different*, the theory of solipsism (which is based upon a high-grade interpretation of what is meant by *ipse*) would be rejected.

That is my first additional observation on this topic. My second observation concerns the common opinion that certain forms of epistemological argument, including one (I mean Berkeley's) that has been justly renowned in and beyond these islands for more than two centuries, protect and advance the logical transition to an exclusively spiritual ontology.

It is past disputing, of course, that Berkeley maintained that reality consisted of spirits and of their ideas. It is also worth remarking, however, that Berkeley, when he set about to explain *why* the mind was neither figured nor coloured although sensa were figured and coloured, averred that sensa were "in" the mind "not by way of mode or attribute, but only by way of idea".[1] He went on to say, it is true, that "what philosophers say of subject and mode seems very groundless and unintelligible",[2] adding that he himself was tempted to discard all these categories. But he did not discard them when he came to deal with minds themselves. According to him, we were "minds or spiritual substances",[3] and God, also, was a spiritual substance. The inference is that nature, according to Berkeley, was "in" minds in a quite peculiar sense, and that minds and God were not "in" mind in any such way. The qualities of sensa, or the compages of sensa that some men call nature, were not the qualities of minds. Their *esse* was indeed supposed to rest upon

[1] *Principles*, sect. 49.   [2] Later in the same paragraph.   [3] *Ibid.*, sect. 89.

their *inesse* in some mind; but they were not minds or like minds, and I do not think they could properly be described as mentities. Their *inesse* involved a sense of the word "in" that had no parallel elsewhere. It was not the honest sense in which one's tea is in one's tea-cup, and it was not the philosophical sense in which an attribute is "in" a substance. It might be described, with equal appropriateness, as existence *before* a mind, confronting the mind; and that theory would yield the harmless tautology that whatever is related to a mind by confronting it does actually confront it.

In short, for Berkeley as for so many others, the reputed bridge between epistemology and pan-psychism was so very frail that we should not, I think, trust it at all. Consequently in passing, as I now do, to pan-psychism, I propose to consider those arguments, and those arguments only, that are independent of epistemology.

The chief such arguments, I think, are (*a*) the argument from universal interiority, (*b*) the argument from universal continuity, (*c*) the argument from indefeasible thinghood.

(*a*) Idealism prides itself, very often, upon being the metaphysics of inside information. We are external observers, it is said, of everything except ourselves, and have to keep our distance, even if it is only our "psychic" distance, from everything else. But, according to pan-psychists, we do have inside information about ourselves and we do know, in the interior way, "what it is to be a subject" to be "in oneself and for oneself".

Consequently the pan-psychist's question is whether it is reasonable to suppose that this in-and-out predicament is a peculiarity of minds. He thinks that it should be presumed to hold, in some form, of all existence. Although Professor Alexander was not a pan-psychist his terms are convenient here. Why should we not say that everything that exists "enjoys" itself in the interior way and "contemplates" other beings in the exterior way? There would be a serious difficulty, it is true, if (as some would interpret Alexander) a being that contemplates must contemplate what is lower than itself. In that case something would have to be incapable of contemplating, since it would have nothing lower to contemplate. Nevertheless, it might "enjoy" itself and there would be no logical impossibility in holding that the lowliest of beings might contemplate what is higher than itself (in a stupid and dazed apprehension) and might contemplate its peers with less vacuous ineptitude.

This seems to me to be a very weak argument. In our own case, as I argued in the last lecture, we do have reflexive acquaintance with ourselves and we also have transcendent acquaintance with other things (as well as, I think, with ourselves). I also maintained, however, that it was imprudent to try to generalize this situation much beyond the conscious quality of our waking experience. I see no reason to retract that opinion. If we could show that everything that exists should be presumed to have transcendent apprehension of other things I allow that there might be a specious inference by analogy to a universal capacity for reflexive self-apprehension. Such a presumption, however, is just the presuming of the truth of pan-psychism. A being that had transcendent apprehension would have to be some sort of psyche, or at least a psychoid.

Few philosophers want to assert that minds are natural miracles. If, however, the alternative be to deny that minds have any distinctive powers that are peculiar to them, there is something to be said for this extremely chastened form of nature-miracle. We may agree with Alexander that there is a universal relation of "compresence" between all the entities in nature; but such "compresence" neither is nor implies mutual apprehension or co-cognition. Such an idea (as Alexander himself affirmed in a way) is far too slight and far too viewy to be constraining. If there were substance in it, that substance would be derived from the second argument, the argument from universal continuity, to which I am about to proceed.

Before doing so, however, I should like, briefly and parenthetically, to mention two matters. The first concerns the meaning of the phrase "inside information" in this connection.

G

Plainly the "internality" is metaphorical and has to be distinguished from the literal sense in which it is true to say that a man has private information regarding his own insides, information that no foreign observer can have. Regarding such literal internality I am inclined to adhere to the opinion I expressed in the last lecture, namely that organic sensa have the same status as other sensa and, like the others, are transcendently and not reflexively known. My second parenthetical observation concerns the opinion of M. Bergson and of some others that "inside information" includes all that is covered by the term "sympathy".[1] Although we cannot get inside another man's skin, we can, according to this philosophy, get inside his mind in the same metaphorical sense as that in which we "get inside" our own minds. A theist might similarly speak boldly of suspiring with deity or of being transessentiated into God.[2] Here I cannot agree either with Bergson or the theists, but I shall not discuss such problems now. We shall meet them again.

(*b*) As I have said, the second argument in support of panpsychism is drawn from the supposed implications of the general continuity of existence.

In the widest way, it may be affirmed that the All is "all of a piece". Consequently, we are told, the mere idea of a radical pluralism in the *kinds* of things is always an evil fantasy.

If so, the argument "There are minds, therefore all is mind" might certainly be used. It would seem, however, that the argument "There are bodies, therefore all is body" would be equally legitimate, as well as the contentions that all must be alive since there is life, and that all must be divine since there is a God or Gods many. In other words, pan-psychism, in terms of this argument, might not seem to be in a stronger position than pan-somatism, pan-biosis or pantheism. The Cartesian *Dubito ergo sum*, it is true, may here be impressed into one of its many philosophical services. We may doubt whether material

[1] And also by "empathy".
[2] Cf. J. Maritain, *The Degrees of Knowledge*, Eng. trans., pp. 454 and 456.

things exist, whether living matter exists, whether God exists. But the existence of a doubt implies the existence of something mental. Mental existence in some sense may therefore be held to be indubitable; and if everything is of the same kind, panpsychism, in some sense, would be a consequence.

I do not think it is necessary to linger over this supremely general argument. It depends upon the denial of ultimate pluralism in the kinds of things, and this denial does not stand to reason. We may ask, however, whether the argument may not be stronger in some more special form.

A favourite contention in a more specialized form of the theory is derived from speculations regarding the origin of minds. Streams, we are told, cannot rise higher than their sources. That I believe is true about streams, unless they are fountains at the source; but I should not be inclined to say that skylarks cannot rise above their nests. If we suppose, however, that our metaphysics in this matter should be governed by the behaviour of streams and not by the behaviour of skylarks, we obtain the result that mental beings must arise from mental beings, "it being as impossible", said Locke, "that things wholly void of knowledge, and operating blindly, and without any perception, should produce a knowing being, as it is impossible that a triangle should make itself three angles bigger than two right ones".[1] There has been a great mass of philosophical testimony to the same effect. Listen, for example, to Professor Dixon in his recent delightful lectures in this University. "To regard the advent of consciousness", he affirmed in one of many eloquent passages to the same general effect, "that is the world's coming to a knowledge of itself, the awakening of a soul in nature, to take this unexampled overwhelming fact as of course and for granted, as no singular event, or anything out of the way noteworthy or surprising, or again as a thing of accident among other accidents, were for me no easier a thought than the notion of the Himalayas giving way to laughter, or the ocean writing its own autobiography. When you begin to suppose

[1] *Essay*, IV, chap. x, sect. 5.

such things you make a clown of reason and adorn it with cap and bells."[1]

Locke, as it happened, used this argument to show that men's cogitative power must be derived from God's cogitative power. Professor Dixon (despite his insistence on the overwhelming singularity of mentality) used the argument as an intimation of the truth of pan-biosis rather than of the truth of pan-psychism. For him, life is a convenient middleman between mind and matter, capable (as experience seems to show) of coming to consciousness, and also capable, like the despised Himalayas, of becoming too sleepy to laugh. I mention the divergence in order to show that this argument is very nearly as elastic as the supremely general one we have just considered. If you insist on the indubitable existence of minds and also insist that like must arise from like, you obtain the conclusion that minds must always have existed. By the same argument you would also prove that the pre-mental in nature must have had the rudiments of laughter and of penmanship in it, even if certain particular aggregates of apparently non-mental atoms, such as the Himalayas, do not seem to laugh, and if other particular aggregates, such as the ocean, are too old to afflict the world with their autobiographies.

The essential premiss in the argument is that like must come from like. That, in its turn, is a more special case of the general principle that causes and effects are always and necessarily instances of the equivalence of similars. In the first series of these lectures we had occasion to examine that principle pretty closely, and we were unable to accept it. In the past, so far as we know, there appears to have been a certain continuity in all the changes that have occurred. We may reasonably expect the same of the future. Such continuity, however, has not prohibited the emergence of radical differences. All we can do, and all that we need to do, is to explore the patterns of change. We are not entitled to set bounds to the degree of novelty that such patterns may show. Therefore we are not entitled to say that if souls

[1] *The Human Situation*, pp. 383 f.

were novelties when they first arose, the thing would be inconceivablè. Therefore in so far as pan-psychism is said to be built upon this circumstance, its foundations are insecure.

The same has to be said of the common argument that pan-psychism gives the only possible solution of the mind-body problem. There is obviously the appearance of interaction between mind and body. A lecturer voluntarily uses his voice (which is physical) and this physical event may arouse attention (which is mental) in his hearers. This being admitted, if we hold that minds and bodies are too dissimilar to interact, we have also to hold, in some way or other, either that all so-called minds are really bodies, or that all so-called bodies are really minds. The suggested alternative of parallelism (that is, that mind acts on mind and body on body and that the two just correspond) is an absurdity unless it is regarded merely as a provisional rule of method. Metaphysically speaking, it would be a miracle on the grandest scale unless the meaning were that minds and bodies were different aspects of the same thing, in which case everything would really have a psychical aspect, that is to say, would really *be* psychical. The entire argument, however, depends upon the alleged similarity (or identity) of cause with effect. Without that premiss, *cadit questio.*

(*c*) The third way of defending pan-psychism is to argue from the implications of indefeasible thinghood. Minds, it is held, are the only possible substances, and nothing but a substance can exist.

The principle of substance has often found favour in Western philosophy, but has sometimes fallen out of favour. Even its enemies, however, would have to admit that it is a stubborn, if eradicable, principle, and that in some of its possible senses it is quite peculiarly stubborn. Therefore if it could be shown that minds were the only possible substances, in some stubborn sense of substance, the fact should not be disdainfully entreated.

One argument of this kind is closely connected with what I have just said about mind and body. It is held that *no* two substances can ever interact. Each substance possesses only its own states. No substance can transfer any of its states to any other substance. Therefore either there is only one substance, to wit reality as a whole, or else the appearance of interaction between different substances of whatever kind must really consist of the concomitant variations in the states of the several substances and of that only. *Tertium non datur.*

The most celebrated and, as many think, the most persuasive form of this metaphysics is a Leibnizian pan-psychism. I shall deal with it in a rather general way.

Consider what Leibniz said about the clocks. Suppose that the universe were an immense assemblage of clocks, each ticking away on its own account but all keeping time, or, in other words, synchronizing and so corresponding. In that case the clocks, without influencing one another, would vary concomitantly and so would present the appearance, but only the appearance, of causal inter-relation.

But why should the clocks agree? The thing would be a miracle or, in Hegel's kindlier language, a philosophical romance if no explanation of the agreement could be given. According to Leibniz, God pre-established their harmony. The trouble is that God, in terms of the theory, could do no such thing. The divine substance *is* a substance. Therefore all its changes and all its acts are, by hypothesis, confined to itself. In other words, deity could neither make the clocks, nor act as a synchronizing master-clock, nor correct the clocks by hand like a college porter.

According to Leibniz and to many of his modern admirers the main difficulty could be solved by remembering that we are dealing not with clocks but with minds of various grades of sleepiness whose business is to represent. Each natural thing has "no windows"[1] or, as we might say with greater accuracy, has no *open* windows. Each is self-enclosed by a metaphysical necessity. It is not, however, precluded from mirroring or

[1] Cf. the tolerant Queen Elizabeth, who "would make no windows into men's souls".

representing what is not itself. That it can do at home without stirring out of doors. Therefore if all substances are minds, we do have a tenable theory.

Since we seem to have the capacity of thinking or of representing entirely within ourselves, this part of the theory seems intelligible. But is it? If there were not merely no *open* windows but also no windows at all, the mirrors would not work. Let it be replied that although mirrors wouldn't work, minds would. I say they wouldn't. Representation, I allow, is something that a mind does. I shall further allow that a mind's representations are its own, and I shall suppose, although I don't believe it, that a theory of non-transcendent representation is quite satisfactory in the epistemological way. The correspondence between the representations of the different natural beings would still have to be explained. God would have to signal to them all and he could not signal because, like all the rest, he would be just a system of irrevocably stay-at-home mirrors.

In short, the theory is impossible without God and impossible with him. It requires him to do what it expressly precludes him from doing.

Before passing to another and (I think) to a stronger form of the argument from indefeasible thinghood I should like to interpolate a remark of some importance. It is natural to interpret theories of Leibniz-like pan-psychism as if their meaning was just that the things we believe to exist (say, neutrons and protons and positrons) really had certain mental potencies very naturally disregarded in common physics. The theory, however, could take other forms and it would, for instance, be rather like Berkeley's if it held that reality consisted of a select company of high-grade spirits, each of them rich in feelings and sensations. On that view, neutrons, positrons and the like need not be supposed to exist at all. They might just be sensory representations experienced by (that is to say, within) the aforesaid select company of minds.

The stronger argument in support of pan-psychism of which I gave notice above asserts that any substance, to be a substance at all, must possess a high degree of unity and integrity, and that nothing except a mind fulfils this requirement.

On the ground that only the whole can be complete and self-sufficient, many philosophers have inferred that the whole is the only genuine substance; but these same philosophers have frequently jibbed at the idea that the whole is a mind. Their own psychical integrity, they think, forbids absorption in the substance of the Whole. Tennyson's lines are appropriate:

> Dark is the world to thee; thyself art the reason why:
> For is He not all but that which has power to feel "I am I"?[1]

Such philosophers often attempt to distinguish God from the Absolute on the ground, principally, that God is a mind but that the Absolute is not. It is super-mental, they say.

As we have seen, however,[2] "all that there is", or "all that there has been up to the present moment", need not be a complete, integrated, perfect totality in the sense of this argument. Indeed, a monistic pan-psychism conceived along these lines is vulnerable at several points. A pluralistic pan-psychism, however, might be less vulnerable. Its substances, up to the present moment, may not have been "complete" in all relevant senses, but they might still be as complete as any substance could be, and it might still be argued that only minds could be the "substantial" members of a reality that had "substantial" constituents.

Indeed, a pluralistic pan-psychist may appear to have rather an easy journey so long as he is attacking his opponents. His principal enemy is material substance, living or dead, and here he can use familiar and not ineffective arguments. Corporeal substance, if it existed, would be extended spatially and temporally. But extension contains *partes extra partes* to infinity. It has therefore no ultimate units, and if, *per impossibile*, there were such units, any corporeal substance composed of them would lack what Leibniz called the *vinculum substantiale*, its inner bond of coherence. The psyche, it is said, provides a *vinculum spirituale* that is also a *vinculum substantiale*. If anyone

[1] In *The Higher Pantheism*.   [2] In the first series.

knows of another or of a better *vinculum*, let him produce it. If he cannot, it is reasonable to hold that minds are substances, and that we know of nothing else that could be a substance. For the comfort of the timid it should here be remarked that such a pan-psychism does not necessarily imply that there are no bodies. All it asserts in this connection is that there cannot be any merely material bodies. What is material, if anything is material, must be immaterially united by a psychic *vinculum*.

The positive part of this contention seems to be much less impressive than the negative. The *vinculum substantiale* has the important office of ensuring substantial persistence through a period of time. It is just here that the *vinculum spirituale* is weakest. If pluralistic pan-psychism is interpreted in the light of human waking experience, sleep and trances seriously perturb the theory of a persistent conscious self. It is difficult not to invoke the persistence of the body.

Accordingly, the inference would seem to be that the proof from the indefeasible integrity of substance is not a solid foundation for pan-psychism, even supposing that the conception of "substance" has all the metaphysical importance that is claimed for it in these arguments. As I explained at the beginning of this lecture, however, the principal aim of the lecture is to consider the extent to which idealistic theories should transfigure our conceptions of nature, human personality, and deity if they were accepted. I have therefore to examine this question with regard to pan-psychism.

Let us, firstly, consider "nature" in the sense of that word which excludes human nature and the divine nature.

As I remarked, almost incidentally, in the earlier discussion, there would seem to be two principal forms of pluralistic pan-psychism. These may be roughly described as the Leibnizian and the Berkeleyan.

According to the (usual) Leibnizian form of pan-psychism, the entities that we commonly consider material, such as protons, or positrons or genes, are really souls. They have a low grade of appetition and of perception of a *very* "sub-conscious" type, and are self-maintaining continuants so long as they endure. There is more in them than physics reckons with, although physics, for its own purposes, may legitimately and accurately neglect these additional features.

Therefore, if the theory were true, there would be a metaphysical (but only a metaphysical) transfiguration of the usual beliefs of common sense and of positive science. For atoms and the like would be more, and might be much more, than they seem to be. On the other hand, the hopes that idealism seems so often to excite need not be fostered. What is hoped in so many quarters from a "spiritual view of reality" is that spirits of the higher grade, and especially spirits of the human order, are not the children of "a thousand chances 'neath the indifferent sky", temporary intruders in a neutral and callous environment, but are dominant in what we sometimes call "the scheme of things". The metaphysical transfiguration of electrons and their like into an incredibly stupid sort of "soul" has no tendency to mitigate the empirical contrasts on which, say, the fear of human extinction, human helplessness and human insignificance ultimately rest. If what we fear is that the higher type of spirit may starve, suffer and die, that its candle-life is brief and precarious, how are these fears allayed if we are assured that the "indifferent sky" is composed of very stupid souls, and not of wholly apsychic units of energy? Is an earthquake less terrible if it is low-grade souls, not *mere* stones and dirt, that swallow us up? If a man is dying of typhoid, is he comforted by the reflection that *living* things, viz. bacteria, are working his ruin and are enjoying their brief proliferating lives? If, as Lord Russell once said, "the whole temple of man's achievements must inevitably be buried beneath the débris of a universe in ruins",[1] what man and what kindly angel would be cheered by the thought that the débris would be composed of psychic nit-wits subconsciously triumphant, unconsciously and unconscionably busy?

It may be suggested, indeed, that there is always a certain promise in pan-psychism that is absent from other theories.

[1] In his essay "The Free Man's Worship."

The Implications of Idealism

These low-grade spirits may develop higher powers. That, I suppose, is possible, but it is also possible that the higher grades of spirits might deteriorate and become even stupider than a stone, even more somnolent than the Himalayas. Again, if pan-psychism were false, but if it were true that the cogitative could arise from the incogitative, the doors of hope would not be barred. The cogitative has arisen, and might arise again. Therefore the death of civilization and of other temples of the spirit need not be permanent, pan-psychism or no pan-psychism.

The second species of pluralistic pan-psychism is, broadly speaking, Berkeleyan, and holds that reality consists of high-grade minds that have ideas. In Berkeley's form of the theory the highest mind of all, namely God's, created finite spirits and guaranteed the order and stability of what Berkeley called their "ideas of sense". This form of theism contains enormous difficulties (We shall notice some of them later.) It creates philosophical embarrassments that heavily off-set the services to philosophical theism that it is supposed to render. For simplicity of exposition, however, we may, for the moment, omit the theism of the theory. In that case what any man calls "nature" would be a name for the ideas of sense that are "in" his mind, and reality, as I have said, would consist of high-grade spirits each having "ideas" in his own mind.

The difficulties in such a system are prodigious. To mention but one, we could hardly have evidence of the existence of other people unless some of our "ideas of sense" testified to the existence of something not ourselves that was *not* an idea of sense. Even if, by sympathy or in some other way, we were acquainted non-sensorily with the minds of our fellows, we do interpret what we call "their" gestures and "their" words as evidence of *their* mentality. It is surely most odd to believe that what we call a clap of thunder, say, is *only* an "idea of sense" in some human auditor's mind, but that what we call the clapping of hands is an "idea of sense" that testifies to another man's enthusiasm. If the second "idea" conveys transcendent information, why not the first? Indeed Berkeley introduced his sketchy and embarrassing theistic theory precisely because he saw that some such transcendent evidence must be supposed to be given by *all* ideas of sense.

Let us waive the difficulties, however, and consider only the *difference* that such a spiritual theory of reality would make to our common views about nature. As it seems to me, the difference, although it is a metaphysical difference, would be very profound. "Nature", it is true, would *look* the same to one of Berkeley's converts as to his impenitent opponents. Visible grass would be visibly green; tangible velvet would be soft to the touch. There would, however, be a very great difference. Water could not drown us, or bread nourish us. Both would be our own products, and could neither make nor undo us. Their existence could not precede ours. If we perished they would perish too. We could not be servile to skyey influences. On the contrary, what we call the skies would be our own mere creatures.

On the other hand, the same objections to the rosier hopes of idealistic theory would have to be made to this Berkeleyan type of pluralistic pan-psychism as to the Leibnizian type. Take any instance we choose. By hypothesis a man need not fear the unfriendly ocean. It could not kill him. Nevertheless, he would have the experience of suffocation if, as we say, he fell into it, and he could also infer that such an experience was the prelude either to his own extinction or to the beginning of the new life that succeeds what we call death. Is there anything friendlier about a "nature" so interpreted than about the "nature" in which men commonly believe? There is no evidence that our (involuntary) "ideas of sense" are less to be dreaded or more malleable according to this metaphysics than according to any other metaphysics. Actually there is very little evidence that the belief in propositions such as "There is no pain", "There is no tedium", does much to alleviate pain or boredom; but, in any case, sorrow and pain have never been the more welcome because they were believed to be "in" the mind. As for death, what most men resent (if they do resent it) is the loss of experience, the finality of becoming nothing at all; and that particular loss would be just as likely to occur if all "nature" were "in" minds as if none of it were.

Empirical differences of that kind would remain on any theory, including the monistic forms of pan-psychism. That would be true if monistic pan-psychism resembled a transfigured naturalism, incorporating a higher dimension into electrons, bacteria, cups and stars, and declaring that the Whole is the prius of all its parts. It would also be true if the Whole were interpreted as a great mind in which "nature" was an assemblage of ideas or of clusters of ideas. If there were just one Whole, in some sense a minding or a mind-laden Whole, the hopes and fears of particular men and women, or of other particular finite spirits in whatever planet they may reside, could hardly be supposed to be of great cosmic or meta-cosmic importance. Much in their experiences would be said to be "merely personal" in the derogatory sense of that phrase. But that is a topic which we may conveniently postpone.

Our second question concerns man. Should pan-psychism transfigure our beliefs concerning *human* nature?

By contrast at least, this question was prominent in what I said about the relation between pan-psychism on the one hand, and earthquakes, the ocean and the inhuman part of nature on the other hand; but I may add some reflections.

If pluralistic pan-psychism, in the first (or Leibnizian) form discussed above, clings tenaciously to the view that every psyche is a substance, and that all that is said to happen *to* a substance must really happen *within* it, an important consequence would be that there can be no literal compounding of psychic substances. In that case the most plausible account of a human mind would be given by the theory that such a mind is a high-grade soul that appears to govern the lower-grade souls that we call the cells of the human body (because there is, in fact, a hierarchical correspondence-relation that looks like such government). If, however, this view of substantiality were rejected, and the compounding of souls into an over-soul were admitted to be possible, the union of certain cells (which would, of course, be psychoid cells) might be just the human being (which would therefore be bodily but also mental).

In the second or Berkeleyan form of pluralistic pan-psychism, the usual assumption is that any finite mind is, metaphysically speaking, an ultimate entity whose "ideas of sense" are its own and cannot be transferred to any other substances. If so, even a God could not transfer his ideas to us, and Berkeley's account of this matter seems to have been quite naïve. Of that, more anon.

Our third and last question is whether pan-psychism, if true, would transfigure our ideas of God. About that I should like to say something now, as a preliminary to various discussions in later lectures.

If every substance, by an ineluctable metaphysical necessity, is wholly self-contained, that must be true of the divine substance. Therefore God could neither beget nor create anything other than himself. He could neither pre-establish the general harmony (supposing that there is such a harmony in what is not God) nor set anything other than himself agoing in such a way that a harmony (or, failing that, a tolerable *modus vivendi*) could later be achieved. The choice for theists would be between pantheistic monism, on the one hand, and, on the other hand, an ultimate pluralism in which God, like any other substance, has no outside influence. The only other possibility would be atheism.

If, however, it were allowed that substances could produce other substances and could have transactions with other substances, no such consequences would ensue. On that assumption, the liveliest question in the present context would be whether the denial that non-mental beings exist is more congruent with theism than the belief in their existence. Of this I can only say that the problem seems to me to be quite indeterminate. Some would say, it is true, that it is more appropriate for deity to create spirits in his own image than to create stocks and stones that have no similitude to anything spiritual. That, however, seems a superficial idea. *Ex hypothesi*, anything other than God, and the whole company of what is other than God, is very much inferior to God. Consequently the problem of all problems is why God should produce any inferior beings *at all*. That problem is of such crucial import that nice calculations about the degree of inferiority seem quite misplaced. Alternatively we may ask how we can be sure that nature, if it be non-mental, is *not* somehow in the image of God? Pantheists would say that it is, and those who admire what Matthew Arnold admired in Goethe:

> For he pursued a lonely road
> His eyes on nature's plan:
> Neither made man too much a God
> Nor God too much a man

perceive the need for caution in these regions. (Yet it seems fair to ask how the repulsive appetitions and perceptions of the *spirocheta pallida* preserve God's image?)

The other, or Berkeleyan, type of pluralistic pan-psychism that I have discussed would be consistent with the view that deity is the name for the society of spirits that constitute the entire substance of reality. If so, it would be as much a monism as a pluralism, and McTaggart, who held this view of the constitution of reality, maintained, in order to defend the pluralism in it, that his philosophy was atheistic.

In Berkeley's philosophy deity was held to be essential to the whole conception of reality. God's volitions, Berkeley said, created men's minds and prevented men's involuntary ideas of sense from occurring at random. For the former opinion, however, there was no evidence except Berkeley's piety, and the latter contained quite exceptional and rather exceptionable difficulties. According to Berkeleyans, each man's ideas of sense were his own. A man could no more transfer his ideas of colour to another man than he could transfer his toothache. If what any man calls "nature", therefore, were really *God's* idea it could not, on analogy with any known principles, be transferred to a *man*, and there would be nothing except the dogma of creation to support the theory. Add the difficulty that Berkeley, to retain his orthodoxy, had to hold that "God perceives nothing by sense as we do".[1] The consequence would be that it is only the *archetypes* of human sense-ideas that could be said to exist in God's mind.[2] Such archetypes might be eternal; but there is *no* persistence of any human sense-ideas beyond the passing moment.

Indeed, it is rather difficult to say how far Berkeley's conception of deity involved *any* transfiguration of any common notions of God. Berkeley held, to speak briefly, that all God's works were just what we perceive them to be, but that they were not accomplished by means of the useless intermediary of material substance The consequence would be that the status of *nature* was profoundly altered, but it is not so plain that the traditional conception of the divine creative spirit would be altered at all. There would just be a simplification of the ordinary accounts of the way in which God set to work when he created the choir of heaven and the furniture of earth.

A monistic pan-psychism would either be a pantheism, or would hold that Absolute Spirit was greater than and included God as well as human spirits. In the latter case God would be finite, although he would be so great in comparison with any man as to appear infinite. Both these views would make a very great difference to what many theists believe about God.

If selves could be united into a greater self, a "personal" God might be identical with the spiritual community. He might live and move and have all his being in *us*. On such a theory, the apparent independence of finite centres of personality might be admitted even if pantheism was also accepted. We may note, however, that Bradley, although he held that "it is better, on the whole, to conclude that no element of reality falls outside the experience of finite centres", freely admitted that the question provoked more "ultimate doubts" than most others.[3]

If selves cannot intermingle into greater selves, if they cannot disintegrate into sub-selves that still are selves, and if God be a self, theism cannot take the form of monistic pantheism, and

[1] *Hylas and Philonous*, 3rd Dialogue, Fraser's ed. (1901), I, 459.
[2] *Ibid.*, 458.   [3] *Appearance and Reality*, 2nd ed. (1908), p. 528.

God, whatever else he may be, cannot be the Whole. This conclusion is very welcome to certain theists who prefer to regard the deity as a magnified non-natural Roman Emperor. I do not suggest that these theists are wrong, but I would like a little space to pursue the question in subsequent lectures.

IV

Omniscience

In the first series of these lectures we discussed several of the attributes generally ascribed to deity by Western and by some other theologians. Among these were omnificence, ubiquity and eternity, the removal of all limitations in respect of power, or of space, or of time. We did not, however, specifically consider one of the most important of all such attributes, God's omniscience, the removal of all limitations to his knowledge and wisdom.

The delay was intentional because the idea of an All-knower is suffused in so many of our philosophies[1] with pan-idea-ism, pan-ideatism and the other epistemological theories which, according to plan, we neglected provisionally in the first series of lectures, but have examined rather closely at the outset of the second series. There is now no occasion for further delay, and the time is opportune for a discussion of God's omniscience. That attribute has a close connection with the enquiries that were undertaken in the last three lectures; for these were concerned, in the main, with the interpretation of knowledge. The discussion of it is also an appropriate prelude to the examination of divine personality and of divine providence with which the subsequent lectures of this course will be very largely concerned.

Indeed, so long a delay has always been regrettable, because the attribute of omniscience (or something very like it) is nearly always tacitly presupposed in the other divine attributes. A blind omnificence, a heedless omnipresence, an anoëtic eternity is seldom if ever what is contemplated by Western theologians

[1] Including Indian and Persian, as well as European.

when they discuss these matters. A world-designer is assumed
to know his cosmic business. He for whom all power is claimed
is held to control, order and integrate all his works, all his
emanations and all his own being with a knowledge and understanding that never fail him. A limited deity might indeed be
limited in his cognitive powers. He might be rather stupid,
deficient in insight, deficient in correlating the data with which
he had to do. But such conjectures are usually regarded as idle,
or as irreverent, or as both.

Accordingly I shall now proceed to the discussion of divine
omniscience, but I should like to make two explanations at the
outset. In the first place, although I shall use monotheistic terms,
I do not want to prejudge the question whether an omniscient
God might not be, more strictly, a society or, as it were, a
university of high gods, collectively not severally omniscient.
I shall use monotheistic terms simply for convenience in the
present lecture, and not with any ulterior purpose, pious or
sinister or piously sinister. In the second place, I should like
to say that I know that complaints may be made about the
attempt to consider any of God's attributes separately. In the
case of human beings the intellect and, more generally, all cognitive powers are constituents of what we call personality, and
there may be over-abstraction if the circumstance be forgotten.
A similar charge of vicious abstraction, it may be said, may be
laid against the conception of God's personality itself—the
theme of later lectures. That I fully admit. If, however, it is
further averred that the divine being must be held to be of
complete and utter simplicity, and that we may *know* this truth
(in some sense of the word "knowledge") although we can never
explicate it without destroying the said simplicity, I should like
to enter my respectful dissent. If these statements were true we
should have the choice between unlimited iteration of the word
"simplicity" on the one hand and utter speechlessness on the
other hand. The former alternative has many disadvantages. The
latter may have fewer. But the separate discussion of God's
knowledge is at least as legitimate as the separate discussion of

his power, or of his love, or of his righteousness; and all these discussions *are* legitimate.

On the whole it appears to me that we may reach the heart of this question, or at least its pericardium, most readily and most directly if we ask two questions in succession. The first is whether we *must* believe in the existence of an omniscient being. The second is whether the existence of such a being is so much as credible.

I

When it is said that we *must* believe in the existence of an omniscient being (i.e. that our reason coerces us into that belief) the argument usually assumes the tones of a piece of metaphysical intimidation. The contention is that unless there were an omniscient knower, nothing at all could be known. Unless someone knows everything, no one could know anything. In the language of the seventeenth century, the question would be whether an atheist would be logically entitled to the possession of any piece of knowledge whatever.

Such attempted proofs of omniscience, in their turn, usually have (in the West) taken one or other of two forms which may be very closely conjoined. These two forms are the Proof from the Sovereign Essences and the Proof from the Eternal Truths. I shall examine each of them separately.

I read with some amazement in Flint's *Theism*, a work whose considerable merits are still admitted, that these arguments belonged to the "proofs which are as catholic as the conclusion which they support".[1] In other words, Flint regarded these proofs as demonstrations that convinced the common man, and not, like the Ontological and other *a priori* proofs, as arguments that appealed only to highly trained specialists, if they appealed to anyone at all. Flint's assumption, I suppose, was cradle-Platonism, the *anima naturaliter Platonica* supposed to reside in every human breast; but even so his opinion seems to be oddly confident. Until I read him I had always supposed that these proofs were

[1] 8th ed., p. 277.

as metaphysical and as esoteric as any in the entire theological armoury; and I still think so. On the other hand, these proofs have certainly been often propounded in responsible quarters, and they continue to be used today, whether their appeal be to common or to uncommon sense. As von Hügel[1] said, "God is no pedant."

Let us, then, examine the Proof from the Sovereign Essences.

I have spoken about cradle-Platonism. So far as I can, however, I shall try to avoid the historical question whether Plato was a Platonist, whether he was not the critic rather than the father of the theory of Forms, Essences or Ideas, whether the Plotinian and Augustinian developments of such a philosophy were not glosses on Plato rather than the recovery of Plato's indwelling spirit. These at least are not questions for cradle-Platonists. They exact most of the life-work of certain historians. Speaking generally, however, we may say that the knowledge-situation, when conceived in terms of the Sovereign Essences, is understood in the following way: A reason, it is held, can always be given why anything is what it is. The solution is that anything is what it is in virtue of the Essence that makes it what it is. Its *ratio essendi* is identical with its *ratio cognoscendi*, and there is nothing that is without its adequate and constitutive *ratio essendi*. Therefore, we are told, nothing can be unknowable, and God's omniscience may be inferred if it can further be shown that anything that is knowable is "knowable" only because it is "known".

That, to my mind, is just the difficulty. I doubt whether there are many, even among cradle-Platonists, who seriously believe that it is wholly absurd to suppose that it is for ever impossible for anyone to come to know anything that nobody knew before, and yet, in the ordinary sense of language, had been *true* before anyone had thought of it. Plato himself, in at least one celebrated passage, appreciated the point, although he put forward alternative hypotheses in other places, for instance when he suggested in the *Meno* that all coming-to-know, on the part of slave-boys and other persons *in statu pupillari*, was a reminiscence of pre-natal knowledge.

The celebrated passage to which I refer occurs in a thoroughly enigmatic dialogue, the *Parmenides*, but is itself very lucid. Socrates[1] asks Parmenides what he thinks of the suggestion that every Form (εἶδος) is just a thought (νόημα) existing only in souls (ἐν ψυχαῖς). Parmenides replies that a thought (νόημα) cannot be a thought of nothing (νόημα οὐδενός) but must always be a thought of something, a νόημα ὄντος. The alternatives, according to Socrates's suggestion, would be either that everything thinks (πάντα νοεῖν) or that thoughts (νοήματα) are anoëtic entities (ὄντα ἀνόητα). It is later stated in the dialogue[2] that such thoughts (νοήματα) cannot be "in us" (ἐν ἡμῖν) since, if they were, they would be contingent and not absolute essences.

This argument of the *Parmenides*, it is plain, refers primarily to the thoughts in someone's mind. It may have been directed (as Mr. Taylor, following Grote, suggests) against Menedemus and other Eritreans who held that qualities were mere personal notions (ψιλαὶ ἔννοιαι). In that case it might be interpreted as a prophetic repudiation of conceptualism and of subjective idealism or personal mentalism. It would not refute, and indeed, would not touch rational phenomenalism. Taken generally, however, Plato's conclusion was strongly opposed to the view that the Essences must be someone's thoughts, whether that someone be man or deity. For any such theory would imply a certain limitation of the absoluteness of the Essences, whether they were *mere* notions, or were notions without the derogatory qualification.

Plato himself distinguished God both from the Forms and from their unity. He held that there was an Essence of all Essences, namely the Idea of the Good; but the Idea of the Good was not God (who was only a soul, that is to say one of the beings whose nature was constituted by Constitutive Essences). For Plato, therefore, God was subordinate to the Essence of all Essences. It follows that, if Plato was right, the argument

[1] 132 c–d.   [2] 133 c.

to the necessity for an omniscient knower, so vigorously maintained by so many professing Platonists, is not a piece of ultimate metaphysics.

Certainly it may be argued, as Mr. Taylor does argue, that whatever Plato may have meant by "God", theologians, speculating on Platonic lines, may have reached the un-Platonic truth of Plato's majestic theme. "The distinguishing characteristic of the Form of the Good", Mr. Taylor says,[1] "is that it is the transcendent source of all the reality and intelligibility of everything other than itself. Thus it is exactly what is meant in Christian philosophy by the *ens realissimum* and is rightly regarded as distinct from and transcendent of the whole system of its effects or manifestations. And, as in the *ens realissimum* of Christian philosophers, so in the 'Form of Good' the distinction valid everywhere else between *essentia* and *esse*, *So-sein* and *Sein*, falls away. In other language, it transcends the distinction, too often treated as absolute, between value and existence. It is the supreme value, and at the same time it is, though 'beyond being', the source of all existence. . . . Thus as it seems to me, metaphysically the Form of Good is what Christian philosophy has meant by God and nothing else."

In other words, Mr. Taylor holds that the Idea of the Good in Plato's philosophy is so developed as to be the precursor of the Ontological Proof that there is a God, that it is the proof, in Leibnizian language, of an *extramundane* God, and indeed of a God "beyond *existence*" as well as merely beyond the *world*. Mr. Taylor further asserts that this proof, like the Ontological Proof in general, is best expressed in terms of a revision of the usual distinctions we draw between "value" and "existence". I shall deal with the last of these contentions in a subsequent lecture. Of the others I shall only say that I do not propose to return to a discussion of the Ontological Proof. I am content to have shown that the argument from the Sovereign Essences need not imply that these Essences must always be known by some mind, or known in their unity by an omniscient mind.

[1] *Plato: the Man and his Work*, p. 289.

They are knowable because they are intelligible, but the language in which we express their intelligibility may easily beguile us into making precarious and unnecessary inferences.

I may add, although I do not think that the point is at all important, that the Idea of the Good belongs to advanced and not to cradle-Platonism, and so that it could not reasonably be expected to impress the plain man. In Plato's last years, Plato's audience, according to Aristoxenus, came to hear about the Idea of the Good, hoping to obtain practical advice. Instead they heard about numbers and the Indefinite Dyad. It is not plain that the entire Academy learned very much more. Therefore, if we are to believe that God is the Supreme Essence of all existence-determining Essences, and have Plato to help us, it is unfortunate that Plato's suggestions remain so very indefinite. We should be unreasonable if we expected an easy theology, straight from the sage's mouth, but we should not be unreasonable if we asked for a proof that there *was* a single Essence of all Essences. The hierarchy of Forms (in arithmetic, say) is scarcely a proof that there must be a single *numerus numerans*, and the idea of a single *natura naturans* would seem to be still more elusive and enigmatical.

Let us turn to the Argument from the Eternal Truths.

This argument may be conjoined with the Argument from Sovereign Essences, because truth and intellectual or notional essences have the closest intimacy. Nevertheless, the Argument from the Eternal Truths contains features peculiar to itself, and was elaborated in the seventeenth century by Descartes, Leibniz and other great philosophers with a taste for theology. I shall later consider some of these questions of history, but I shall begin by making certain general observations.

Truth, as I have said, is closely connected with concepts and essences; for every proposition, even if it is of the type "It is raining", "There is a noise", contains a notional or conceptual element; and truth is always an affair of propositions. This latter statement, it may be said, is of itself highly significant for our present theme. For even if the notional constituents of propositions could be unminded entities, ὄντα ἀνόητα, propositions themselves (we are told) must always be mentities. According to some philosophers propositions are *statements*, that is to say, wordy things, and therefore symbolic tokens. For words (as opposed to mere sounds) have meaning and are therefore a kind of mentities. This opinion, it is true, is disputed by other philosophers who hold that statements and other symbolic tokens *express* but do not *constitute* propositions. They are said to be the marks of propositions, not the reality of propositions. On that interpretation of them, however, it might still be held that propositions could not be true unless they were affirmed, and that affirmation is clearly a mental performance.

Consequently, the way might seem to be paved for an argument to the following effect: Propositions always involve a relation, covert or express, to some actual mind. Propositions are the sole currency of truth. Therefore all truth implies some actual mind. But (we are told) there is a totality of true propositions and we know (from our logical experience?) that no valid inference can be drawn unless all the relevant premisses are apprehended by one and the same mind. The totality of true propositions therefore implies the existence of a single mind that knows the totality, that is to say, it implies an omniscient mind.

Another argument sometimes used in this connection, and developed by Leibniz in a dialogue of 1677,[1] is based upon the mutual relations of truth and falsity. According to this argument, falsity plainly pertains to thoughts and not to things, since there cannot be any false things. Propositions, however, may be either true or false. They therefore cannot be things, and it would be quite absurd to hold that true propositions could be non-mental although false propositions are always mental. This argument might indeed be disputed on the ground that a true proposition has valid trans-presentational reference, while a false proposition only appears to have a valid reference of that kind. It has in fact (we may be told) only mental (or intra-presentational)

[1] Quoted by Russell, *The Philosophy of Leibniz*, p. 289.

reality and has no valid trans-presentational standing. The reply would be that in that case true propositions have intra-presentational reality as well as trans-presentational reference, and so that they *are* mental.

Several distinct problems are raised in these arguments. We should ask (1) whether nothing but a proposition can be known: (2) whether nothing but a proposition can be true: (3) how the answer to these two questions affects the actuality of omniscience.

(1) The word "knowledge" is used in various senses, some of them very wide and others intentionally very narrow. In the wider sense our acquaintance with ourselves, or our sensory acquaintance with colours and tastes, would be accounted "knowledge". In that sense of "knowledge" it would not be true to say that all "knowledge" was of propositions. We do not taste propositions when we taste bacon and eggs, and if, strictly speaking, it is not bacon but the taste of bacon with which we are acquainted in the sensory way, the taste of bacon also is not a proposition. In narrower senses of "knowledge", however, it would commonly be said that there is no knowledge unless there is truth, that neither bacon itself nor the taste of bacon is "true", and that any knowledge that has to do with the taste of bacon or with bacon is a knowledge of propositions based upon an acquaintance with bacon or with the taste of bacon (*although* that is not itself knowledge). In short, the view would be that our knowledge of things and even of sensa is always mediated by propositions. It might be added that nothing escapes the propositional net in any respect whatsoever.

(2) These statements have trenched upon our second question concerning truth. Just as the range of the term "knowledge" is debateable, so there are different views regarding the range of the term "truth". On any theory, truth must be examined in connection with falsity. If, then, we include illusion and confusion under "falsity", it would have to be admitted that we commonly hold that the senses and the memory may be confused and mistaken. When they are not mistaken it is not unusual and it might seem to be legitimate to say that they are "true",

although sometimes a term like "correct" or "veridical" is preferred.

Accordingly there are senses of "truth" in which something that is not a proposition may be "true". On the other hand, it is not unusual to restrict the terms "truth" and "falsity" to propositions. Much depends upon the definition of "truth".

(3) The answers to the above questions have a distinct bearing upon the problem of the nature and reality of divine omniscience. One of the chief of them is that if all knowledge be restricted to propositions, God's knowledge must also be restricted to propositions. God could not know what is unknowable. *Ex hypothesi*, therefore, he could not know what is non-propositional. If all the so-called knowledge of things must be mediated by propositions, God's knowledge of himself, and of human souls and of other things, must similarly be mediated. If there is any sort of acquaintance that escapes the propositional net in any respect, such acquaintance, whoever has it, must also escape an "omniscience" that is confined to propositions.

That is a matter of some theological importance. Another matter, however, may seem to most of us to be of even greater moment. When we speak about the truth of propositions, e.g. of the truth of the proposition that $a^m \times a^n = a^{m+n}$, the reference to any actual knowing is often covert and elliptical. Our meaning is that such a proposition would be known to be true if anyone grasped it with adequate intelligence. It follows that there would be no "truth" if there were no minds, but what we usually mean by such a "truth" certainly does not imply that the proposition in question owes its character and validity to its discovery at any particular time. Similarly it does not imply that nobody can come to know a "truth" of which he was formerly ignorant, unless someone else, or he himself in some pre-existent condition, had already grasped it.

Such an opinion is only a fantastic conceit. The first alternative, namely that what anyone comes to know must have been already known by someone else, is reducible to the argument that the only way of learning anything is to be *told* it. If so, who would tell God? It is useless to say that the learner knows the mind of the teller. He would have to be *told* that too; and if he knew the mind of the teller, he would then know something in a manner of knowing that contradicts the hypothesis. The second alternative is equally forlorn. It would reduce all insight to the memory of insight, one's own or someone else's. What then of the first piece of insight?

More generally, I submit that from the mere fact (which I admit) that there could not, strictly speaking, be *truth* if there had never been any knowing minds, it cannot be inferred that eternal or timeless truths imply the existence of eternal or timeless minds, still less the existence of a single eternal or timeless mind.

A subordinate but important question is whether and in what sense these arguments should be based upon *all* truths or only upon the *eternal* truths. In this matter we may continue to examine some of Leibniz's views.

Regarding the eternal verities, Leibniz, while following Descartes rather closely, made highly significant reservations. Writing to Mersenne in 1630 Descartes said: "God produces the eternal verities *ut efficiens et totalis causa*, for he is the author of the essence as well as of the existence of his creatures, and his essence is just the eternal verities."[1] According to this argument all truth was God's creature, including geometry, algebra and the still more general logistical science of Descartes's dreams, the *characteristica universalis*. Similarly in his reply to the sixth set of objections to his *Meditations*, Descartes argued that the reason why we should hold that it was better that the world should have been created than that it should not have been created was simply that God did create it, and not, as some theologians falsely averred, that God created it because he saw that its existence was better than its non-existence. In the same way and in the same place Descartes maintained that the reason why the angles in a triangle were equal to two right angles was simply

[1] A. T., I, 152.

that God had ordained it to be so, and not, conversely, because the fact was unalterable even by God.

The question here at issue was the fundamental scholastic and pre-scholastic problem whether God would be limited by the eternal verities if these had to be regarded as true in their own right, and not by the grace of God. Verbally at least Descartes's view subordinated truth to God's mere power and volition. Leibniz, on the other hand, vigorously maintained that what made the eternal truths true was just God's being and nature, and *not* his will. They did not govern God's nature by an outside limitation but *belonged* to his nature. God *was* these truths, although Leibniz cautiously added that "we ought not to say with some Scotists that the eternal truths would subsist even if there were no understanding, not even God's".[1] According to Leibniz, what depended on God's will were the truths of mere fact, not the eternal verities; and the truths of fact had a sufficient antecedent reason in God's choice of the best.

These contentions (which are a master's conclusions after a long historical controversy) contain several important features. In the first place Leibniz accepted the ultimacy of the distinction between God's voluntary actions, such as creation, and God's nature. Similarly he maintained that there was a corresponding distinction between the truths of fact and the eternal truths; for the former resulted from God's creative fiat while the latter did not. In the second place the theory that God *was* the eternal truths and that these eternal truths would not subsist without him is indistinguishable, in the end, from the apparently less provocative assertion that such truths evince the nature of ultimate reality, and do not limit that reality in any sense except the absurd one in which there is said to be "limitation" of a thing if the thing is just what it is.

While the second of these features may be innocuous, the first raises a host of difficulties, some of which I may mention briefly.

In much Platonic theory the sovereign and eternal essences

---

[1] Quoted by Russell, *The Philosophy of Leibniz*, p. 289.

were said to be the *fons totius entis*, but it is not clear that the same could be said of the "eternal truths" when these were effectively distinguished from mere "truths of fact". Such truths of fact, according to Leibniz, were contingent upon the fact of creation, and creation, the work of God's volition, might have been withheld. It is true that God, if he had not created the world, would have refrained from doing what was best. There-fore, said Leibniz, we may be certain that God *would* not have refrained from the labour of creation, although, metaphysically speaking, he was a free agent who *could* have so refrained. On the other hand God must be supposed to have known what all the possible worlds would come to, *if* they were created. There-fore, although he created only the best of the possible worlds, there must be some sense in which something that never existed, namely the internal implications of the rejected possible worlds, did eternally subsist. The opinion of the despised Scotists was not unsubstantiated.

To some extent Descartes's view may have been easier to maintain consistently than Leibniz's, but it was an intruder in the Cartesian system and, philosophically speaking, a rogue. The Cartesian system was based upon clear ideas and upon their clear implications. Descartes claimed invincible clarity for the *Cogito* and for certain other so-called intuitions. If, however, these "invincible" clarities were ultimately vincible in respect of their clarity, being matter-of-fact propositions about God's actual power and not ineluctable intuitions into the nature of reality, the clear and distinct ideas would, in the end, be dethroned.

There is some interest in the kind and degree of knowledge that these authors kindly permitted the atheist to have. Leibniz allowed that an atheist might be a geometer, but maintained that the atheist would have nothing to know, since, if there were no God, there would be no object of geometry.[1] The atheist, I think, might fairly reply that on Leibniz's own assump-tions, he, the atheist, would actually be dealing with the actual

[1] Russell's *Leibniz*, p. 289.

geometry in God. He might further retort that, unless Leibniz could show that the geometrical part of the divine essence logically implied the rest of the divine essence in the same sense as geometrical propositions imply other geometrical propositions, an atheist would be logically free to be *only* a geometer.

Descartes treated the atheist rather differently. In his reply to the second set of objections to his *Meditations*, he said that the atheist might have clear geometrical knowledge, but that such knowledge would not be "true science" since its metaphysical weakness would leave room for doubts. The atheist might retort that his geometrical ideas were absolutely clear and wholly free from doubt; or, again, that Descartes's demonstrations of deity were said to depend upon clear ideas and their geometry-like union. Did not Descartes himself define a clear intuition as "mentis purae at attentae tam facilem distinctumque conceptum, ut de eo quod intelligamus, nulla prorsus dubitatio relinquatur",[1] and did he not, *inter alia*, cite a geometrical instance? If it were replied, in one of the usual Cartesian ways,[2] that the atheist might have clear geometrical intuitions but no geometrical demonstrations (since demonstrations are lengthy things and depend upon a fallible memory), the atheist might reply that memory *was* fallible even if theism were true, and that the Cartesian demonstrations of God's existence really did profess to be *demonstrations*.

In any case it is not even plausible to maintain that no one can know anything unless someone knows everything. Yet that is what is supposed to disturb the atheist. Even if the atheist were wrong in believing that the light of his reason could shine at all unless it were reflected from above, he is surely entitled to say that it does shine in fact, and that he knows that it does.

With these remarks I shall end my discussion of the argument to omniscience from intimidation, that is to say, from the attempt to show that unless somebody knows everything, nobody could know anything. The threat does not seem to me to be formidable, and although I have been burrowing in the remote past (of Greece

[1] A. T., X, 368 f.   [2] *Cf.* Keeling, *Descartes*, p. 77.

and of the seventeenth century) in my search for solid arguments to examine, I am not very penitent about that. Modern statements to the same effect seem to me to be much more impetuous and also much weaker. Thus when I am told in a book published in the present year that "awareness of a world common to all experients belongs to finite minds only if they are differentiations of a universal mind",[1] I should be disposed to say that I might just as well assume that ten men could not be aware of the moon unless the ten men were really one man.

II

So I shall pass to the second principal question raised in this lecture. It is the opposite of the first question. We are now asking whether the existence of an omniscient being is so much as credible.

An omniscient being—let us say, some Mazdah, the All-wise in Zoroastrian theology—might be supposed (*a*) to know every-thing that *is* known, or (*b*) to know everything that *could be* known. This distinction corresponds to the distinction that may be drawn in the case of an Almighty being between omnificence on the one hand and omnipotence on the other hand. I shall subdivide the discussion in terms of this principle. Many other distinctions, however, will also enter. We have to remember that the term "knowledge" is used in various senses, and that the circumstance affects our discussion. We have to ask whether an omniscient being has (1) only a special (and sufficient) *kind* of knowledge of or about everything, or (2) whether he has *every* sort of knowledge of or about everything. We have also to ask the familiar question whether the removal of all limitations or "imperfections" from the notion of a knowledgeable being leaves a determinate or merely an indeterminate notion of that being and of his knowledgeable works and ways. Throughout the dis-cussion it should be clearly understood that our question is not whether there is a God, or whether God be supremely wise.

[1] G. R. G. Mure, *An Introduction to Hegel*, p. 91 (1940).

Omniscience

The question is in what sense, if any, God should be believed to be, strictly speaking, omniscient.

(*a*) Let us ask, then, in the first place, whether it is credible that there should be a being who knows all that is known, and, for simplicity's sake, let us further suppose that this question, in its turn, concerns the existence of a being who knows all that is known at any given time, and all that has been known up to that time.

It will be convenient, I think, if we take the distinction between what is reflexive and what is transcendent in knowledge as our cue in this matter, and examine God's omniscience with respect (α) to what may be supposed to be *his* and *our* reflexive knowledge and (β) to be *his* and *our* transcendent knowledge.

(α) I tried to show in a former lecture that the conscious quality in each man's waking experience has a reflexive dimension. There may, I admit, be disputes about the question whether our reflexive self-acquaintance is or is not to be called knowledge. Even if it be not itself "knowledge", however—and the denial that it is "knowledge" would seem to be finicking and pedantic—believers in divine omniscience would have to face a difficult problem if reflexiveness were essential to and the peculiar basis of a certain kind of "knowledge". That problem is whether a man's reflexive self-acquaintance is not immitigably private, and therefore inaccessible to any other being, even to a Mazdah. If reflexive knowledge were immitigably private, Mazdah would *not* know all that is known, and therefore would not be literally omniscient in the sense of that term at present under discussion. Since divine omniscience is generally held to include a most searching acquaintance with the human heart and mind this necessary ignorance on God's part (if it *were* necessary) could not be held to be negligible. If pure phenomenalism were the truth about these matters, all knowledge and also all reality would consist of self-luminous entities that showed all that they were by the mere fact of existing. An omniscient being, on that hypothesis, would be the totality of such entities at any given time. *Prima facie* there is no contradiction in that idea, but the relation of the constituent self-luminosities to the self-luminosity of the whole would groan under heavy burdens. If each of the constituents is self-luminous, can it be inferred that the totality of them is reflexively self-luminous as a totality? If, as some philosophers hold, the individual phenomena are transmuted in the Whole (or, to be more accurate, would be so transmuted if they were not what, in fact, they are, viz. distinct individual phenomena) what becomes of the professed phenomenalism of the theory? If the phenomena are scattered into finite centres, what precisely is their totality? Would they be scattered as dust may be scattered into little whirling eddies that nevertheless may be parts of a dust-storm?

I have argued earlier that pure phenomenalism is an untenable theory. Let us therefore renounce it here. In that case, in this affair of reflexiveness, we are left with the reflexive self-acquaintance of individual minds "at the very moment". Here, empirically, each mind seems to be its own self-reflector, and indeed to be reflexively aware of itself, at any given moment, without any psychic interval between knower and known. Some, it is true, would favour a certain speculative possibility, viz. that each of us may be supposed to be made up of sub-selves each of which might have reflexive acquaintance with itself. There is, however, only the vaguest and most disputable empirical evidence (if there is any at all) that *we* have reflexive acquaintance with any such sub-selves. This consideration has much theological importance. If God's omniscience includes all that *is* known reflexively, it must include all that *we* know reflexively. If knower and known are identical in reflexive self-acquaintance, God must be identical with us in so far as *he* has *our* reflexive self-know-ledge. There is no empirical evidence that such a thing could be, and it is at least legitimate to deny that *any* evidence favours the idea. Certainly God, on this hypothesis, might and probably would have reflexive self-acquaintance with his own great mind, just as we have reflexive self-acquaintance with our own small minds. He might also, in *some* way, know all that we are and do; but not, it would seem, in the reflexive way.

These conjectures may seem to be profoundly unimportant. If the All-knower knows everything, what does it matter how he knows it? Does not the assumption that the *mode* of knowing is relevant to these matters itself imply the fallacy that there are epistemological objects, and have we not repeatedly and vigorously repudiated that fallacy?

This reply, I think, is essentially sound. Nevertheless, if it were true that certain things, or certain features of certain things, could *only* be known in a particular way, then, if *we* knew something in that way, and if God could not know it in that way, it would follow that he could not know it at all. Such views are often expressed. It is said, for instance, that no one who has not experienced pleasure or pain or pity in himself can know what pleasure or pain or pity is, and it is often said, further, that pleasure and pain and pity are reflexive experiences. According to many Christian theologians it is naïve and even blasphemous, a foolish humanizing of deity, to hold that God can experience these or any other emotions. In any case, if pleasure or pain or pity can only be known reflexively, and if there is an incommensurable distinction between divine and human emotions, God could not experience *our* joys, or wretchedness or compassion, and so could not "know" them in one of the relevant senses of "knowing".

The same argument would hold of sense-acquaintance if sense-acquaintance be reflexive. This question has been debated a good deal. It may here suffice if I revert to what Berkeley said about it. His most explicit statement was the following:[1]

"*Hylas:* But you have asserted that whatever ideas we perceive from without are in the mind which affects us. The ideas therefore of pain and uneasiness are in God; or, in other words, God suffers pain: that is to say, there is an imperfection in the divine nature: which you acknowledged was absurd. So you are caught in a plain contradiction.

Philonous: That God knows or understands all things, and that he knows among other things, what pain is, even every sort of painful

[1] *Dialogues between Hylas and Philonous*, Fraser's ed. of *Works*, I, 458 f.

sensation, and what it is for his creatures to suffer pain, I make no question. But that God, though he knows and sometimes causes painful sensations in us, can himself suffer pain, I positively deny. We, who are limited and dependent spirits, are liable to impressions of sense, the effects of an external Agent, which, being produced against our wills, are sometimes painful and uneasy. But God, whom no external being can affect, who perceives nothing by sense as we do; whose will is absolute and independent, causing all things, and liable to be thwarted or resisted by nothing; it is evident that such a Being as this can suffer nothing, nor be affected by any painful sensation, or indeed any sensation at all. We are chained to a body; that is to say, our perceptions are connected with corporeal motions. . . . But God is a pure spirit, disengaged from all such sympathy or natural ties. No corporeal motions are attended with the sensations of pain or pleasure in his mind. To know everything knowable is certainly a perfection; but to endure, or suffer, or feel anything by sense is an imperfection. The former, I say, agrees to God but not the latter. God knows or hath ideas; but his ideas are not conveyed to him by sense as ours are. Your not distinguishing, where there is so manifest a difference, makes you fancy you see an absurdity where there is none.

This argument of Berkeley's depended on the assumption that divine knowledge, like the entire divine nature, must be wholly "active" and in no sense "passive". A possible reply (among others) would be that the terms "activity" and "passivity" apply only to the cause or to the origin of certain experiences, and not to the nature of any experience. In that case Hylas's difficulty might be held to be unreal for a different reason from the one that Philonous gave. On any showing, however, it is not at all clear how an impassive or, in technical theological language, an *impassible* being could have reflexive acquaintance with our "passive" experiences. I can see nothing in Philonous's rejoinder that touches the point. What he said was that God "knew" pain but did not feel it. That is no answer if the *feeling* of pain *is* the reflexive knowledge in question.

(β) Let us turn from reflexive to transcendent knowledge.

Among human beings transcendent knowledge, at any rate

in one of the usual senses of "knowledge", would include memory-apprehension and conceptual apprehension. According to certain philosophical theories of sense-acquaintance (although not according to the theory we have just considered) it would also include sense-apprehension.

With regard to memory-apprehension and conceptual apprehension, it would seem to be entirely possible that all that is not reflexive in them might be known by *any* knower, and therefore that a single most knowing being might know whatever is known in these ways. By the word "memory", it is true, we are accustomed to designate something personal. None of us remembers what *he* has not experienced. To that extent there is at least a suggestion of reflexiveness about memory. There is no contradiction, however, in holding that two or more persons might have transcendent retrocognition of *the same event*, and so that a Mazdah might be acquainted retrospectively with all the past events that anyone remembered at any time. Similarly there would seem to be no contradiction in the theory that an "all-knowing" being might know all the propositions that are known at any given time, that is to say have all the conceptualized knowledge that is known to be true at any given time.

It must be conceded, indeed, that, according to many philosophers and theologians, the divine understanding is supposed to be undividedly intuitive. God is supposed to perceive *all* truth in a single act, and so to differ infinitely from man. For a man, at the best, can grasp but a few simple clarities in this intuitive way, and these one at a time. It would seem, however, that the unity of such intuition need not affect the *verity* of the propositions that are intuited in any way at all. When Spinoza, for instance, set what he called the "third" way of knowing (namely, the intuitive) above the "second" way (namely, step-by-step demonstration) he expressly denied that the second way was false. The example that he gave, namely that a gifted mathematician can intuit the fourth proportional that a less gifted mathematician has to infer, does not suggest a different but only a quicker (indeed an instantaneous) grasp of the truth. A familiar example would be found in the way in which some skilled mathematicians are able, at a glance, to disarticulate the number of a passing motor-car, factorizing its prime numbers on the instant. The magnification of such powers without limit would not seem to involve any theoretical difficulty, for the simple reason that the speed of such knowledge does not affect the content of the truth that is known.

On the whole, the case with regard to conceptual knowledge is clearer than the case of memory if only because memory may be the memory of sense-experience, and sense-experience, even if it be transcendent, may still raise difficulties for the theory of omniscience. One interpretation of the transcendence of sense-experience in mankind is that men's sensa (even if it is held that at bottom they are personal phenomena reflexively known), are supposed to be the vehicles of a transcendent reference to things. They are usually believed to convey a message about foreign bodies, a *message* that is public although the *sensa* are not. In that case an all-knowing being might be able to read the messages without himself experiencing or being able to experience the sensa. Moreover, if it were maintained, as some realists hold, that our sense-acquaintance, when it is not illusory, selects from the field that confronts us without altering its "objects," it might seem that an omniscient being would sense all that men select, and much that men don't select, all at once. I think that is probably the correct conclusion, supposing this realistic hypothesis to be admissible.

Nevertheless the matter is disputable, even when the selective hypothesis is followed. It may be objected, firstly, that allowing our sensa to be selected and not to be illusory, the fact that they *are* selected and are limited in that way is absolutely essential to their very being and nature. A sixpence is just a sixpence whoever has it, but if it is a poor man's last sixpence it acquires a property in the poor man's experience that distinguishes it from a rich man's sixpence without making it either more or less than sixpence. Similarly, perhaps—I do not say that the analogy is very good—the removal of all private limitations to the selection of sensa might be said to rob the sensa of much that was indefeasibly theirs. Secondly, and rather more cogently (although not, I think, conclusively), it may be said that our own experience is hostile to the opinion that the sensing of an omniscient being could simply and tidily include *all* the sensa of private men. A man, for instance, who takes a wide view of what he subsequently sees in detail, or makes a microscopic examination of what he formerly saw with the naked eye, can scarcely be supposed to have the sort of perception that would occur if the minuter sensa were simply pieced together into a wider whole. Hence there would appear to be some difficulty in the notion that an all-seeing being could simply and quite literally see all that we see (and more), that an all-hearing being could simply hear all that we hear (and more). And similarly of the other senses.

Summing up, however,[1] we may say that the existence of a Mazdah who knows all that anyone knows *transcendently* (and more) may not be wholly incredible, but that the existence of a Mazdah who knows all that any one knows *reflexively* is, to speak mildly, very hard to believe.

Continuing our discussion of our second principal question, viz. whether it is so much as credible that a being exists who knows everything that either *is* known or *could* be known, we may enlarge the question by asking whether there may not be much that is literally unknowable, not by us only but also by any conceivable knower.

Quite frequently this question is simply dismissed on the ground that it is self-contradictory to try to speak knowledgeably about the unknowable, and even that it is self-contradictory for *us* to try to speak knowledgeably about what *we* cannot know. To avoid the absurdity of declaring ineptly that knowledge contains some inherent ineptitude, or sphere of impotence, it is said, we must maintain precisely the contrary. We must strongly assert that in accepting knowledge we accept something that is insatiable and invincible in principle, something that

[1] I.e. summing up (*a*) and (*β*).

is not content to ask for bread carefully kneaded and made conformable to it, but is itself conformable to all things. In such audacity lies sanity and safety.

It is clear, I think, that any such assertion is specious rather than tenable. It is not absurd to admit certain inherent limitations, known to be such, to human knowledge; and it is a legitimate question whether it is only the limitations of our *humanity* that prescribes these boundaries.

There is profit, I think, in recalling some of the things Locke said about human ignorance, and in asking (as Locke did not ask) whether there would not have to be a similar ignorance on the part of an omniscient being, if there were one.

When Locke discussed the "extent of human knowledge"[1] he argued in detail that our experimental knowledge of natural philosophy was very imperfect because we never could discover the sort of "visible necessary connection"[2] between substances and their properties, or between causes and their effects that we find in the more highly rationalized sciences of geometry and algebra. Locke's comment seems to have been just, but it leads to a further question. Why should we deny that the absence of such *visible* necessary connection is due, not to our finitude and our blindness, but to the absence of any such connection, visible or secret, in the facts themselves? If that were the truth, omniscience itself could not discover "secret" bonds where there were none. This possibility should always be remembered in metaphysics. It is a danger-signal in philosophy, a moniment that is a warning against confusing *idola specus* with the necessities of fact.

Locke further suggested that want of ideas, want of a discoverable connection between the ideas we have, and want of tracing and examining our ideas, were among the primary sources of *human* ignorance.[3] We should further ask whether, in some of these respects, there may not also be *divine* ignorance.

Want of ideas could scarcely be suspected of an omniscient being, but in Locke's very catholic sense of the word "idea"

---

[1] *Essay*, IV, chap. iii, *passim*.   [2] *Ibid.*, sect. 10.   [3] *Ibid.*, sect. 22.

there are problems (as we have seen) regarding what Locke called "ideas of reflexion" and also regarding the "ideas" that he called sensations. Regarding the latter, the conjecture that we should have incomparably more knowledge if, like Voltaire's Micromégas, we had, not five, but a thousand senses, would raise interesting speculations regarding omniscience, although it might not affect any vital point of principle.

Among the many questions that Locke discussed under the second and the third heads mentioned above, one of rather special interest is his suggestion that much of our ignorance depended upon our failure to discover the appropriate "intermediate ideas"[1] by which a demonstrative chain could be forged. That is plainly important for our mathematicians and for all the rest of us, but it raises the query whether there always *are* such intermediate ideas, or whether omniscience also might not be at a loss to find them. I do not know whether it is possible to show that there could not be a formula for all prime numbers, but I would suggest that there would be no absurdity if there were no such formula, and no "intermediate ideas" on which it could rest. Mathematics itself has its curiosities, its "brute" and, in a sense, its empirical facts. There is no sufficient reason for believing that there would be no "brute" fact for omniscience.

Again (but, this time, to run far ahead of Locke) it might be remembered that certain philosophers have maintained that God must be "beyond knowing" as well as "beyond being". Certain mystics, like Meister Eckhart, have maintained, in consequence, that the majesty of the ultimate receives its proper reverence only when it is worshipped as the last refuge, not of *our* ignorance only, but also of *its own*.

But let us leave the mystics and consider the more mundane problem of ideas about the future.

If it is true, as I have frequently suggested in these lectures, that what we call "the future", at any given moment, is indeterminate before it occurs, then it is wrong in principle to talk about knowledge without enquiring *when* the knowledge occurs.

[1] *Essay*, IV, chap. iii, sect. 30.

The eternal or timeless truths may not obviously offend this principle; they are the same at all times; but the truths of temporal fact would obviously offend it. If "the future", before it occurs, is indeterminate it cannot, before it occurs, have the determinate characteristics that later events acquire. Therefore an all-knower, a Mazdah, could not know these determinate characteristics before they occur, because, before they occur, there would be no such thing to know.

This question, as I have also observed, should not be confused with the problem of determinism. The thesis of determinism is that every future event is inferable with certainty (in theory) from the knowledge of a sufficient set of past and of present events, such data (in theory) being always discoverable in their sufficiency. If determinism were false, it would be quite legitimate to maintain (as many philosophers do maintain) that although the future is not *inferable* in this way, it might still be *foreknown*, not by inference, but by some sort of clairvoyance, just as the remembered past need not be *inferred* (as the past often is) but is directly known. In that case a Mazdah would *know* all the future at any given time but could not *infer* it. What I am suggesting, however, is something much more radical than this. I am saying that if these views about the future are true, an omniscient being could not know the future before it occurs in any way at all. He could guess, like the rest of us; but he could not fore*know*.

Consider, again, infinity. I do not suggest that infinity is intellectually inapprehensible, and if the fallacy of identifying Knowing with Being be avoided, it seems to me to be negligent to assert that a finite being, just because he is finite, must be gravelled by the infinite. The thought of the infinite is not an infinite thought. On the other hand, as I have formerly observed, a finite infinite is a contradiction, and the partisans of omniscience should be wary lest they contradict themselves in what they say about the Infinite Being's knowledge of his own infinity. An omniscient and infinite being might indeed be able to number all the hairs on all the heads that (up to the moment of his census) had ever been hairy—but only if that number were enumerable, that is to say, finite. He could not count a *countless* number. In the case of infinity, therefore, it is futile to suggest that *our* finitude is the fountain and sole origin of all our perplexities about infinity, and that a reverent psychic blindness in such matters is all that should be expected of a thinking being. These problems also affect an omniscient knower.

More generally, let us examine some traditional questions regarding the divine intellect.

Certain philosophers have maintained that divine knowledge must be super-intellectual on the ground that intellectual knowledge is a linked affair and not a perfect unity. That contention itself is highly problematical. Reality might *be* a linked affair, and so would be falsified if the links were supposed to be fused. Again, if it is permissible to speak of divine knowledge at all, and to contemplate deity *sub specie veritatis*, a distinction has already been drawn within the unity of divine experience or divine selfhood. It is therefore too late nervously to attempt a restoration of the riven unity and simplicity. In any case it might reasonably be held, as we saw that Spinoza held, that step-by-step intellectualism need not be false even if the divine *scientia intuitiva* is nobler and stronger.

Accordingly we may legitimately consider the possibility of intellectual omniscience, and the allied question whether, if everything were known intellectually, there would be "omniscience" in every relevant and important sense of the word.

Those philosophers who maintain that there is an "alogical" element in reality correctly infer that a merely intellectual knowledge of everything would fall short of omniscience. This belief cannot be summarily dismissed as false. I allow that if it meant that anything real is *contra*logical, it need not be seriously examined. Various reasons may be given, however, for holding that much that is real may escape the logical intellect without contradicting it flatly. In that case much may be "alogical" even if its escape is only partial.

Apart from nervous monistic apprehensions regarding affronts to the "seamless unity" and "translucent simplicity" of reality, the principal argument of this type is that the intellect deals with concepts and with propositions, and that *something* in the real escapes concepts and therefore escapes propositions (which always contain a conceptual element). The reason is that all concepts are general, but that whatever exists is particular. If we could accept the principle of the identity of indiscernibles, i.e. if it were certain that there can be no difference where there is no *conceptual* difference either in a relation or in a quality, we should have to reject the possibility of the "alogical" altogether, even in its most attenuated sense. There is nothing illogical or anti-intellectual, however, in denying the principle of the identity of indiscernibles.

As we have seen, it may be consistently asserted that all intellectual affirmations and denials are ultimately existential affirmations and denials. It may also be true that *certain* intellectual notions may determine *ad unum*. In general, however, it seems to be true to say that unless the principle of the identity of indiscernibles must be accepted, many particulars cannot be wholly intellectualized in their full particularity, and so, in a measure, escape although they do not contradict logic. If, therefore, we do know particulars, and can recognize the distinction between certain beings that are intellectually indiscernible, it follows that something that is known would escape an intellectual being who knew everything that could be known but only in the intellectual way.

This may be a defensible view of the limitations of any intellect, even God's, and it does not imply what it is often falsely supposed to imply, namely that there must be a third estate of concepts and propositions that are neither knowing minds nor known things. On the contrary it is fully consistent with the realistic theory that the intellect selects from reality in *its* intellectual way just as other cognitive faculties select in *their* characteristic ways. The intellect selects the general features of reality that are intellectually discernible. Our present question is simply whether this intellectual selection (or everything that may be expressed in terms of intellectual selection) does or does not exhaust the reality that is known. The question is complicated by the circumstance that all our language is conceptual. When, say, we describe some particular (e.g. a red cross) we use the same terms as when we say that we perceive its redness. The perceived particular, however, is a single entity, while the proposition that expresses it contains more than one term. I am therefore prepared to allow that there may be a limitation of this order in the case of every sort of intellection, human or divine.

In the concluding part of this lecture, discussing the question whether it is credible that a being exists who knows *everything*, I have elected to give most attention to the problem of the types of our knowing and of their relation to such alleged omniscience. My choice may be censured on the ground that it gives, at the best, a rather oblique answer to the question put. If, however, a more direct answer is wanted, there is no great difficulty in supplying one. We concluded, at an earlier stage in the lecture, that it was very hard to believe that there was a being, or a community of beings, that knew all that was known in all relevant senses of "knowing". It follows (or, rather, it is a pleonasm) that it is very hard to believe that there is a being who knows all that could be known. And "everything that could be known" may not be quite *everything*.

In a general way, it is surely quite plain that the apparently simple statement that there is a being who knows *everything* is much less simple than it looks. That, indeed, is so plain that it could be demonstrated in a line or two. I have taken a whole hour to develop the theme because the incidentals of the question seemed to me to be worth following up. My regret now is that I have not pursued them further.

On the whole the most interesting questions for most of us are whether it can be shown that when any man knows it is God that knoweth in him, and that everything that any man comes to know must be something that some God or divine community has known from all eternity. I have tried to answer these questions, and have answered the second of them definitely in the negative. In concluding the lecture, however, I should like to repeat what I said at an earlier stage. I have not been trying to discuss whether there is a *supreme* being, supereminently wise and of an understanding unsearchable by man. I am asking only whether such a being *must* or *could* be held to be literally omniscient, and in what sense.

V

Divine Personality

IN this second series of lectures, treating of "Mind and Deity", we have been concerned, up to the present, almost exclusively with the attributes of mind that are shown in knowledge, ideas and the like. This plan, indeed, was almost prescribed for us, since one of our aims was to consider whether the provisional realism of the first series of lectures should or should not be abandoned by a more adequate philosophy. Can we do justice to the strength of theistic argument if we remain realists in our philosophy?

To examine that question was primarily to examine pan-idea-ism, pan-ideatism and such-like theories. Even pan-psychism, a wider theory, has been often supposed to be based, very largely, upon the implications of an adequate theory of knowledge.

It is clear, however, that when we speak of "minds" we commonly assume either that minds are selves or that "mind" is a name for certain functions of selves, their mental functions. It is also clear that the conceptions of selfhood and of personality are very closely connected.

Consequently it is at least possible that an enquiry into personality, human or divine, may have something (and perhaps much) to add to the sort of question that has been occupying us recently. In particular, it would be maintained, frequently and very vigorously, that the moral attributes that are often supposed to distinguish theism proper from mere deism, and all the arguments that support the attribution of moral properties to deity, cannot be effectively considered except in connection with the conception of God's personality. This part of our subject is obviously quintessential to it. In the opinion of many, it alone, in Hume's words, "affects human action or forbearance". On it man's hopes are often centred. On it his destiny may be thought to depend.

The rest of our enquiry will be chiefly about such matters, and should be introduced by a discussion of the nature of personality.

I have to confess to some surprise when I read in Dr. Webb's *God and Personality* that the doctrine of God's personality is a latish interloper in Christian theology, that it is scarcely distinguishable from the Socinian heresy, and that English divines in particular seldom spoke of God's personality before the middle of the nineteenth century. I had heard, I may say, of the doctrine of the Trinity, and of the obtuseness involved in dividing the substance or in confusing the persons of the Godhead. The obvious inference, however, had escaped me, I mean Dr. Webb's inference that, according to the logic of the Trinitarian doctrine, there is personality *in* God, but not, in strictness, *of* God.

I make this confession with becoming shame, and I shall not try to excuse it. I was, however, one of a numerous company. Which of us has not been told by ever so many preachers and apologists that Christian theism is opposed to pantheism, and to much of the theology of the East, precisely because Christian theists conceive God to be personal? As Bowman would say, Christian theism has checked the "drift towards the impersonal", a drift that is supposed to have begun with man's dissatisfaction with the primitive animism of his prehistoric world-view. The ascetics of the Yoga system believed that they had left God behind, because Ishvara was *only* a personal saviour of persons.[1] He was earth-clogged like all persons because his office was to rescue the earth-bound. Christians, on the contrary (we were told), look to God's personality as the goal of all their seeking.

In such statements it is the personality *of* God that is nearly always asserted.

[1] Vide Söderblom, *The Living God*, p. 45.

Divine Personality

Since we are not here concerned with Christian apologetics, and cannot even pretend that the doctrine of the Trinity is a possible consequence of mere natural theology, we have no direct interest in the relation of our views to this part of Christian doctrine. If, however, the Christian doctrine of the Trinity is subtler and more carefully guarded regarding divine personality than the modern talk about a "personal God" would indicate to all except perhaps a very few, the fact, I think, is encouraging. It may even be heartening to those who believe that the future of religion has little promise unless some at least of the barriers between the great historical religions are less intimidating than they seem to be.

Hence I am rash enough to adventure another laic comment here. It seems to me that the sense in which one of the "persons" in the Christian Trinity can be said to be *a* person is very obscure indeed. I gather from *Doctrine in the Church of England* (pp. 93 ff.) that the Holy Spirit should not be regarded primarily as a charismatic effluence, but chiefly as the continuing inspiration and unwearied bond of fellowship in the Christian Church. The explanation is interesting. The one thing that *looks* certain about the early manifestations of the Holy Spirit at Pentecost was that it *was* a charismatic effluence, a mantic "possession" or *epipnoia* similar in very many ways to the voluble frenzies of many mystery religions.[1] The same might readily be said of the "Spirit of prophecy", the "Spirit of miracle" and so forth. Let us grant, however, that it was also quite peculiar and let us dispose ourselves to accept the statements of these Anglican writers as accurate. How could it then be inferred that the Holy Spirit is a distinctive person? Again, when I read further from the same pages that "God cannot be a merely unitary personality because personality, as we know it, always requires for its own completeness personality other than itself",[2] I am sceptical about the soundness of the reason given, but interested in the implied

---

[1] Cf. Joel ii. 28 and 29, the history of Montanism in Phrygia, *c.* A.D. 150, etc. In the second century Athenagoras said, "The Holy Spirit is an effluence from God as light from fire". [2] P. 96.

admission that the sense (if there is one) in which God is a person must be very different indeed from the sense that would usually be collected by the common mind.

In the present lecture I shall consider two questions. The first is whether it is credible that God is a person. The second is whether those who do not believe in God's personality must on that account alone renounce any intelligible form of theism. Each of these questions implies that the meaning of "being a person" is fairly clear. I have therefore to examine that topic first of all.

I have said a good deal about "mind", and have remarked that there is a pretty close connection between "mind" and "personality". The terms, however, are not interchangeable, for "mind" is in one way a wider and in another way a thinner term than "personality". It is wider, for instance, because we may legitimately speak of "the animal mind" but not of "animal personality". It is thinner because the "mind" of a person refers primarily if not exclusively to that person's knowledgeable powers. The terms "spirit" and "self" and "ego" do not have this kind of thinness, and in their common use may be little (if at all) wider than "person". I shall employ them quite frequently without distinguishing them explicitly from "person", but I shall also try to indicate the nicer flavour of meaning that is usually supposed to permeate the word "person". I shall not say much about "souls", for although that good old-fashioned word may be mouthed with more relish than many of the others, its primary sense is vitalistic or biological.

It must be confessed that we frequently speak of "personality" very vaguely indeed. Thus I read in *The Times*[1] that the President of the Royal College of Organists, discussing the relations between organists and certain other important people, said that "apart from his technical equipment, an organist needs to possess personality in large quantities". I think I know what was meant, but I shall not stay to define that meaning. I shall also not discuss what we mean by "merely personal reasons",

[1] January 24, 1938.

and shall neglect the sense of the word "person" in which a man's "person" is his body. Since the word "person" is frequently used in a concrete rather than in an abstract sense, I shall sometimes use Coleridge's term "personeity", despite the irregularity of its formation, when I want to refer to the abstract property or set of properties with which we are here concerned.

By "personeity" we should mean primarily a certain type and level of manhood or womanhood that the lower animals cannot evince, that imbeciles never attain and that, in children, is only in the making. The man is a body-mind, just as a colt or a baby is, but his personeity describes a certain level of body-mindedness; and in the main connotes the characteristics of what is called "responsibility" in a forensic or in a moral way, although a man's distinctive individuality—the *style* of him, as in the phrase "le style c'est l'homme"—is also sometimes what is meant. Among human beings, therefore, personeity has to be acquired, but there is a presumption (which might be rather difficult to justify in detail) that nearly all human beings do acquire the quality when they grow up. When they acquire it, there is a further presumption that mind and moral character take the lead and, as we say rather picturesquely, "govern" the body-mind in question. On the other hand, we apply the word "person" to the whole concrete being, and not to a mere capacity —the "personal capacity"—of that being. Accordingly the etymological sense of *persona*, namely an actor's mask, and, in a transferred sense, a "capacity" or an "office", is substantially irrelevant to the modern use of the word.

It is plain that personeity, so understood, raises many problems. The implied doctrine of *mens una in corpore uno* may itself be challenged, and so may the doctrine of an inner *imperium in imperio*. We shall have to take account of some of these problems in due course. For the present it may suffice to indicate the general character of a few of them.

Speaking in a rough way, we have to say that other people identify a man by identifying his body. Their testimony, in general, coincides with the man's own. His private acquaintance with his own body corroborates their external evidence. He has to admit that he was at Charing Cross Station when others say that he was at Charing Cross Station. Nevertheless it may be doubted how far these foreign identifications would be accepted by each private man if hearsay as well as his own experience did not enter into his general presumption. Most of us have *no* intimate retrospective acquaintance with "our" body of twenty years ago, and would not accept finger-print evidence or even a photographer's evidence, except by hearsay. Consider, again, a common plea in many trials. The accused remembers that he shook the woman but professes to have no recollection of subsequent events, although he may be prepared to infer with other people that his were probably the hands that strangled her. Such a statement, although so often suspect, might sometimes be true. In short, there are many lacunæ in the ordinary working theory of this matter.

These remarks may give a rough indication of what we mean by personality in man. We have now to ask whether it is credible that God should be a person.

If man is made in God's image, or if, as the irreverent say, God is made in man's image, there must be a certain resemblance however immense the interval between them. Hence we are often told that, since personeity marks man at his highest, there must be a resemblance in point of personeity if man's vaunting claim to be in the image of deity contains much of substance. That, for example, was why Chesterton held that Christian was superior to much Eastern theology. He applauded "the idea that personality is the glory of the universe and not its shame, that creation is higher than evolution because it is more personal, that pardon is higher than nemesis because it is more personal",[1] in short, that the time had come "when we were worthy to be anthropomorphic" in our beliefs about God. Others similarly might suppose that the time had come when we could afford to be theomorphic in our beliefs about man. To a third party it might seem that there is better hope for piety and greater scope

[1] *Blake*, p. 48. Quoted by Webb, *Divine Personality*, p. 99.

for philosophy if we neither anthropomorphize God nor theo-morphize man.

There is an obvious difficulty regarding what is sometimes called the corporeal basis of human personality. Some would say outright with Dr. Strong that "the subject is the whole organism or self".[1] Others would hold with Stout and William James that human personeity is a property of an embodied self, primarily known from the inside by cœnæsthesia or bodily "warmth and intimacy".

If so it would follow that "divine personality" would be a thoroughly misleading phrase unless the divine person were either a body or an embodied self, not merely as the temporary historical incarnation of a being who had the divine as well as a human nature, but also essentially and always. I do not think, however, that those who believe in God's personality need be affrighted at this consequence. God's ubiquity is a defensible theological doctrine, and the Lutherans in their doctrine of consubstantiation assert the extreme mobility of the body of the risen Christ. In short, God may be embodied.

On the other hand, if deity be embodied, his body cannot reasonably be supposed to be at all similar to a human body. Few would now suppose that the prophet Daniel had a true vision when he wrote "I beheld till the thrones were cast down, and the Ancient of Days did sit, whose garment was white as snow, and the hair of his head like the pure wool: his throne was like the fiery flame, and his wheels as burning fire".[2] In brief, it is incredible that God's body should be similar to ours, whether his body be the world, or a part of the world, or a spiritual body distinct from the world and from all its parts. It is puerile to imagine that the divine embodied personality has any visible semblance of the human shape or of human nerves and arteries. To be sure, there is a vast difference between inner cœnæsthesia and the outward visible frame, but it would be a wild surmise to conjecture that there is any close or detailed correspondence between human and divine cœnæsthesia.

[1] *A Creed for Sceptics*, p. 26.   [2] Daniel vii. 9.

We have to conclude, therefore, that if God be embodied, his body does not resemble ours in the look of it. That, however, is scarcely a proof that both he and we are not persons, even supposing that personeity is an attribute of a mind-body. I am further of opinion that two other obstacles that are supposed to stand in the way of a belief in divine personality are not insurmountable.

The first is this: Men and women, it is said, acquire personality through the discipline of a physical and social environment and with reference to that environment. Therefore, we are told, the removal of these conditions and limitations of human personality would slit any thread of analogy between man's personeity and God's. We might believe in the existence of an impersonal and limitless deity, or of a personal and limited deity, but not in the existence of a deity both personal and unlimited.

This argument sets out to show that if God be personal he is limited. That, no doubt, would be an important conclusion; for many theologians insist that God cannot be less than the Whole. Thus Dr. Webb maintains that God, in Tertullian's phrase, is *Totum quod sumus et in quo sumus.* That is an explicit assertion of the truth of pantheism, although Dr. Webb also holds that "the God whom we worship must be the Highest" and must be conceived to respond, almost as a friend responds, to those who worship him in sincerity of heart. These statements may indeed be inconsistent, but they are evidence of extreme reluctance to admit any sort of finitude in the deity.

The argument itself, however, despite the importance of its goal, seems to be rather frail. I do not see how it could be demonstrated that a not-self (including other selves) is essential to the existence of a self, and if the contention be that because our personeity is acquired, therefore God's personeity implies that he too is a growing being, I think we should say that the inference is feeble and that, in any case, God *may* be a growing being. To speak more generally, no one denies that the differences between divine and human personality must be very great. The question is only whether it is either inconceivable or incredible that both man and God should be persons.

The other argument that I take to be insufficient is used by Bradley, Bosanquet and by some others, and is to the general effect that personality is altogether too juristic and too moralistic a conception to be applicable to deity. "A God that can say to himself 'I' as against you and me", Bradley remarks,[1] "is not in my judgement defensible as the last and complete truth for metaphysics." The world of personality, Bosanquet says, is a world of "claims and counter-claims", a world in which the members defend their rights and fulfil, or are dragooned into fulfilling, their obligations. God, however, is not a litigant among other litigants, and he cannot either bind himself or be bound by others in the way that is implied by a legal or by a moral obligation. Therefore, according to Bosanquet, he is not a "person" in the forensic-moralistic sense which alone is appropriate to that appellation, and we demonstrate our poverty of imagination if we speak of him in these terms.

These contentions are unconvincing. The forensic interpretation of responsibility is primarily concerned with the limits below which a man is judged unfit to plead or to understand the sort of expiation that legal punishment is supposed to entail. The presence of lower limits need not establish the presence of upper limits; and although the conception of deity as a magnified non-natural judge need not indicate much delicacy of theological perception, it is not any ruder in principle than the conception of deity as the friend of man. In this and in other cases the supreme difficulty is to conceive God as the Highest and also as the Whole. Similarly the objection to moralistic rather than to forensic conceptions of deity does not seem to be solid. Even if, as Kant thought,[2] the notion of *duty* or of moral obligation is inapplicable to a holy will that is without bonds, or sanctions, or temptations, the conception of *righteousness* is not inapplicable. Righteousness is not a mark of imperfection although the form of it that we call moral obligation may imply the possibility of vagrant and peccant inclinations that have to be subdued in man, and do not exist in God.

[1] *Essays in Truth and Reality*, p. 432.   [2] E.g. *Fundamental Principles*, sect. 1.

These difficulties, I submit, need not overwhelm us. On the other hand, if God be a person and also *Totum quod sumus et in quo sumus*, his personality must include all finite personalities. That is among the hardest of all hard beliefs; but it stares us in the face. I propose to examine it now, that is, to ask whether it is possible for selves to be part of a greater self. I shall begin by considering such empirical evidence as we have, and shall go on to discuss less empirical arguments.

In a recent discussion Mr. Broad has said: "I suppose that no one has ever suggested that one human self could be part of another."[1] In saying so he seems to have been, for once, inadvertent. Indeed he himself entertains (although he does not accept) the suggestion on his very next page where he discusses certain views regarding so-called "multiple personality". Again, on a later page,[2] he admits that all traducians have held some such doctrine. Moreover, as Mr. Broad knows very well, those who believe that selves are loosish groups, or bundles, or colonies of experiences have frequently been willing to infer that the members of such bundles may be either recompounded, or actually are simultaneously compounded, into other bundles that are selves.

In any case there may seem to be empirical evidence for the compounding of self-like bundles into other self-like bundles, and we may conveniently consider the empirical evidence under two heads. The first will deal with the possibility of the compounding of selves within the same body, the second will deal with the possibility of a many-bodied self composed of single-bodied selves.

As we have often noticed, careless talk about the sub- and un-conscious might seem to support the belief that each of us is many-selved, having an "unconscious" and a "fore-conscious" self as well as a self-conscious one, and perhaps having many others. It seems plain, however, that even if there is a multiplicity of these psychoid levels, there is no reason to suppose that each such level is a distinct *self* that can struggle or live in

[1] *Examination of McTaggart's Philosophy*, II, 154. [2] *Ibid.*, II, 613.

amity with the waking self. The more usual interpretation is that all the levels are levels of the same ego, although they may have to be tapped in devious and expensive ways. That indeed seems to be the therapeutic revelation of psycho-analytic theory. The loch becomes sweet and calm when the monster is induced to rise to the surface.

If it could be shown, however, that some of these psychoid levels beneath the threshold of waking retrospective self-acquaintance are capable of an independent development of thought, and will, and memory, doubts about the general question might begin to emerge. Such doubts, again, might be supported by a counter-attack designed to show that the unity of what we are accustomed to call *the* ego in any given body may be a good deal looser than we often credulously suppose. This line of argument was rather sedulously pursued a few years ago in the considerable literature about so-called "multiple personality", especially in the most careful and skilful book on the subject, Morton Prince's presentation of the Beauchamp case.[1]

Consider the fable of Philip drunk and Philip sober. Philip has to get drunk again if he is to find what he hid when he was drunk before. In itself, Philip's hard drinking might seem to be just a mnemonic device, like tying a knot in his handkerchief. So let us expand the idea. Suppose, for instance, that Philip is something of a poet when he is drunk, but very prosy when he is sober, and that his voice, and mannerisms, and religiosity and moral tone differ characteristically in the two conditions. The supposition is now approaching the conditions required for a Jekyll-and-Hyde story, although all the steps in it are easy. Now suppose just a little more, namely, that there is a definite memory-barrier in all respects between Philip drunk and Philip sober, and that the traits of style and of character before mentioned attach themselves in opposed ways to these uncommunicating memory-systems. What grounds would you then have for denying that Philip drunk and Philip sober were two different persons?

[1] *The Dissociation of a Personality.*

Your grounds, I submit, would be pretty weak if you rested the case upon Philip's retrospective self-acquaintance plus his distinctive mannerisms, that is to say, if you used the ordinary criteria. True, you might claim that a hypnotist might discover a unitary Philip, and that a shock might do by chance what a hypnotist would do by design. Philip's double personality, in other words, might be a temporary condition, traumatic in origin, remediable by another trauma or destined perhaps to fade gradually back into singularity. These, however, are surmises. Even if the two Philips could be reunited, would it be at all clear that they were not two before the reunion? Might not the two Philips die first and be extinguished in the so-called reunion? And if the two Philips were reunited, might not the truth be that two human selves had become one human self?

I have described these possibilities conjecturally and in a parable, but it must not be supposed that the entire idea is imaginative. There have been classical instances, Félida X, Ansel Bourne, Mary Reynolds, Louis Vivé, the Rev. Mr. Hanna, the Beauchamp family and others—fictitious names for actual cases. In most of these cases, it is true, the evidence for disintegration is a good deal stronger than the evidence for the existence of a discriminable family. That should be said in the Beauchamp case of the temporary conditions that the investigator labelled B I, B IV and B IVa. These were exclusive memory-conditions with associated mannerisms and traits of character. Morton Prince claimed, however, that "Sally" Beauchamp *was* a distinctive personality that had to be obliterated in order that "Miss Beauchamp" might live in health.

"Sally's" claim to be a distinctive personality in all relevant respects except in respect of her body is unique in the literature; and one instance is scarcely enough to build upon. The analytical implications of this type of empirical evidence, however, are very important. If it be said that all the instances are extreme cases of disintegration of personality, and that there is just one self in each body all the time, the consequence is that selfhood is consistent with so much disintegration that it must be held to be a very loose type of psychic unity. If it be said that the instances show that personality may disappear from waking life altogether although psychical functions and experiences remain, the consequence would be that personality in man is something much narrower than we commonly suppose and that it may be much less usual. If it be said that the so-called dissociated personalities may be redintegrated into one personality it would not follow that they had been just one personality all the time. Moreover, the possibility of the compounding of personalities would seem to be conceded.

My own opinion on these matters, for what it is worth, is that there is very little empirical evidence in favour of the view that a personality may be disintegrated *into personalities*, or that several personalities in the same body may be integrated *into another personality*. That is the special question with which we are now concerned. The empirical evidence, however, does not prohibit and, in a small way, may even suggest the possibility of a body that is many-selved, and it is seriously disturbing to our ordinary blunt conviction that the unity of a single self in a single body may be taken for granted.

I can afford to be briefer, I think, about the familiar contention that in every society or community, minds and selves are united, *de facto*, into group-minds and group-selves, and consequently that every church, every nation and every committee is a many-bodied mind or self. The sufficient objection to all such views is that while they may prove the existence of spiritual groups, they do not even begin to prove that any such group is *a* mind, or *a* self, or *a* person. It is true that the chairman of the committee may say "Gentlemen, what is your mind?" or "Gentlemen, what is your will?" If he said so, he would be using the words "mind" and "will" in a sense that applies to groups. It is perfectly plain, however, that the specific sort of unity that we believe to be characteristic of selfhood is not to be found in the committee or in any other such group. The committee, as such, does not remember. To return to a stock illustration, if one of its members, A, has a certain piece of information, and if another of its members, B, has another piece of information, the *committee* cannot unite these pieces of information by inference, association or other such processes unless A and B communicate their information to some at least of the several minds in the group. In short, a group of selves need not be a group-self.

Such spiritual communities may show a type of unity that is greater or, as Aristotle said, is "nobler and more divine"[1] than selfhood. In comparison with their greatness and worth the greatness and the worth of every private man may be feeble and poor. That is a serious reflection for those theists who are inclined to argue, as so many theists do, that God must be a person because personality is "the highest thing we know". The personality of individual men and women may *not* be the highest spiritual thing that we know empirically. No doubt it may be replied that spiritual groups *may* be of lesser worth than private men and women. There is often more stupidity than safety in numbers, and the best thinking may be done in solitude. In short, we must hold that a spiritual group *may* be superior and also that it *may* be inferior to any of its members. In any case, the argument, taken in bare abstraction, proves very little. A parallel contention would be that the Highest cannot be thumbless, since the human thumb, empirically speaking, attains a unique pitch of excellence in its kind.

On the whole, then, there is little empirical evidence in favour of the view that selves can be compounded into a greater self, although the evidence from multiple personality may not be entirely negligible, and although the integrity of empirical selfhood is frequently suspect and is an easy prey to conflicting definitions. I propose now to turn to less empirical arguments.

Among recent discussions, McTaggart's in *The Nature of Existence* is more confident than most. McTaggart emphatically denied that one self could form part of another, and that two selves could overlap. "When I contemplate what is meant by a cognition, an emotion, or any other part of my experience", he

---

[1] κάλλιον καὶ θειότερον, N.E. 1094b.

said, "it seems as impossible to me that such a state should belong to more than one self, as it is that it should not belong to a self at all. And this impossibility, like the other, seems to me to be an ultimate synthetic proposition."[1]

The trouble about "ultimate synthetic propositions" is that, being ultimate, they permit of no proof, but that, being synthetic, they may be denied without contradiction. McTaggart claimed to have reached ultimate certainty where many other philosophers remained doubtful. He even claimed to be able to indicate the sort of erroneous grounds that prevented these other philosophers from seeing what he himself so clearly perceived.[2] But there was nothing more he could do if his opponents persisted in their incredulity.

In general these claims to final synthetic certainty are made at the end of prolonged analytical argument, and profess to be beams of indestructible clarity that have broken through when the mists of muddled thinking were dispelled. That is a fair description of the context in which McTaggart made these confident assertions. It is impracticable here to attempt to supply McTaggart's whole close context, but attention may be given to some features of it.

McTaggart believed he could prove fairly easily that the animate body is never the substance of the self, and that his principal business was to refute Hume's "bundle" theory of selfhood, revived in some of its principal features by F. H. Bradley, a philosopher whom McTaggart esteemed more highly than any of his contemporaries.

McTaggart agreed, up to a point, with Hume and Bradley since he believed that what he called "awarenesses", "cogitations" and "perceptions" were parts or constituents of some ego. He differed from them, however, because he believed he could prove that there must be acquaintance with the ego as a whole as well as with such "parts" of it. According to McTaggart, if anyone can truly affirm "I am acquainted with this awareness", he must be acquainted with the ego that has the awareness as

---

[1] *The Nature of Existence*, II, 82 f.   [2] *Ibid.*, 84 f.

well as with the awareness in order to know that the entity that has the awareness is the entity that is making the judgement. He must be able to perceive the whole as well as the parts (and McTaggart believed that, in the extreme case, it is possible to perceive a whole without perceiving *any* of its parts).[1]

"The quality of being a self", McTaggart said, "is a quality which is known to me because I perceive—in the strict sense of the word—one substance as possessing this quality. This substance is myself. And this quality is simple. We can perceive no parts or elements of which it is composed, any more than we can with the quality of redness. Like redness it is simple and undefinable."[2] According to his theory, however, the *substance* does contain parts, namely what McTaggart called "awarenesses". Therefore his contention seems to have been that the whole possessed a simple quality that the parts, or some of them, did not possess. He would also appear to have held that all of us in childhood, in maturity and in our declining years perceive this same simple quality of selfhood as often as we are aware of any of our experiences.

I think it is very difficult to believe that we have any such power, but if we had some such power I do not see that McTaggart's case would be established. The possession of such a faculty would not prove that there can be no experience that is not the experience of a self, but only that when anyone perceives that *he* has an experience, *he* is also acquainted with himself. Again, it does not seem to be true that these contentions of McTaggart's refute the "bundle" theory of selfhood. What McTaggart maintained was that when anyone is acquainted with an experience that *de facto* and to his knowledge is part of a "bundle" [i.e. is united with other experiences that he also calls *his*] he is always acquainted, in addition, with himself [i.e. with a particular entity that owns this bundle of experiences and has *his* unique "quality" of simple selfhood]. Let it be so. What, in that case, would prevent the members of this bundle, either collectively or separately, from belonging to other bundles

[1] *The Nature of Existence*, II, p. 69.   [2] *Ibid.*, p. 76.

attached to some other self or selves? *Ex hypothesi,* no given ego would be acquainted with any other ego, but that would not prevent the experiences that are said to be among its "parts" from being parts of other selves. McTaggart may have had reasonable empirical grounds for believing that he himself was never aware of any experience except an experience of his own, and also that his own self-acquaintance seemed opposed to the theory that his own experiences formed a rather loose bundle of constituents that might have other ties. That, however, would not be a sufficient proof that each bundle and each member of each bundle must belong, as a piece of ultimate metaphysics, to one ego and to one ego only. That view may be true; but McTaggart, I think, did not establish its truth.

There is another comment to be made on McTaggart's views. He assumed in all his arguments that his acquaintance with himself and with his "awarenesses" was a sort of "perception", that is to say, was a piece of transcendent knowledge.[1] That contradicts the position I have tried to defend in former lectures, namely that our self-acquaintence, although it is often transcendent (as it must be when, for example, it is retrospective) has *reflexive* non-transcendent knowledge at the roots of it. It may perhaps be thought, however, that if McTaggart had accepted such a doctrine of non-transcendent self-acquaintance his conclusion would have been firmly established. If, in reflexive self-acquaintance, knower and known are one, would it not follow that each of us, in so far as he knows himself reflexively, is aware of nothing except himself, and so that *such* self-acquaintance excludes all other selves by the mere fact of occurring?

I think this is a very strong argument, but it does not seem to me to be absolutely conclusive. I have argued in former lectures, it is true, that our reflexive acquaintance with ourselves "at the very moment" is acquaintance with something very complex, and that it is imprudent to try to enlarge the conception much beyond the boundaries of our actual experience. I have also argued that the reflexive self-experience of a universal mind

[1] "Prehension," Mr. Broad would call it.

should be held to be self-acquaintance with that immense totality, and so would be different from our private self-acquaintance, even on the assumption that our minds were parts of God's mind. I have also maintained, however, that some of our experiences may be pure phenomena, that is to say, that certain of our experiences would show what they are and be what they show if they existed quite alone. In other words, the reflexive dimension of our waking consciousness at any given moment does not necessarily imply that our complex selves at that moment cannot contain constituents that themselves have the reflexive property.

If this be true (and I am not convinced that it is false) the point of principle would be settled in a way that is adverse to McTaggart's metaphysics. A reflexive whole might contain reflexive constituents. If so, it might be possible that self-like unities of experience might have the reflexive property and yet be parts of a wider whole that was also a self-like unity of experience. From this there would be only a short step, and not a prodigious stride, to the theory that a larger self might include lesser selves. I am not suggesting that this is a probable theory. I am not claiming empirical support for it except of the vaguest kind. I am not asking anyone to believe it. All I am saying is that it is not wholly inconceivable.

Mr. Broad, in discussing these views of McTaggart's, remarks, as I suppose we would all admit, that the important philosophical question is not whether a human self could be part of another self of the same order, but whether it could be part of another self of a higher order; and he refers to the interest that the Society for Psychical Research might legitimately take in the matter. In making a suggestion of his own, he uses the useful term "sympsychic experiences" instead of Hume's "bundle of perceptions"; and that is a gain in point of accuracy and in point of avoiding provocative expressions. His suggestion is that if selves were composed without residue of sympsychic experiences these might readily be compared to a set of points which, in a certain relation, comprised a circle. Concyclic points, he goes on to say, have a close formal relation to co-spherical points. There-fore personality of a higher order might fitly be compared to a sphere that contained the circles of human personality on its surface.[1]

This analogy must be admitted for what it is worth, but it may not be worth very much. It is not unusual to speak of lines being generated by points, and of volumes being generated by areas. Such language, however, is frankly metaphorical. We might hold, with at least equal correctness, that two-dimensional figures and three-dimensional solids are strictly incomparable, that a sphere is not made up of circles (although there are circles on its surface), and therefore that God (in terms of the analogy) would *not* be a self or a personality. His unity would be more than sympsychic by a whole new dimension of being, and even if he were a sympsychic unity it would not follow that our selves were sympsychic *parts* of the divine sympsychic totality.

Let us now turn to the second question that was put at the beginning of this lecture. Do those who deny or decline to admit that God is personal renounce every intelligible form of theism by doing so?

According to Boethius, quoted with approval by Dr. Webb, *Persona est naturae rationabilis individua substantia.*[2] In its intel-lectual aspects this statement must be taken to mean that a person or rational substance is a being that can think and infer, and this interpretation agrees with our earlier conclusions regarding the nature of mind. We have also argued on several occasions that the legibility of the book of nature does not imply that someone is always reading it.

What an impersonalistic theist would naturally say to a personalistic theist, I think, would be something like this: "What you regard as the *mark* of the activity of a divine person is to me the substance and the reality of theism itself. That is what I believe about the rational order of the universe that, according to you, redounds so signally to the glory and majesty

[1] *Examination*, II, 154, cf. II, 179.
[2] *Contra Eutychen et Nestorium*, chap. 3, see Webb, *God and Personality*, p. 47.

of God. I allow that we live in a universe and not in a multi-verse, in a cosmos and not in a chaos. If you will, I allow that reality is a book with divine homilies on every page. But where you speculate freely, and, if I may say so, where you talk rather glibly about the personal cause of this order, I, for my part, am disposed to maintain that the fact of order itself is the fact of deity. God, for me, *is* the deiformity of things. Order is just what God is. It is not his signature. There is no need and there is little excuse for seeking anything more ultimate than this, and then another 'ultimate', and then another still. There is a more delicate satisfaction (as Hume might have said) and there is a far sounder philosophy in restraining one's intemperate desire for supposing secret foundations that needn't be supposed. *Something* must be ultimate. In my view the orderliness of which you speak *is* what is ultimate, and theism, in this aspect, is just the recognition of ultimate fact of order, conformable to a tidy intellect. There is nothing behind this veil, and it is not a veil at all. To assume that it is a veil is just to forget God."

I submit that there is nothing absurd and nothing negligent in such a theism. On the contrary, it would seem to me that in so far as theism has to do with the orderliness and the inferable inter-connections of existence, this form of theism is preferable to most others. I allow that a question may be made whether the orderliness of reality has the majesty, the glory and the divinity that Malebranche, Berkeley and so many other philo-sophical theologians have ascribed to it. If and so far, however, as the theistic argument rests upon the inferable inter-connected-ness of existence, it rests upon the very deiformity of existence that so many theists believe to be supra-mundane. It was this orderliness *itself* upon which the philosophical theologians of the new age should have relied when they took Francis Bacon's hint and tried to show that while a little of the new science seemed to lead men away from God, depth in the new philo-sophy led them back to God. And the new science, even if it has become still newer, is with us today.

Divinity, in this aspect of it, may be impersonal rather than personal. It need not be the ungodly only who, as the Psalmist thought, say corruptly, their eyes standing out with fatness, "How does God know? and is there knowledge in the Most High?"[1] Lean-eyed and pious men may ask the same question. Perhaps they should not be afraid of the answer.

As we have seen, neither selfhood nor the personeity of self-hood is merely intellectual or cognitive. It is more than "mind" (in that sense of "mind") although it may not be capable of being less than "mind". We have also seen that, in the main, what we think of when we think of personeity is a certain level of selfhood regarded in terms of moral and forensic responsibility. I do not say that this notion is complete in itself or exhaustive of all that we may legitimately mean by the personeity of a person. Character may be wider than responsibility. Compassion, loyalty and loving-kindness are moral attributes but seem to exceed the forensic minimum of being in one's right mind and knowing the accredited and more unsubtle distinctions between right and wrong. Again, as we saw, a man's personality may be taken to mean the individual *style* of him. I think, however, that a discussion of the forensic sense of personality and of impersonality should sensibly advance our investigations in the present place.

We asked in the last lecture whether the logical interconnectedness of reality had to be governed or constituted by some orderly personal mind. We may now raise a similar question regarding the righteousness of reality, interpreting the word "righteousness" rather widely, and including under it something more than the stern but elusive property that we call justice.

A large part of the remaining lectures in the present course will be concerned with precisely this problem, and I shall not try to do more than introduce it in the present lecture. I shall try, however, to say something about the nature of an impersonal theory of divine benevolence, and of an impersonal theory of divine justice.

[1] Psalm lxxiii. 11.

Let us, then, consider an impersonal theory of divine "benevolence".

We are often told that it is better for man's moral nature that physical nature should itself be quite non-moral. If God should take sides he should not take sides in that natural way. It is better for self-discipline and for self-reliance that men should have to work for their bread than that manna from heaven should be given them in nice proportion to the virtues of the recipients. It is well for man that rain should fall upon the parched fields of the unjust as well as upon the thirsty acres of the just, that tempests and pestilence are avoided by the prudent rather than by the righteous, and not always by the prudent. This line of argument may be pursued almost without limit. It may be applied to earthquakes in Anatolia, to sand-buried villages in the east of Scotland, to lives cut short in the past that medicine could save today, and to lives cut short today that medicine may learn to save tomorrow. In short, it may be applied to all the perils of nature, whether these are preventable to-day, or will later be preventable, or will never be preventable.

If there is soundness in these arguments (and I cannot think they are wholly corrupt) the inference would be that the righteousness of the universe is not inconsistent with the absence of a certain kind of moral discrimination respecting much that exists. If that, however, were the end of the story, we should not have learned very much. The "ethical neutrality" of physical nature, as it is sometimes called, is consistent with atheism, and also with the several forms of theism. It is consistent with atheism because the theory may be that physical nature is the basis of everything and has itself no moral properties whatever. It is consistent with the belief in a detached deity who keeps wholly aloof from so petty a thing as conscience either in man or in any other being. It is consistent with the sort of belief that some deists may have entertained, namely that God is an intellectual giant, but a moral imbecile. It is consistent with the belief that a moral deity does not care to take sides too crudely or too obviously. Still, if the "ethical neutrality" of physical nature is allied with benevolence, we must suppose, theists say, that God is a *benevolent* neutral, and therefore that he is neither indifferent to morality nor un-moral. What should we say about that?

The word benevolence implies a benevolent wish and will. It suggests and it may even imply the wish and will of a person or of a society of persons. Nevertheless what we call the fruits of benevolence may grow on quite unbenevolent trees. If the fruit is there it may be eaten whether a benevolent philanthropist or the jungle has produced it.[1] In other words the operative part of the supposed benevolence might just be beneficence; and beneficence rather than benevolence may be the heart of the problem.

If such beneficence, in respect of physical nature, means simply that nature is propitious to man and to some other finite beings that are rather like him, such beneficial action does not imply any personeity in the beneficial agent. The sun and the weather may be beneficial in this sense. In so far as theism stands for the propitiousness of physical nature to mankind a propitious meteorology would be as good as a benevolent ruler of the seasons.

Again, if the complaint be that the happiness of man and of other similar beings would be merely episodic in an "ethically neutral" universe, the question may at once be raised whether man's existence, and the felicitous course of that existence, *are* merely episodic. It is not the impersonality of reality that forbids the belief that the propitiousness of physical nature to mankind cannot be stable, or, for that matter, unending. According to the personalistic interpretation of theism, Man's prospects are rendered secure, or relatively so, by a benevolent personal agent who has the power to see to the issue. If, however, the deiformity of the universe were, among other things, a name for the security of such prospects, the prospects, *ex hypothesi*, would *be* secure. It might well appear that the security is the important

[1] From the Chinese *Book of Deeds and Rewards* Kan-Ying-P'ien, "The heaven and the earth give to all creatures life and growth. If you harm them, you do not imitate the kindness of the heaven and the earth."

matter, and not the way in which it is brought about. We have further to note that an argument of this type may go far beyond human comfort and happiness and agreeable sensation. It applies generally to the security of human existence, and of any existence like the human. The security itself is the thing. If, for example, the immortality of finite spirits, or of finite spirits of a high order, were held to be essential to such security, then, if the immortality of such spirits could be proved, it would be irrelevant whether the immortality occurred in a universe that as a whole was personal or was impersonal. Man's physical body dissolves, or most of it does; but if, as some think, his spiritual body does not dissolve, or if, as others think, he becomes a pure bodiless spirit at death, his immortality is naturally and, it may be, metaphysically secure.

In short, neither the propitiousness of physical nature to man's happiness nor the stability of his spirit in a fluctuating world depends in any logical way upon the personeity of reality as a whole or on the personeity of its governing part. In so far, therefore, as the substance of theism is supposed to stand for the conservation of spiritual existence and for the stability of a modest and irregular but genuine measure of happiness it is consistent with an impersonal as well as with a personal interpretation of the constitution of reality.

An obvious retort is that *such* "beneficence" is a very small part of the substance of a truly moral theism. The discipline of the moral character is of far greater moral account than the abundance of the means to comfort and pleasure. If physical nature is morally of service it is of service as a place of moral opportunity, a place in which duty may be done, aspirations may be furthered, and souls may be saved. As Luther said in his *Great Catechism*: "A God is that whereto we are to look for all good and to take refuge in all distress; so that to have a God is to trust and believe him from the whole heart." Is it credible, we may ask, that such things should be believed of God if reality were impersonally constituted?

I would suggest, although with great diffidence, that it is not incredible. If man's environment did perform and would continue to perform these services, hope and confidence as well as acquiescence might be directed towards it. The environment would be dependable and, in that sense, trustworthy. It might be reverenced, admired, extolled and even worshipped. Affection might be felt for it as well as trust. It might be loved unless, in the English way, we restrict the term "love" to the sort of feeling that can only be felt for another person. There have been nature-worshippers who were not primitive but enlightened as well as sincere.

Most people would say, and I think correctly, that a physical environment, undiscriminatingly beneficent, could never have the subtle spiritual properties that would be essential to a righteous universe. Therefore if an impersonal theism referred to physical nature *only* it would be inept. Reality, however, is not merely physical; and if moral beings are not merely episodic in the constitution of things, the objection comes to have a significantly altered look. The objector says that reverence, affection and admiration, except of a tepid and watery kind, could not be felt for physical nature, unless by inadvertence or mere illusion. Suppose that this statement is substantially true. We have still to remember that a spiritual community, i.e. a spiritual unity that need not itself be a self or a person, may and does inspire such feelings. Consider the possibility that the Holy Spirit, understood impersonally, is the principal agent in the Christian life. Consider the possibility that human history, despite so much in the past and despite nearly all in the present, is the gradual achievement of a heavenly republic, and is not a passing episode on the surface of a precarious planet. Such theories are impersonal but theistic. What right has anyone to say that they are quite absurd?

Men have said that they reverenced their bodies. By how much more may they not reverence the art of a noble epoch, the blood of the martyrs, the ethos of Greece in her prime? If we exclaim against the futility of the worship of mere humanity, the cause of our dissent is not that there is *nothing* in humanity that might be worshipped, but that worship at its highest stretch seems to be devoted to something deeper and stronger and finer. *Such* worship, many think, should be kept for the high gods. If, however, reality itself were a unity in which spiritual beings must be born and must live, this species of objection would have lost all rational support. Empirically speaking it is *not* plain that every Englishman is greater than England, that Socrates (even) outsoared the whole Pythagorean brotherhood, in short, that a spiritual group may not have finer properties than any individual person. *Some* high properties may attach to persons and not to groups; but that circumstance, in itself, proves very little.

I spoke above of *undiscriminating* beneficence, and it seems clear that discrimination is a property of a discerning mind. What is discriminated, however, is relevant differences, and minds do not *make* such differences or their relevance. Accordingly, unless special reason to the contrary can be given, we should infer that even if an impersonal reality could not discriminate, it would be righteous if it responded accurately to distinctions of righteousness. Righteous is as righteous does. If the pattern of things were moral in the sense that relevant moral differences were incorporated in the pattern, the pattern itself would be a pattern of righteousness. It is true, I think, that sub-personal beings are not moral beings. Nevertheless the law of righteousness might be the pattern that an impersonal reality assumed when it grew into persons. There is no need for assuming that the *im*personal must be *sub*-personal.

A morally *discriminating* beneficence is justice in one of its aspects, the aspect that we call distributive justice, and is closely connected with the notion of moral desert. This circumstance facilitates a transition from beneficence to justice.

Mr. Bevan has recently remarked that "such a common exclamation as 'Hard lines!' is altogether meaningless except on the supposition that there is such a thing as desert, that is, a nexus of appropriateness between wrongdoing and pain".[1] His sentiments are surely very odd. We do not usually say "Hard

[1] *Symbolism and Belief*, p. 225.

lines!" when a man is sent to jail for robbery with violence, and we do say it very often on the golf course where the "nexus of unappropriateness" refers to a disproportion between skill and result without any reference to moral character. More generally, we do not hold either with regard to distributive or to retributive justice that all pain and all misfortune are a penalty for sin, and that all joys, all success and all good health are the reward of moral virtue. Theists used often to think so, but Western theists seldom think so now.

That is one of the reasons why an old and very familiar doctrine of the impersonal righteousness of the universe, the doctrine namely of Nemesis or of Karma, may seem to be defective. The conception, some would say, is altogether too rigid and too crude, even if it be developed in such a way as to explain why the apparently wobbling scales of merit and retribution in a single life may be held to be precisely balanced in a long succession of reincarnated lives. Dr. Oman compares the conception of Karma to the dynamical principle that action and reaction are equal and opposite[1]; and he thinks that such a simple and rigid principle is incapable even of lisping the accents of theism. Similarly it may seem plausible to say, as Chesterton said in the passage I quoted from his *Blake*, that mercy and pardon are higher than Nemesis. Believing as we do that a few rigid and inflexible rules cannot measure the niceties of moral desert, we are inclined to hold that a judge with a large (and, still more, with a plenary) discretion has a greater capacity for justice than the abstract rule of Karma. For that abstract rule, the classical expression is the following: "If a man speaks or acts with an evil thought, pain follows him, as the wheel follows the foot of the ox that draws the carriage. . . . If a man speaks or acts with a pure thought, happiness follows him, like a shadow that never leaves him." (But it should be remembered that Karma is more discriminating and even more personal than a doctrine of transferred merit, such as the Atonement.)

It is clear on reflection, however, that these criticisms are very

[1] *The Natural and the Supernatural*, p. 221.

superficial. There is no reason why an amended doctrine of Nemesis or of Karma should not refer, not to all crude suffering or success, but to the special sort of suffering or success (if there be any) that really is appropriate to moral desert. The *exactitude* of Karma or of Nemesis, again, is surely not an objection to the principle, and the theory does not imply that the scales are rough and merely approximate. There is no good reason for limiting the nicety of Nemesis, simply because the reality of Nemesis is admitted. The same holds of the discretion of a judge. Justice may be the better served if the judge has such discretion; but only on one condition. The condition is that the laws that the judge administers are rough and approximate. If they were fine and precise there would be no such implication. As for mercy, I cannot see that the quality of mercy is consistent with retributive justice unless it is shown only to those who repent, and then only because the penitent sinner is supposed to be suffering a more appropriate pain than a ruder penal system would exact irrespective of his penitence. Indeed, it is quite absurd to maintain that such impersonal moral laws of retribution *could* not attain an ideal exactitude, although the superficial facts of the moral world may well induce doubts regarding the reality of such a doctrine. A theist who held that the laws *were* exact, despite the cruder appearances, would not be saying anything that contained the slightest internal contradiction. "Coldly sublime, intolerably just", a poet complains. But why should we endorse the complaint?

The inference is that if the pattern of an impersonal universe were such that moral selves began to live and continued to live within it, and were such that the pattern of their existence included a very nice proportion between their moral deserts and their welfare or ill-fare, no inherent contradiction or major difficulty could be found in the conception, however hard it may be to believe that such a nice proportion really does exist. In other words, retributive and distributive justice, if they existed, would not be an obstacle to an impersonal moral theism. The plausibility of opposing views (I am convinced) is due to the belief that there is no such proportion in the nature of things, but that all punishment and all reward has to be artificially compassed, that it is compassed, empirically speaking, by men, and not by nature, and that if it is compassed on a cosmic scale it must be the result of the overruling of the cosmos by a hyper-cosmic moral man-like being. I cannot see that this solution would diminish the difficulties of theism, but what I am now saying is only that the assumption on which it is based is not indisputable.

As a mere introduction to a large subject these remarks may have some weight, and they tend to show that an impersonal theism would not necessarily be deficient in some at least of its moral aspects. For myself, although I believe in justice, I do not believe that so-called retributive "justice" is a defensible moral principle, and the whole conception of moral desert seems to me to require very close scrutiny. I am therefore not likely to make the mistake of supposing that a discussion of retributive justice exhausts the subject of justice itself, and I admit that, following tradition, I have chosen the easiest instance for illustrating what might be meant by an impersonal law of righteousness.

It would not be difficult, however, to summon similar arguments to the aid of some other principle of distributive justice, for instance, in favour of the communistic principle that each should be supplied according to his needs, rather than punished or rewarded according to his deserts. Again, the matter might be illustrated by larger conceptions of justice than simply distributive justice.

Consider for instance the suggestion regarding the implications of a just universe that is contained in the following passage from *Doctrine in the Church of England*, at page 54: "Plato speaks of the principle whereby like is drawn to like, so that in the end each of us would be associated with the same moral type as ourselves; so also there is the law that when we defy the eternal values we lose sensitiveness to them, and conversely, that as we live by the light we have, we receive fuller light."

Such principles, if they are sound, refer to what is held to be morally appropriate to human nature. They do not require a theistic hypothesis, but they are congruent with theism of an impersonal type, as well as with a personal sort of theism. To the same effect a Cambridge Platonist, Benjamin Whichcote, may be quoted: "A proud man", he said, "hath no God: an unpeaceable man hath no neighbour; a distrustful man hath no friend: a discontented man hath not himself." One of the Rabbis wrote: "The reward of a sin is a sin, the reward of a transgression is a transgression"; and few can forget the teaching of the *Gorgias* and other dialogues that degradation and corruption, not the tyrant's whip, is the terrible and also the moral sequel of wrong-doing. "The greatest penalty of evil-doing is to grow into the likeness of bad men."

VI

Providence

DIVINE providence has the closest possible relations with the theme we discussed in the last lecture. According to many philosophers it is God's providence that marks the essential distinction between a mere deism "evacuated of all moral content" and a moral theism. We distinguish between the theory of a demiurge that plans and schemes on the one hand, and, on the other hand, the conception of a God who, in his planning, cares for that which within the plan is subtler and finer than the rest. We turn our minds towards a deity that, as we think, does not merely order all things but also, as the Book of Wisdom says, "ordereth all things *graciously*".

That is one connecting tie between the present lecture and the last. Another tie is the obvious fact that the doctrine of divine providence is usually expressed in a personal if not even in an anthropomorphic manner. That may not be essential to the doctrine. Indeed in such a document as Seneca's *De Providentia* we find that personal and impersonal doctrines jostle one another. While Seneca, for the most part, was concerned with an anthropomorphic conception of divine providence, there are other parts of his rhetorical essay in which personality and design would seem to be out of place. On the one hand we read about *magnificus ille parens* who trains his children in a hard school, but pampers slave-boys and other unworthy mortals, encouraging the licence of their vulgar wit. On the other hand Providence also appears in Seneca's pages as an impersonal but unchallengeable Nemesis.

Accordingly this lecture, like its predecessor, will be largely concerned with the conception of a divine person, and with the objections to that conception as well as with the evidence that supports it. It will be a transitional lecture in the scheme of this course. Later we shall turn to more general and to more abstract metaphysical considerations.

I shall begin by remarking the distinction between God's general and his special providence, or, in a pleasant phrase that Herbert of Cherbury used, between God's "common grace" and his "special grace".[1] Further subdivisions might, of course, be drawn along the same lines. I have seen mention made of God's "universal, general, particular, special and most special" providence;[2] but refinements so elaborate seem to be more curious than useful. The broad distinction between common and special grace may be of greater moment and I propose to use it. The doctrine of *special* providence includes, *inter alia*, miracle and prophecy, the answer to prayer, the forgiveness of secret sins. But it may include more than that, and Herbert said of it: "When in a moment of intense faith we make a special appeal to God and feel within us his saving power and a sense of marvellous deliverance, I do not doubt that the mind is touched by grace, or particular providence, and that since some new aspect of God is revealed, we pass beyond the normal level of experience."[3] Some have thought that *special* providence, and it alone, raises peculiar philosophical problems. What is called general providence, on this view, is secular rather than sacred. That was the burden of the revived Epicurean debate in a celebrated essay of Hume's.[4] Others hold that if so-called divine providence were not special as well as general, it would be a maimed and feeble thing, unworthy of its august appellation. For the time being, however, I propose to postpone the discussion of God's *special* providence, and to deal only with the philosophy of his *common* grace. I shall return to the theme of his special providence (as it is called) at a later stage of this lecture; and I shall not forget St. Thomas's saying: "Gratia non tollit naturam sed perficit."

[1] In *De Veritate, passim.*
[2] Article, "Providence" in *Dictionary of Religion and Ethics.*
[3] *De Veritate*, trans. Carré, p. 311.
[4] *Enquiry concerning Human Understanding*, sect. xi.

Providence

On the whole it seems appropriate to begin this discussion of God's common grace by enquiring into the positive evidence in favour of that conception. By doing so we shall supplement a part of the argument in the last lecture. In that lecture we saw that if certain things could be shown, for example the propitiousness of physical nature to certain finite spirits, *then* a theist would be confronted with sundry possible interpretations. We are now asking *whether* such things can be shown.

In discussing this worn but tenacious theme, I shall deal, rather narrowly, with man and his place in the cosmos. This restricted treatment may indeed be parochial, but unless our standards of value have no general significance (in which case the question falls) we are bound to test our general theories in the instance in which the issue seems plainest, and that is with reference to man. For I believe man is the bearer of the highest values with which we have any empirical acquaintance. Again, since the human parish is so very wide, it seems better, because it seems sufficient for present purposes, to limit the discussion to two features of the problem of evil (as it is called) and to discuss, on the one hand, suffering, and on the other hand, sin. There are other "problems" of human evil, such as the "problems" of human transience, ignorance, ugliness, weakness and poverty of opportunity. Some questions may be begged and some answers stolen when the problem is restricted in the way in which I intend to restrict it now, but its general outlines, I think, should not be appreciably dimmed.

What, then, is the theological "problem" of suffering? What bearing has our suffering upon providential and upon anti-providential arguments?

There is no problem if the last word on the subject must be simply that suffering occurs, and there is no problem if suffering be not an evil. Again, there is no problem if God be altogether omnipotent and also wholly good, for in that case the existence of any pain whatever (if pain be evil) entails a plain contradiction. Such a God could always bestow the palm without the dust. On the other hand there is a problem for those theists who admit that some at least of the suffering that exists is a genuine evil, and do not renounce every possibility of talking sense about the question by committing themselves to a childish interpretation of "omnipotence".

Philosophers with a Stoical bent have often argued that pain is not an evil. So said Seneca—among other things. According to him,[1] the genuine recipients of divine favour were stalwarts like Mucius who kept his hand in the flames, Regulus who preferred Punic torture to un-Roman bad faith, Cato re-opening the self-inflicted wound that had failed to bring him the honourable release of a vanquished patriot. This grim picture would seem to present Seneca with an insoluble "problem of *pleasure*". For pleasure also exists. According to Seneca it is the base coin with which the high gods repay base natures, giving unworthy mortals something that they desire but also giving them something that, unlike pain, *is* an evil.

It is needless, however, to pursue the point. Whether or not pleasure is an unworthy thing, suffering is an evil, for all Seneca's moral rhetoric. It is evil unmitigated unless it is necessary for an ulterior good that swamps or annuls its evil. If, using anthropomorphic language, we were to say that God was indifferent to suffering as such, we should be saying that God was callous. If he applauded the suffering, like the saints in heaven who have sometimes been thought to applaud the sufferings of the damned in hell, he would be cruel.

Accordingly we are usually told in the theodicies that pain is not purposeless, but is a salutary warning in matters of health and is our schoolmaster in matters of moral education. The doctrine is still pretty grim, but it might be true for all that, and it is consistent with the belief in a non-omnipotent providence. The implication, however, would be that *no* suffering is purposeless, and it is hard to suppose that such is the truth. In the case of animal suffering, for instance (where the moral discipline of the sufferers cannot be a relevant consideration), it is difficult

[1] In *De Providentia*.

to believe that the suffering of slaughtered animals before humane killing became general was justified in terms of this argument, and also that the diminution of animal suffering after humane killing was generally practised is likewise justified. In the case of human beings the same difficulty would arise in connection with advances in our knowledge and use of anæsthetics. We all know of the arguments that have been raised about the use of anæsthetics in childbirth. More generally, there would be a similar problem regarding the moral effects of a rise in the standard of comfortable living.

Obviously, however, it would be unreasonable to expect that every instance of pain that could be cited conveyed a clearly intelligible benefit either to the sufferer or to some other being, or else had to be adjudged to be an instance of finally unjustifiable evil. "Nothing would be more alarming in reality", von Hügel said, "than to find that religion, when pressed, could give us nothing but just what we want."[1] If the line of argument mentioned above supplied the rudiments of an answer to the question set it would have done a great deal; for the argument itself has the widest ramifications. If, however, it be assumed, as is not unreasonable, that what appear to be close factual connections should be held to be metaphysically stubborn if not even indissoluble, the above type of argument has strength and soundness. I have spoken of the palm without the dust, but no one seriously supposes that it is possible to win a race without running it, or to run it without a quickened pulse and bursting lungs. That should be clear as a matter of course, and the argument may be persuasively extended in the way that is commonly done. We are told that the conquest of perils and the overcoming of obstacles imply the reality of the perils and of the obstacles. In a psychological way, perhaps indissoluble, it may be said to imply the reality of fears, and doubts, and depression, and actual anguish, if not inevitably, at least generally in the course of nature. In this sense there are joys of earth that would have no place in a sheltered heaven, and some of these, say the

[1] *The Reality of God*, p. 15.

M

explorer's zest or the romantic lover's or even the struggles of an ambitious author, may be sweeter and keener because of the risk and because of the painful struggle. It might further be argued that there would be no risk if there were not, sometimes, an actual disaster.

Such arguments, then, must be accorded a certain weight, but although they are empirical they are also rather high-handed in what they say of empirical fact. We find empirically that some (perhaps much) suffering has a beneficial function, and we are entitled to surmise that frequently, when this beneficial function is not apparent, it may nevertheless occur. On the other hand, it would also be legitimate to surmise that some of the apparent benefits of suffering are illusory; and in any case we should be flying a very speculative kite if we maintained that *all* suffering must be beneficial because we know that *some* of it is.

That would have to be said even if we admitted that the very audacity of a hypothesis may be one of its better motives to credence. It may, for instance, be more plausible to explain the hurly-burly of our sensations by supposing that permanent physical objects exist and act than by making suppositions that keep closer to the whirling impermanence of our actual sensory experience. Such ideas outstrip the evidence of our senses (according to many interpretations of that evidence) by a mile; but we are all accustomed to make them. So here. The bolder flights of theistic optimism may seem safer and better credible than a more timid resort to whatever gods there may be. The boldness of these flights, however, should not take the form of suppressing or of denying the anti-providential arguments. Courage of that kind is neither hard-headed nor empirical.

An equally familiar objection to the providential hypothesis is that even if all suffering had *some* beneficial office, it would still be impossible to defend the *amount* of suffering that exists. Cancer may give an occasion for fortitude and for a certain melancholy dignity, but, in its case, anodynes are better than dignity and most of the suffering is sheer waste.

In the instance of cancer, this argument may be very forcible, but it relies on a general principle that seems to be exceedingly dubious. How can anyone who holds that the existence of some (and of much) suffering is consistent with the government of a benign providence take it upon himself to say *how much* suffering there ought to be? With what measure does such an one compute the permissible quota of suffering? How, for that matter, does he compute the amount of suffering at all? But if he could compute the amount of suffering that exists, how could he determine whether or not this computed quantum of suffering (with or without taking its relation to joy into account) either demanded or was opposed to an explanation in terms of a beneficent providence? It seems to me, as I have suggested in an earlier lecture,[1] that the problem is quite indeterminate, and that, because it is indeterminate, we have no business to speak with confidence either about the need for inferring the existence of a providence on these grounds or about the success of the anti-providentialists in maintaining the opposite opinion. That, I think, is the decisive feature of this affair.

It is not impressive, I allow, to argue that the pain in the world is of small account. The well-known Epicurean tag that pain is brief if it is severe, and tolerable if it is prolonged, is not very accurate and is not very profound. Agony need not be very brief. If it is brief it may recur. Years of dull misery, seldom alleviated, have often to be borne. Similarly it is difficult to have patience with the shallow view that there are always compensations for the most shocking events, and that the compensations really do compensate. If that argument were pressed to its extremities, the conclusion would be that it is all one whether cancer is conquered like leprosy and smallpox, whether women are widowed in war or raped in peace, whether torture and flogging persist in a judicial system, whether poison gas is or is not to be used. There is a great deal of pain in the world, and much of it is peculiarly revolting, but I do not see how we are able to conjecture whether there is more of it, or less, than a divine regimen would permit.

[1] Lecture IX in the First Series.

In the large, I believe, it is reasonable to hold that there has been and that there is a favourable balance of pleasure over pain on this planet. I think it is true, speaking broadly, that life is sweet and that while there is life there is hope. If the latter statement is true, the former could not easily be false. For hope is glad. If some Miserrimus Doleful tells us that we are the dupes of hope, that, looking back on our lives, we should always say "Never again" if we were candid, that the sight of a healthy little child should always make us sad, thinking of what the poor little mite will have to go through, the answer is clearly that hope is not the less pleasant because it is illusory. The hopefulness of our vitality may not be very creditable to our intelligence, but it is very comforting to the heart.

That, I think, is what we should say on the whole, however true it may be that we are often tempted to think like the Chorus in *Murder in the Cathedral*:

O, late, late, late!, late is the time, late too late, and rotten
   the year;
Evil the wind, and bitter the sea, and the sky, grey, grey, grey.

So far as I can see, however, this argument is just another illustration of the impossibility of arguing with precision to or against the existence of a benevolent providence from the credit-balance of happiness over suffering. Let it be held that the positive correlation between vitality and hopefulness is something inevitable and in the long run preponderant. It follows that wherever there is life there will be hope, and so that there is some reason for expecting a favourable balance of joy over pain. But life exists. Therefore, by hypothesis, this favourable balance exists whether we are to say of our sorrows, with Seneca, "veniunt non incident", or, contrariwise, "incident non veniunt". The assertion is that a preponderance of happiness is an inevitable characteristic of life as such. That assertion, however, is not evidence that a providence must have contrived the favourable balance that exists in fact, and it is not evidence against that view. The inference to a providential cause of the favourable balance is neither helped nor hindered.

Let us now pass from the problem of physical evil (i.e. of suffering) to the problem of moral evil (i.e. of sin).

The problem of sin is more intricate and more difficult for a theist than the problem of pain, but rather similar arguments are frequently employed in both cases.

Very few theists suggest that sin, if and where it exists, is not an evil. In this respect the Stoics contrasted vice with pain, for they said that depravity and dishonour were genuine evils although mere pain was not. Again, if anyone were disposed to doubt that sin is an evil, he might be reminded that even the illusion of sinfulness is itself an unworthy thing. A hyper-sensitive conviction of sin is not so good as sinlessness. Apart from that, many sins are plainly most foul. Moreover sin seems often to be a sort of rebellion against the right and the good, and so, in a host of ways, to be thoroughly anomalous in a supposedly moral universe.

Notwithstanding these special features of the problem, how-ever (and notwithstanding many other special features that I shall here neglect) the writers of theodicies are usually disposed to attempt a solution of the problem of moral evil on the same lines as they try to follow in the case of the problem of suffering. Sin is implied, at least indirectly, they say, if high moral char-acter is to be won. There must be a certain liberty to sin (and, therefore, sometimes the actuality of sinning) if moral achieve-ment be genuine. Providence would not be gracious to man if he denied man such opportunities. There must be moral evil if there is to be moral good.

Such an apology for *actual* sinning seems to be rather weak. In the first place it raises difficulties concerning some of the moral virtues. For example, it seems to involve a theory definitely inconsistent with what we usually believe to be true concerning the virtue of purity. Granting that a man may be pure if his heart is cleansed, it is not at all apparent why a garment that is cleansed should be whiter than a garment that has never been stained. Again, even if there ought to be a certain liberty to make mistakes it surely does not follow that there ought to be any liberty to become thoroughly vicious and depraved. Consider, once again, what we commonly hold when a man has been victorious in some terrible moral struggle. We praise his resolution and respect the toughness of his moral fibre, but we do not usually regard him as an ideal man, any more than we think that the conquest of some physical disadvantage is better than physical fitness that had no such disadvantages to overcome. Indeed, I think we might say generally that the struggle with evil tendencies is not a necessary prerequisite of saintliness. That is what Christians have to maintain when they accept the dogma of the Master's sinlessness. They *are* asserting dogmatically (whether or not the Gospels[1] expressly assert Christ's sinlessness) that the highest moral character does *not* imply a struggle with vicious tendencies. Passing to lighter instances, I should say that there is a certain plausibility in Plato's suggestion[2] that the best doctors are those who are themselves rather delicate, but that there is nothing like a metaphysical necessity about that circumstance.

These comments refer to the peculiar characteristics of many sins and to the heinousness of certain sins rather than to the simple fact of sin's existence. Therefore they lead to the second point in the parallel between misery and wickedness, namely whether, allowing that there may or must be *some* sinning in a righteously ordered universe, there is any sufficient reason for believing that, in such a universe, there could be *as many* sins and as revolting sins as there are in this universe. As in the case of suffering it seems to me that the problem put is quite indeterminate and does not admit of an answer. How can we pretend to say how much sin there would be if God's common grace abounds, but does not always bring good out of evil? If we

[1] John viii. 46 is obviously not decisive. Outside the Gospels, Hebrews iv. 15 is evidence only of the writer's theology, and similarly of Hebrews vii. 26. The same should be said of Paul in 2 Corinthians v. 21, and of John in 1 John iii. 5. It should be noted that Matthew v. 28 forbids us from holding that serious temptation without actual sin is possible. [2] *Rep.* 408 d.

cannot say whether the actual universe favours human morality more than a secular universe would do, how could we say that a providence either should or should not be supposed?

Consider the Christian tradition. If God's common providence is held to describe "nature", and if human nature (or even the important constituent of human nature that we call the flesh) is held to be corrupt, making for perdition, a decaying thing whose wages is death, then it is usual to invoke supernatural grace, a providence beyond God's "common" providence, to purge that "nature" and to destroy what is offending and diseased. There must be a second birth to redeem the first. If, on the other hand, it be held that the natural man does "by nature" the things contained in the law of the Gentiles, the *cursus ordinarius* of human nature would be supposed to be moral in principle, just as our bodies may be said, for the most part, to be healthy in principle although they do not escape disease and decay. On the latter hypothesis, supernatural grace might be required in order to lift men above common morality, but would not be necessary either to instigate or to sustain a moral level that, even without it, might be very high. There are all sorts of intermediate positions between these extremes, but all the divergent conclusions depend upon certain initial premisses regarding the virtuous potentialities of "mere" human nature. I have illustrated the question by a contrast within Christian theism, but the same problem would be apparent if human nature and its bent towards morality or away from morality were interpreted secularly. From the mixture of moral good and evil in our experience (which is obvious) and from the premiss that good and evil must be closely intertwined even if the good be prepotent (which we are here assuming for argument's sake) we are not in a position to say whether "nature's" ways are either more or less friendly to moral virtue than "natural" expectations warrant.

On the other hand, just as it is not unreasonable to enquire whether there is normally a favourable balance of pleasure over pain, so we may legitimately ask whether human nature has more

affinity with moral virtue than with vice. I shall say something
about that question, not because I expect a solution but rather
because it raises one of the major questions in our general debate,
the question that may be described paradoxically as the problem
of the possibility of providence without design.

It is very generally allowed that a simulacrum of moral virtue
(if no more) would normally proceed from mere self-interest
mixed with not uncommon doses of common sense, in other
words from a very secular side of human nature. On this simple
basis Hobbes believed that he could justify "the whole law of
Christ",[1] that is to say everything in Christian ethics that could
be accurately described as moral *law*. Men, according to Hobbes,
were not really so stupid that they could not see that it was
better to hang together than to hang separately. He also believed
that "the sum of virtue is to be sociable with them that will be
sociable, and formidable to them that will not".[2] Even a dull
man could perceive that the sort of conduct that we call "right"
is, in general, an indispensable means to comfort, security and
the ways of peace. Here we may agree with the sage of Malmes-
bury. It is true that no one looking at the world with candid
eyes and surveying its history at any period since the collapse of
the Golden Age could maintain that man's practice shows that
he has learned this elementary lesson very well. As domestic
crime lessens the greater crime of collective war seems to have
gathered momentum. On the other hand it is quite absurd to
suppose that Hobbes's principles have no bearing at all upon
actual human conduct, that moral rules of mutual forbearance
and of mutual help do not play an important part in human
affairs, or that there is anything contrary to human nature in
the fact that they do so often prevail.

This argument from the sociable aspect of human conduct,
with its inevitable inclusion of a large part of ethics, is greatly
strengthened if we allow, as most observers are prepared to
allow in a much less grudging spirit than Hobbes's, that gener-
osity and the rudiments of public spirit belong to the raw material

[1] *De Cive*, conclusion of chap. iv.   [2] *The Elements of Law*, chap. iv, sect. 15.

of human nature and fortify the sociability that fairly intelligent self-interest would inculcate by itself alone even if the joys of philanthropy were slight. In that case a large part of human conduct would be "right" conduct. The "generous impulses" would be strong enough to counteract certain at least of the anti-social impulses that, as well as the generous ones, appear to be conjoined with self-interest. If, in addition, a largish proportion of mankind found an intense personal joy in helping its fellows, right conduct would be still more usual. Arguing on these lines Hume, with something less than his habitual caution, maintained that the "particle of the dove" in human nature, *however weak it might be*, must eventually vanquish "the elements of the wolf and of the serpent".[1] It would grow in strength while the wolfish and serpentine elements made for their own destruction. Such optimism may be over-confident; but it is not absurd.

In such ways as these a fairly persuasive utilitarian case may be made out for the thesis that, in general, private vices are neither public nor private benefits, and that, in general, public spirit brings both private and public benefit. Mere utilitarianism, it is true, may not be a sufficient basis for ethics. Morality may be more than an instrumental thing, a means to something else. Many moralists, however, *are* utilitarians, hedonistic, "ideal" or of some other camp; and utilitarian ethics is consistent with the strongest respect for morality in empirical practice.

For us the most pressing question in this region concerns the relation between theological and secular utilitarianism—for example (in the hedonistic tradition of British utilitarianism) between the views of John Gay, Butler (in part) and Paley, on the one hand, and the opinions of a secularist like Bentham on the other hand. For the former writers the clue to utilitarianism was found in the providence of God, his design to ensure the happiness of his creatures. God's commandments, even if they were revealed, were said to be declarations of his providential will, telling the vulgar in simple intelligible language how they

[1] *Enquiry concerning the Principles of Morals*, sect. ix, Part I.

might gain felicity and avoid misery and despair. Philosophers could understand what the vulgar were wiser to accept in an unenquiring and docile spirit. The secularists believed, on the contrary, that they could dispense with all such theological hypotheses; but later writers (such as Henry Sidgwick, to mention but one) were profoundly impressed by the inadequacy of the natural order to protect and sustain moral effort in detail. Therefore they looked to theism,[1] rather wistfully, in the hope that the patent crudities of the natural order might be refined and corrected.

It is not only on utilitarian grounds, however, that the moral optimism of the thesis that good morals naturally prevail among mankind may be defended. Stoical and, as we now say, deontological moralists may argue similarly.

The dominant note in this second line of argument is the good man's independence of the vicissitudes of external circumstance, both social and sub-human. From one point of view, it is true, the good man's independence of external fortune may be regarded as his independence of the common order of God's providence. Yet the good man is also nature's son. Therefore, from another point of view, the fact that the good man exists (although he did not make himself) and is capable, for a brief space, of defying material and social rebuffs, is of itself an argument in favour of the thesis that human nature may be naturally independent of external vicissitudes. If moral integrity be the height of such independence, man's natural bent may be prevailingly moral.

This argument may be developed in a sense that comes very near to bombast. Such is Pascal's unjustly celebrated pæan upon the thinking reed which says to the tempest that will destroy it: "I can think but thou canst not." A parallel argument would be that the thinking reed can be sick with craven fears although the tempest cannot. It would be the summit of tragedy in the thinking reed if, although it could think, it was bound to lose. In a wider way, however, it may reasonably be held that that there is

[1] *The Methods of Ethics.* Concluding chapter.

a natural conformity between man's moral virtue and the heights to which he may rise. A life of ceaseless moral struggle, it is true, seems to be very far removed from the ideal, and rigorists may be sad and broken men, dangerous and hateful to their fellows. On the other hand, a Stoicism that without being flaccid is wiser and more humane than many historical doctrines of this order, has the right to say that virtue tends to bring peace and joy to its possessor, that such high contentment is a reward beyond the rubies of pomp and the warmth of material comfort, and that there is no state so high as the state of loving the right. Morality may be the life in accordance with a man's proper nature, destined, in the natural way, to be radiant and triumphant. "The sense-soul", said Julian of Norwich, "is grounded in nature, in mercy, in grace."

There are therefore many ways in which the doctrine of a temperate but wholly genuine moral optimism may be rationally defended on non-theological and in their way, on "natural" lines. I say this without any reference to the possibility of another and of a better world for human beings after death. "All this, and heaven too", said Matthew Henry when he thought of the good things, and the fine things, of this present world. I am, for the moment, restricting myself to the first part of the famous Puritan's statement.

I may now sum up this part of our discussion. We have been exploring the field of God's common, not of his special, grace, restricting the discussion still further to pleasure-pain and to moral conduct in mankind. There, firstly, (1) we have had to consider certain questions of fact. Does good exist and does evil exist? Is there on the whole more good than evil in human existence? Secondly (2), we have had to examine the bearing of the answers to these questions upon theistic theory.

(1) On the question of fact I have argued that both good and evil exist; and I incline towards a temperate empirical optimism regarding both "physical" and "moral" good. I think that there is more joy than pain in human life, that what we call "common decency" really is pretty common, and that rightness

of conduct, at any rate in a pedestrian way, prevails in the main over wickedness and vice, or tends so to prevail over a long period.

(2) The bearing of these matters of fact upon theology is much more disputable. The existence of evil, I submit, is consistent with any theology that does not assert God's unqualified omnipotence. It is inconsistent with the existence of a God who is both morally good and also omnipotent. On the other hand, the existence of *some* good, physical or moral, is not in itself a proof of theism.

If it be admitted that the world contains some good, and much good; some evil, and much evil; I do not see that we can further argue that it contains too much good to be anything except the result of God's providence or too much evil to allow a belief in God's providence. The premisses on which such arguments profess to be based are quite indeterminate, at any rate in the sphere of what is called God's common grace.

I have stated these conclusions sometimes in the language of the doctrine of providence, sometimes in more general theistic terms. We must now attend more closely to the precise topic of this lecture, namely the doctrine of providence in its relation to other forms of theistic theory. That will be the subject to which we now proceed, in the first instance only with reference to God's common grace.

The Argument to Providence is a special form of the Argument to Design. Providence or πρόνοια implies foresight and provision for the future. It is, as Paley said, "prospective contrivance", and is usually assumed to be personal activity. I have mentioned the circumstance, it is true, that Seneca and some other authors have occasionally spoken of providence in impersonal terms, and in terms of laws or equations rather than in terms of plans and schemes. I have also mentioned the paradox of "providence without design". Strictly speaking, however, "providence without design" is a misnomer rather similar to the sham conception of "purposiveness without purpose". Whatever meaning may be attached to the phrase should be expressed in other language. We should speak not of providence but, say, of a beneficent natural order.

It is important therefore to examine the conception of *providence* and not some other theological theory that may be better or worse but is in any case different. The conception is fairly definite. It is not content with the *quod* or the *quia*, that there is a God or why there must be a God. It describes the *quid*, what God is. According to the theology of providence, God is a supramundane being, having power to order the world, and when he orders the world graciously he does so according to plan. That is the quiddity with which we are now concerned. That, in the West at least, is what the man in the street and even the man in the library mean by the doctrine of divine providence.

I shall try to show, firstly, that the argument to a providence is in some ways stronger than the more general Argument to Design, but, secondly, that in other respects it exacerbates the very grave difficulties contained in that argument.

To take the first point: It is plausible to maintain that the conception of a designing providence is sounder and stronger than the conception of a designer who is not a providence. The idea of God the designer is thoroughly anthropomorphic and may even be industrial. It is the idea of God the potter, God the architect, a God of blue prints, and the type of conception remains substantially the same in these modern days when people think by preference in terms of microphysics and of electricity. In its wide outlines, the idea of a celestial, like the idea of a terrestrial designer, is the idea of one who plans the execution of a future purpose, who has to wait and to adapt in order that some better thing may come in the place of what was formerly imperfect or non-existent.

In terms of these analogies we have to say that a designer who exercised his designing talents for no other purpose than the designing itself might be clever but would not be wise. What would the planning be for? For God's glory on account of the magnitude of the operations? For an æsthetic purpose because of the elegance of the achievement? On grounds such as these we might perhaps say that the Demiurge was a little greater than a common puzzle-solver. In substance, however, he would either be planning without a purpose or planning for a purpose quite fantastically trivial. Even a man would be wiser than that. All the philosophers, from Seneca to Charron, who have treated of wisdom, *sapientia, la sagesse* have discerned much more in human wisdom than elegance, cleverness, or skill. Therefore a wise deity is more readily credible than a merely clever deity. Certainly God's ends might be greater and higher than we can conceive. It is therefore *possible* that his wisdom may be incommensurable with ours, that what we count wisdom he rightly counts foolishness. If so, however, it would be more accurate to say that he is beyond wisdom altogether. To retain the word wisdom but to alter its meaning into something wholly inconceivable is not a contribution to clarity. In that case, surely, it would also be more accurate to say that God is beyond purpose and beyond design.

In brief, if you employ a certain order of conceptions you should stick to them and give adequate notice if and where you intend to abandon them. You cannot reasonably drop them when it suits you and resume them when it suits you. Very well then. If you are talking about purpose, design and providence you are using terms that in a certain intelligible context have a plain and intelligible meaning. In that context action for a purpose is more purposeful and to better purpose if it be wise than if it be simply clever or simply slick.

I submit, therefore, that if deity be the sort of being who can plan and design, it is reasonable to infer that he plans and designs for wise ends. In this context of ends and means, purposes and aims, wisdom is not "evacuated of moral content" and is not a stranger to love. It may therefore be reasonably understood ("theistically") to include God's general providence or common grace as well as ("deistically") to include his ordering skill. A translation of the belief in providence into quite different terms may be so very free a paraphrase of the original as to lose all intelligible identity.

Providence

That is one side of the story. A designing providence is more easily credible than a mere designer conceived after the fashion of simple non-providential deism. Unfortunately for the argument, however, there is another side to the story; and there, as I have said, the providential character of the designer seems to exacerbate the inherent difficulties of the design hypothesis. God would not need to plan and scheme with such care and with such wisdom unless there were obstacles that he had to overcome, and unless the future, at any given time, set him quite peculiar problems. His wisdom would have to be shown in removing imperfections and in a sort of insurance against future calamity. That would be the field of his "prospective contrivance. If these obstacles were within himself, his wisdom would be shown in his own self-discipline and self-culture. He would be bent upon self-improvement and upon preventing deterioration within himself. If he had to contend with foreign obstacles, his business would be to diminish or remove the obstacles and to prevent the disasters that would occur if he withdrew his guiding hand. It is scarcely surprising that a great many theists should vehemently repudiate all such ideas.

Consider, for example, a redemptive theory of the cosmic process. If the world and the spirits within the world who may be redeemed were either a foreign territory that a supramundane God had to reckon with from all eternity to all eternity, or a part of the divine being that could never be absent from his inner nature, the language of gradual improvement would be quite intelligible, although the language of *redemption* on any strict interpretation would be very odd indeed. For what do we mean by the theory of redemption? We mean that the world was created in order to be redeemed, and that redemption at its ideal pitch would occur if the world, once again, were taken up into deity. The goal of the process would be just what there would have been had there been no process, and the process itself would consequently be purposeless. It is common for Christian theists to say that *if* the redemptive process occurred more than once it *would* be purposeless. Would not any Christian theist[1] be embarrassed at the thought of another Eden, another *felix culpa* on the part of another Eve and of another Adam? The problem, however, would be the same if there were but one redemptive process and if God initiated it.

Some people disguise these difficulties from themselves by saying that all will be well in the future. It is true, I dare say, that if we could all look forward to a future in which suffering was triumphantly surmounted and wickedness was overcome, we should then be complacent enough about the past and regard it as something like an evil dream that had vanished with the morning sun. In general there is some reason for supposing that the balance of good being the same, nearly anyone would prefer a progress towards heaven than a retrogression from a Golden Age, although (as it seems to me) many who cannot reasonably expect either a long life or an easy death, nevertheless find sweetness, as Epicurus did, in the memory of their youth and of their prime. Such arguments, however, seem plainly to be irrelevant to the general question of the theodicy of the process itself. If the entire history of the world were an avoidable episode, the nett balance of good over evil might be precisely the same if the episode had been progressive, had been retrogressive or had oscillated in these respects. The sum of things, we are strongly inclined to suppose, would have been better if there had never been an earth. *We* might not greatly care if our own sins and sorrows had become things of the past and would never recur. *We* might shut our eyes to the sins and the sorrows of those who went before us. But a creator who was wise and good could not be indifferent to the baseness, ugliness and misery that had vanished in the end. For what could have been the need for them?

It may reasonably be maintained, it is true, that difficulties of this order attach to *every* form of moral theism, and not peculiarly to the theory of a designing providence. That must be granted, but the theory of a designing providence makes them cry out to the painful earth, and demand the limitation either of God's

[1] Indian theists are not embarrassed.

goodness or of his power with an urgency that other theories may do much to diminish. I shall say something more on this head before proceeding to consider God's *special* rather than his *common* grace.

The main stumbling-block is the idea of divine perfection. Perfection itself is a slippery notion in which the distinguishable and (I think) the fundamentally distinct ideas of excellence and of fulness are forcibly and often carelessly united in some vague conception of an optimum condition. If instead of "perfection" we spoke of value or of goodness, I think we would not find any definite contradiction in the theory that a divine being who was supremely good created a universe of lesser but still of very great value. Indeed those who maintain that "maximizing the good" is the fundamental if not the sole canon of ethics might contend with some plausibility that more good would exist if there were a very imperfect world in addition to God, provided only that there was a favourable balance of good over evil in the said imperfect world. A cryptic passage in Plato's so cryptic *Timaeus* is sometimes quoted in support of this idea, namely his assertion that the reason why the world was made at all is that God was good, and therefore not jealous, so that "being free from jealousy, he declared that all things should be as like himself as they could be".[1] Similarly we may be reminded, as by Mr. Lovejoy, of the scholastic maxim *Omne bonum est diffusivum sui*, or, as by Mr. Nicholson,[2] that according to some of the Sufis creation itself is the first and greatest act of God's bounty.

Such arguments, it is true, are very embarrassing. It can hardly be plain that the "maximization of good" *beyond the optimum* is a valid ideal, and it is at least dubious whether the optimum should be equipped with a grapnel to dredge for other and lesser goods. If this objection were overruled, it could not be directly inferred that all the possible goodness outside God was contained in this present world. Nevertheless the possibility remains that if the more rigid implications of the term "perfection" are modified, it may be true that, supposing God to be

[1] 29 d.   [2] E.g., *Studies in Islamic Mysticism*, p. 80.

supremely good and also supra-mundane, it is better that there should be a world than that there should be no world at all. If so, the language of design and of providence, even if it be inadequate, might not be wholly inappropriate. God would have scope for a certain wisdom and bounty.

The traditional notion of "perfection", therefore, has to be modified and muted if it be conciliable with the ideas of design and of providence. If its "perfection" means its fulness of being —in other words if theism is immanentist, pantheistic or totalitarian—we cannot suppose that the Whole plans or provides for itself. If, on the other hand, "perfection" be a term used to describe, rather loosely, a very high pitch of excellence, God's general providence might be described not wholly inadequately in the traditional language of providence. With respect to God's "common grace", however, it seems to be abundantly clear that the inadequacy of the metaphors and analogies that are used in the traditional Argument from Design are at least as great in the Christian's arguments to a providence as in the deist's argument to a mere designer. The greater apparent persuasiveness of the metaphors and analogies that cluster round the conception of providence have already been remarked in this lecture. But they are often very superficial.

That is a matter of some moment. The doctrine of providence professes to be a doctrine of *quod* and of *quia*, and also a doctrine of *quomodo* and of *quid*. It professes to describe not merely that God is and why God is, but also how God acts and what God is. If the language of providence is said to be only metaphorical, *quod* and *quia* might remain but *quomodo* and *quid* are abandoned. Of the two I admit that *quid* is more important than *quomodo*, and I have not, in the main, been arguing about *quomodo*. I have been discussing the distinctive character of the hypothesis of divine providence in the sphere of what is called God's common grace.

Let us now examine the sphere of God's special grace.

I think it is difficult, at the present time, to be impressed by the traditional arguments concerning prophecy and miracles.

The argument from the fulfilment of prophecy is seldom heard even in our pulpits to-day, for reasons too obvious to need comment. Its traditional use, as Butler said, was "to prove a particular dispensation of Providence, the redemption of the world by the Messiah",[1] and this, according to the tradition, surpassed but was consistent with natural theology (which was supposed to prove God's general providence) since the Messianic dispensation was consistent with (although it exceeded) God's common bounty. As to miracles I have already noted in a former lecture[2] that Locke, who inaugurated so many of our modern views, was so much a child of the past that he regarded miracles as the most conclusive and indeed as indisputable proof of the reasonableness of Christianity. In the next age, after a very lively controversy had raged, Bishop Butler was much more cautious. "It may possibly be disputed", he said, "how far miracles can prove natural religion; and notable objections may be urged against the proof of it, considered as a matter of speculation: but considered as a practical thing there can be none."[3] He also maintained, with great vigour, "that there is certainly no such presumption against miracles as to render them in any wise incredible".[4] The idea of occasional miraculous intervention, however, was wholly opposed to the general conceptions of later scientific theory,[5] and I trust I may assume that we have not gone back upon that, and will never do so unless our theology becomes as barbarous and as retrograde as much in our civilization threatens to become. Let us dismiss the nature miracles, in Christianity or in any other sacred tradition, and interpret the more spiritual type of miracle after quite another fashion—perhaps just as God's gift, as, I believe, the Hebrew word translated "miracle" may be rendered. It is childish to debate whether a Demiurge who constantly meddles with his own machinery is either more or less skilful than one who designs a machine that feeds itself and never needs repairing.

[1] *Analogy*, Part II, chap. i. [2] IX (First Series). [3] *Ibid.* [4] *Ibid.*, chap. ii.
[5] Despite the fact that Mansel in the nineteenth century agreed in substance with Locke.

What may be held with a greater show of reason is that a fatherly as opposed to a merely cosmological deity should be regarded as a particular providence, not simply as a general providence. Common grace, it may be said, could not describe all the relevant facts if divine providence be at all analogous to the relation between a loving father and his children in an unequal but tender and genuine friendship. Indeed it is difficult to avoid being shocked at the lengths to which some apologists for God's general providence have been prepared to go. Thus, when the controversies regarding evolution had reached their most strident phase, and the hypothesis of a gradual improvement of an evolving universe was opposed to the doctrine of the special intervention of a watchful deity, the following argument was produced by Professor Flint:[1] "There is a law of over-production, we are told, which gives rise to a struggle for existence. Well, is this law not a means to an end worthy of divine wisdom?" In other words, the misery and despair of the weaker who groan and starve and die is regarded as an incident, not even regrettable, in an advancing order. Compare the spirit of such a conception with the spirit of the Scripture saying that a sparrow that is sold for half a farthing "shall not fall to the ground without your Father".[2] We know that sparrows do fall to the ground. We know that when they are sold they are very probably dead. We know that nature has teeth and claws. But still we may long to believe that God shows particular care for particular beings. We may recall Blake's poem:

> For Mercy, Pity, Peace and Love
> Is God our Father dear,
> And Mercy, Pity, Peace and Love
> Is man, his child and care.

> For Mercy has a human heart,
> Pity a human face;
> And Love the human form divine;
> And Peace the human dress.

[1] *Theism*, 8th ed., p. 203.   [2] Matthew x. 29.

Providence

> Then every man of every clime
> That prays in his distress
> Prays to the human form divine—
> Love, Mercy, Pity, Peace.

By another route, therefore, we arrive at the same debatable region as was discussed at the conclusion of the last lecture. The argument now is that if divine providence were but general it would be undiscriminating. Therefore God's providence must be special as well as general. If it were not so (we are told) he could not be heedful of private persons in the deep singularity of their individual being.

In the last lecture we noticed that discrimination implies distinctions that are discriminated. It does not make these distinctions. It discerns them. We further suggested that an impersonal moral principle might include the correlation of the nicest moral distinctions and therefore need not be "undiscriminating" in the sense that might seem to be objectionable.

The point may be illustrated by a familiar controversy in ethics recently revived in a vigorous way. If a right action be defined as the action which, in its circumstances, tends to produce the maximum benefit, it is complained that such a standard is negligently indiscriminate. It does not (we are told) distinguish between the recipients, although it certainly should. For some of them deserve well, and others deserve ill. Again, some have prior claims to others, as a man's young children have claims upon his purse that are prior to the claims of any city hospital. I shall not here enquire into the extent to which such objections may be justified for polemical purposes, but I should like to call attention to a very simple point. Respect for prior obligations and for other such moral distinctions may itself be implied in (and be an indispensable means towards) obtaining the maximum benefit. Suppose, for instance (and this is a legitimate although it may not be a correct supposition), that the family system is better for the children and better for the parents than any other, communistic or promiscuous, or what you will. If so, it is an implication of the system that parents should have *special* duties

197

towards their own children, and that children should have special duties towards their own parents. The reason, however, may be quite general, namely that the system which implies these special duties and prior claims is more beneficial than any other, and not that these special duties would attach to *every* system or would be independent of all systems.

In other words, God's general providence, if effective, may require to be specified into distinctive providential ways. In that case it would be entirely possible that what is called his "special" providence was an implication of his *common* grace, and not something additional, supervenient and supernatural.

This brings us to the most familiar and, at the same time, to the most moving of all these problems, the problem of supernatural grace as distinct from and, it may be, as opposed to the common order of nature.

As we have seen so often, all such doctrines rest upon the shifting sands of facile and provisional definitions. "Nature" is regarded, sometimes as merely material, sometimes as semi-spiritual in a mediocre or "wounded" way, sometimes as a mass of corruption, sometimes as healthy but uninspiring. In short, its boundaries yield under pressure or else are conventional lines. The same is true of the distinction between natural and non-natural spiritual powers whether or not the "natural" powers of the spirit are supposed to be corrupt, or merely "wounded" or merely unsanctified. Because of these shifting boundaries, natural theology, like any other theology or philosophy, becomes an exercise in the elasticity of extensible terms. By a suitable manipulation of expression, reality is at one time contracted into a "nature" that is merely starved, at another time "nature" is expanded until it coincides with reality. Thus we are told, on the one hand, that "nature" connotes some deficiency of true being, but that it has supernal filaments. If the filaments are broken the result is verily a "wounded" being. On the other hand, we are told that the ascent from nature to the supernal is itself a natural ascent, an inevitable gradation in reality. *Supremum infimi attingit ad infimum supremi.* Reality is regarded as an ordered harmony, a hierarchical whole whose grades, although distinguishable, are linked each to each by a chain of pure gold.

Similar comments, I fear, have to be made about the doctrine of "infused" or "sanative" grace. I would speak of this doctrine with reverence if I could. If the state of man be such that when he is most sorely tried he tends to acquire strength to endure, that moments of crisis heighten spiritual vitality, that discernment is quickened and character healed when the tension of the soul is at its highest, that in such moments a man seems to himself to be fortified by the ethos of a fellowship with the best in social tradition and with the hidden springs of all reality, this tendency, whether it be the fruit of man's inherent divinity or the gift of a genius or of a God, is something immeasurably precious. The existence of the tendency need not be denied simply because there have been so many failures.

That having been said, it must also be said that the theory of *gratia sanans*, and the language in which the theory is conveyed, are clouded over with the deepest shadows. There is nothing of reverence and nothing of piety in clinging to these shadows, and the order of ideas that casts the shadows can hardly enlighten a reflective mind. The similitude of infused grace to a drug is far too close to be reassuring. The doctrine is a doctrine of celestial pharmacology, and although such analogies should never be taken *au pied de la lettre* they give pause to all who gladly accept the truth of their general tenor. It may be crude to talk about spiritual benzedrine, but it would be dishonest to deny that the phrase has its appositeness.

Let me revert to an illustration I have formerly used. If a layman in medicine were permitted to discuss such matters, he might affirm without gross absurdity (I suppose) that the *vis medicatrix naturae* is a name, among other things, for the fact that the rise of body-temperature and the like is a special life-sustaining reaction at times of crisis. That, in a rough way, might be said to be part of the biological "nature" of man and of some other animals. The effect of drugs, if they are skilfully administered, is to assist and correct the *vis medicatrix naturae* in its critical struggles with micro-organisms or with other menacing conditions. Such timely assistance may save a body that without it would succumb.

Consequently the parallel between God's sanative and his common grace is tolerably exact, and, for that reason, the other side of the story should also be heard. Nothing could be more absurd or more superstitious than the plain man's ordinary attitude towards drugs. Consider, for instance, the columns that fill our Press during the silly season about the legitimacy of a visit to the chemist's before an athletic contest or before an examination. It is vaguely assumed that there are natural and unnatural ways of becoming and of keeping fit, and that the unnatural ways are illegitimate either for ordinary or for competitive purposes although they should be selected in cases of sickness. I allow that there are better arguments than these, but the prevalence of the bad ones is notorious; and it may be doubted whether the better among the common arguments are really so very much better.

I need not stay to point out that any such division between "natural" and "unnatural" is arbitrary to the last degree. It may be wise, in a general way, to try to make ourselves independent of exotic and expensive aids to the ordinary business of living. It may be equitable to prohibit such aids in an athletic competition or in a beauty contest. It may be foolish or even criminal to renounce them when life and health are in the balance. In principle, however, the use and abuse of "drugs" is on the same footing as the use of anything else in the environment. Any other view confuses between magic and medicine.

The doctrine of infused or of sanative grace has similarly to discriminate between what is, on the one hand, "natural" to man, and what, on the other hand, is super-natural or at least non-natural. I cannot see that there are any certain principles in terms of which such a boundary could be assigned with firmness or even with plausibility.

It is notorious that the boundary may be described in frankly magical imagery, splendid though the magic may be. I quote from Fénelon's *Spiritual Letters*: "As the sacristan snuffs out the candles one by one when Mass is over, so must grace put away our natural life; and as his extinguisher, if carelessly used, leaves behind a smouldering wick to melt the wax away, so will it be with us if a single spark of natural life remains."[1]

But enough of that. The principal question we have here to discuss is whether *gratia sanans*, that special grace, implies a *providence*. So far as I can see, the logic of "special" is precisely similar to the logic of "common" grace. Must the graciousness of things, in special critical conjunctures as well as in their common order, be something that is *put* into the world by an extra-mundane God, or may it be a feature of the world's pattern truly and faithfully interpreted? It seems to me that the latter conception might well be true. If this conclusion, in its turn, implies the substitution of an impersonal but gracious deiformity of existence, a *vita convenienter naturae*, for a personal providence, I cannot infer that it should therefore be rejected.

[1] Quoted by Kirk, *The Vision of God*, p. 455.

VII

Value and Existence

A THEISM that puts its trust in a personal and moral deity, gracious, redeeming, just and benign, moves in a region of thought that is almost concrete. It is a warm hypothesis to live by. It may be depicted by the story of the Incarnation. In comparison, all attempts to transhumanize such conceptions tend to be regarded as attempts to de-humanize them, to steal their warmth away, to make them shadowy and still.

Neverthless we must insist that natural theology is not poetry. If the transhumanity of the divine essence be, as many think, not less profound and not less undeniable than God's similitude to anything that is human, the circumstance has to be faced with intellectual detachment and with diligent zetetic resolution. Many Christian apologists, I think, would admit that we should be prepared to de-humanize our conceptions of deity in order the more effectively to transhumanize them; and natural theology has to follow this argument, as well as the other, whithersoever it may lead.

In the present lecture I propose to revert to the more abstract type of argument characteristic of the earlier lectures in the present series. In other words, I shall return to general philosophy, for I shall try to deal with philosophical idealism in the sense in which that idealism, being an affair of ideals, is much more than mere idea-ism, an affair of ideas. I am asking you to give your minds to the sort of theory implied in such a statement as Lotze's: "the true beginning of metaphysics lies in ethics".[1] Indeed, that is now my text.

A summary way of describing the widest metaphysical thesis

[1] *Metaphysics.* At the conclusion.

of this order is to say, as Mr. Taylor does,[1] that there can be no "divorce" between value and existence. I shall later enquire into some of the ways in which this picturesque language about divorce and consortium may be sustained, but I shall begin by remarking upon a general but very important feature of the situation. Existence, as we saw when we examined the Ontological Proof, is not a characterizing property of any real being. Therefore "existence" could not conceivably be connected with any *property* of an existent in the way in which different properties of existing things may be connected together. Such a connection, however, seems to be precisely what is meant when there is said to be an indissoluble union between "value" and "existence". One thinks, for instance, of the indissoluble connection between equiangularity and equilaterality in a certain type of triangle.

As I have already observed on several occasions "to be" means, quite simply *to be*. It can be truly asserted wherever it is true to say "There is", and that statement means neither more nor less than what it says. If any addition be made to the meaning of the verb, the addition really is an addition. That is forgotten in many philosophies. We hear that "to be is to be perceived", that "to be is to be sense-evidenced", that "to be is to be corporeal", that "to be is to be verifiable", that "to be is to be expressible", that "to be is to be expressible in physical language". All such statements are indefensible in principle when they are understood in their plain meaning, viz. that the verb "to be" implies "to be in a certain way". There is never such an implication. Therefore it is never defensible to maintain that "to be" means "to be valuable" or "to be valid" or "to avail".

These statements refer to the verb "to be", but I do not think it is either expedient in the short run or legitimate in the long run to distinguish between "being" and "existence". If there were such a distinction, if, for instance, existence were defined as "corporeal being" or if someone said, like Bowman, that "to exist is to persist" the consequence would be that the statement

[1] *The Faith of a Moralist*, e.g. p. 29

"X exists" would have a different meaning from the statement "There is an X". If existence, for instance, implied corporeal existence, "X exists" would be a compound statement meaning "There is an X and it is a body". If so, since *body* is definable in terms of certain properties, these properties might be necessarily connected with other properties. Corporeity, for instance, might be necessarily connected with "value" although "being" could not. I do not say that the term "existence" is never used in some such sense. It has been so used when Aristotle, together with many Christian, Moslem, Indian and Chinese theologians spoke of what is "outside" or "beyond" existence; and anyone may stipulate that he proposes so to use it. On the other hand, "existence" is commonly and legitimately used in a wider sense ultimately indistinguishable from "being", and it is arbitrary and almost invariably misleading to neglect this wider sense.

These general considerations should prohibit the putting of quite a lot of wrong questions, but we should be careful to notice what they permit as well as to notice what they prohibit.

Let us, for instance, consider the *esse-percipi* formula. "To be" does not *mean* "to be perceived", but if we say, with Berkeley, that "to be a sound is to be heard", "to be an odour is to be smelt", "to be a pleasure is to be felt", our statements (as I said in a former lecture[1]) may very well be true, not because "to be" *means* "to be perceived", but because the sort of thing that is a sound must be something that is heard, and generally because (as some think) all sensations are mentities. Thus it may very well be true that wherever you can say "There is a sound" you are also saying, and mean to say, "Someone is hearing." In a broader way it is *possible* that although the words "There is" mean neither more nor less than simply "there is", it is true, nevertheless, that everything that exists has certain common properties although existence is not a "property" in that sense of "property". If so, although it would be false to say that existence *implies* the common properties that all existents possess,

[1] Lecture II, p. 61.

it would be true to say that these properties are present wherever anything exists.

In this sense it might be permissible to entertain the hypothesis and to try to prove that wherever *est* can be asserted, *valet* can also be asserted, and the hypothesis would not be disturbed unless an instance could be found in which *est* could be truly asserted but *valet* could not. Since it would be significant to ask whether there was such an instance, the affair cannot be one of strict logical implication. If it were, the question of the existence of such an instance could not be raised. On the other hand, no such instance might be discovered, and reasons might be given for holding that it was undiscoverable.

Thus if a man says "Everything that exists is corporeal, either plainly or covertly", and is able to meet the *prima facie* objection that thoughts, imaginations and errors exist (although they may not seem to be corporeal) by showing that they are covertly corporeal, his hypothesis would remain intact. Similarly it might be credible and philosophical to say that *esse* always is *valere*; but it is neither credible nor philosophical to say that *esse* means or implies *valere*.

In view of these considerations the talk about the inconceivability of any "divorce" between values and existence may assume an altered look. Let us enquire.

Indissoluble wedlock implies two inseparable companions. On the side of existence, therefore, it would have to be maintained that every existent has some value and must have it. On the side of value the contention would seem to be that nothing that has value can be non-existent.

The first of these statements is plainly significant, and it might conceivably be true. It might, however, be interpreted in so tepid a fashion as to be quite absurdly trivial. If, for instance, it were held that all existents are interconnected, then, if some one of them were valuable, none in a sense could be "divorced" from value. That would be a proof that all existent things have some sort of connection with something that has some sort of value and would, as it stands, be very trivial. It would be con-

sistent with a state of affairs in which only one existing thing had
intrinsic value and in which the connection of the other things
with this one thing had very little relevance to the intrinsic
value in question. It would not be impressive (would it?) to
hold that because a puppy has some connection with the fixed
stars, and because there is intrinsic value in the fun that the
puppy gets from chasing his tail, therefore the fixed stars are not
"divorced" from value. Something more would be required if
there were anything mordant in the metaphysics of the catholicity
of value, and it seems plain, in the ordinary sense of language,
that there are many things that have no intrinsic value. That is
because we commonly regard a "value" as something that is
rare. I do not say that the alternatives must be between intrinsic
value, on the one hand, and the complete absence of value on
the other, and I do not deny that there may be senses of "value"
in which its rarity is unlikely. I am saying only that if the alleged
indissolubility of *esse* with *valere* is at all important, something
more than a vague general connection of everything that there
is with *something* that is valuable must be asserted.

On the side of value, the denial of any possible "divorce"
between value and existence is usually another way of affirming
that "values" and ideals cannot be unreal.[1] Man, it is said, is an
aspiring animal. The character of his aspirations reveals much
that he *is*. He is in the making, and he may become what, as yet,
he is not, or is not fully. What he aspires to be would be con-
tinuous with his present nature if he achieved it, and this continuity would be integral and not simply or chiefly a piece of
temporal consecution. Man's is a growing spirit, rooted in his
present actuality, but essentially a burgeoning spirit.

These are very important arguments respecting man, and it is
not unreasonable to enquire whether they may not be of equal
moment with regard to all other beings, and to consider how

[1] When von Hügel said: "No amount of *Oughtnesses* can be made to take
the place of one *Isness*" his assumption seems to have been that "oughtness"
or obligation is in itself empty and merely notional. See e.g. *Selected Letters*,
p. 174 and *passim*.

important they are in man's case and in the case of the other beings. On the other hand, they could not show that what a man aspires to be cannot be unreal in the ordinary sense of unreality. Our aspirations may be illusory, an escape-fantasy, a dream. They may be fond and vain and void. Since the aspirations occur, it may be believed that the stuff they are made on is actual and not non-entitative. Even moonshine is something; but not every ideal is capable of being realized. "The presence of the ideal", it has been said, "is the reality of God within us."[1] As it happened, on the day on which I read these words I also read in a novel, "He was not very much, perhaps, but O! he *wanted* so splendidly". The two statements may only be alternative ways of saying the same thing; but they sound rather different.

If it be said that the enemy to be destroyed is the false belief that ideals have only an ideal existence, or are laid up in a heaven that has only an ideal existence, I grant the falsity of such beliefs. What exists does exist and cannot do less than exist. If an ideal or its heaven be a fantasy and no more than a fantasy, then existence includes the existent fantasy and nothing else that is relevant. Similarly, if any ideal is more than a fantasy it really is something more. It is requisite and necessary to enquire into the status of ideals, but it is absurd to pretend that high metaphysics can demonstrate that ideals cannot be illusory. "What I aspired to be" may be "what I *was not* and never could be".

Similarly, very little can be inferred from the truth contained in one of Die Vernon's sayings. "Rather than any good action", she said, "should walk through the world like an unappropriated adjective in an ill-arranged sentence, he [Rashleigh] is always willing to stand noun substantive to it himself." All good deeds, we allow, are good things and, being actual, exist in some actual agent. But nothing that is relevant follows regarding the alleged indissolubility of values and existence.

Another very obvious point has to be remembered in this connection. The term "value" may be used in a sense in which

[1] A. S. Pringle Pattison, *The Idea of God*, p. 246.

it includes disvalue or in a sense in which it excludes disvalue. In the first sense it is a general name for value-or-disvalue and excludes only what is neither good nor bad. In the second sense it is contrasted with what is bad. Both senses may be convenient in different contexts, but care should be taken to remember the difference between them. If it be declared, for instance, that theism stands for the ubiquity or the sempiternity of values, and is based on the indissolubility of value and existence, it might be embarrassing to remember that what is asserted in the first part of the statement may be the ubiquity and sempiternity of God's *goodness*, while what is asserted in the second part of the statement is that all existence must be *either good or bad*. Yet the above is a very common argument. Again, if it could be shown that all existence is either sentient or effectively related to what is sentient, and if sentience is always either agreeable or disagreeable, we should have a proof of some sort of "ubiquity" of pleasure-pain; but we should have no proof at all of a comfortable optimism. The same would be true if it could be shown, for instance, that everything that *is* should be held to be sense-evidenced, and that all that is sensed has æsthetic properties. We should then have proved the ubiquity of the beautiful-or-ugly, but would not have begun to show the non-existence (or the half-existence?) of what is discordant and revolting.

To be sure, it might be maintained with some show of reason that if the ubiquity or sempiternity of value-or-disvalue could be proved, certain rays of hope would emerge. *Veritas praevalet*, not error. Error can exist only when there is truth to rob, just as forgery can succeed only if there is a credit system. Evil, similarly, may be the parasite of the good. There is no attainable or conceivable maximum of deterioration and corruption. Even a band of robbers must have something of honour and of justice in their banditry.

Such arguments may be admitted for what they are worth. They do not apply at all to pleasure and pain, for pleasure is as likely to be parasitic upon pain as pain to be parasitic on pleasure. I do not think that they apply to the contrast between beauty and ugliness; and although there is more to be said in favour of the parasitic character of moral evil, the remarks about the robber band are not at all persuasive. If it is justice and honour that strengthens these knavish fingers and fists, then justice and honour, so far, would be something to be deplored. That is as it may be; but no such arguments can abolish the clear distinction that has to be remembered so frequently.

Up to the present in this lecture I have spoken very freely of "value" and of "disvalue" without attempting to explain what I mean by these terms. I must now attempt to repair the omission, the more particularly because, in discussing teleology in the first series of these lectures,[1] I spoke of "value" in a sense that may seem to be very remote from the arguments and from the illustrations in the present lecture. To be brief, I maintained, while discussing teleology, that utilizing, accommodation and self-maintenance are value-functions, have a wide application in nature, and are not restricted to conscious experience. These I shall now call "maintenance-values" and I retain the opinion that maintenance-values do exist and are values.

The plainest and the most serious objection to this opinion is that these "maintenance-values" (so-called) are only means to an end, and that a means, although beneficial, need not itself be good at all. My answer is that maintenance-values do not seem to me to be means to an end. I cannot see, for instance, how human life can be said to be a *means* (say) to happiness when what one understands by happiness is just happy living.

It is abundantly plain, however (I submit), that a proof of the ubiquity of maintenance-values would have no tendency at all to establish the ubiquity of what we are accustomed to regard as the "higher values"—truth, righteousness, felicity, beauty and perhaps some others. The tragedy of existence, as many philosophers see it, is that the bearers of these higher values stumble and fall at the assault of things that have no such exalted aims. There is maintenance-value on the part of streptococci, but if a man dies, his high capacities perish with him. The unwilling

[1] Lecture VIII.

host is the victim, and there is nothing high about his unwelcome guest.

These higher values might be called axiological values, to use a neologism that seems to have come to stay although its classical pedigree may be dubious.[1] I shall speak of axiological values when I think it is necessary to underline the distinction between axiological and maintenance-values. The common practice, however, is to speak of values *simpliciter* when axiological values are meant, and indeed to deny that what I have called "maintenance-values" are "values" at all. In general, therefore, it will be sufficient if I give notice that when I speak henceforth of "values" I mean "axiological values" unless I refer explicitly to "maintenance-values" and call them by that name. I shall be chiefly concerned with the familiar triad, the true, the beautiful and the good.

Accordingly we have to ask whether it is necessary or reasonable to believe that all that exists is characterized by some or by all of these values. *Omne ens est verum*, that is to say, Whatever is, is true. *Omne ens est pulchrum*, Whatever is, is beautiful. *Omne ens est bonum*. Whatever is, is (morally?) good. What should we say about these and such-like propositions?

Let us consider the statements *seriatim*, at the price, if necessary, of a certain repetition of matters discussed in earlier lectures.

(*a*) *Omne ens est verum*. It may be objected that this statement cannot be true, since there are false beliefs. That particular objection, however, is fallacious. When false beliefs occur they really do occur. They may be examined, and the truth about them may be discovered. They are something about which true statements may be made, just as true statements may be made about a forgery, or about a hoax, or about false trails or about red herrings.

Assuming the relevance, and, *pro tanto*, the success of this rejoinder, however, we are not at the end of our difficulties. As

---

[1] In its classical origin the term seems to have referred to material reward. I don't know whether that is what Wordsworth meant when he signed his first poem—a prize-poem—"Axiologus".

we have seen, philosophers usually hold that only beliefs, or judgements or propositions can either be true or false, and few would suppose that everything that exists is a belief or a judgement or a proposition. That is plain if beliefs or judgements are mental processes. It is also plain if a proposition be regarded as a mental proposal rather than as a propositum. Again, if by a "belief" one means "that which is believed", one has to avoid the fallacy of supposing that "epistemological objects" are actual things.

To say that everything is a possible term in a true proposition may be very good sense. It is another way of saying that true statements may be made about anything, but there is neither truth nor sense in the statement that everything *is* a proposition —food and clothes and haberdashers, and loyalties, and electrons, and church mice. An "epistemological object" again (as we have seen so often) describes the status of some *ens* in relation to an apprehending mind. It is *res judicata, res percepta, res ficta,* and so forth. None of these is a natural thing.

The same type of argument would apply to the view that perceptions, let us say, or some other cognitive processes, may be "true" or "veridical" as well as judgements or beliefs. Apprehensibility is an extrinsic denomination of any entity, and I shall not separately discuss the various types of apprehensibility. The most that could legitimately be urged on such lines as the above would be that if anything has the extrinsic property of being apprehensible, it must also possess all the intrinsic properties that are implied by its capacity to be apprehended. There would seem, however, to be no *other* special property that is implied by this one, unless the property of not being self-contradictory. However that may be, unless we affirm that every entity has the properties, whatever they may be, that fit it to be truly apprehended if there were a mind to apprehend it, we are not entitled to affirm that it is "true" in an absolutely straightforward sense of that word. Certainly we are accustomed to use the adjective "true" with only a covert reference to the possible presence of an apprehending mind. We say, for instance, that it is true that two and two make four, and hence may speak negligently about what would be true if there never had been any minds. A convenient ellipsis, however, is not a serious piece of metaphysics.

These obvious considerations are specially relevant when truth is regarded as a "value". To say that the proposition "two and two make four", since it is true, must be a "value", and so would have to be a value if there never were anyone who could count, is not a statement that could or should appeal either to the lay or to the expert mind. Indeed, it seems to be very clear indeed that when we speak about the value of truth we are always thinking about the value of true belief or of knowledge-able insight. It is the truth in the soul, the mental state of clear-headedness, insight and intellectual mastery that is the value, and the only value, in the case.

Some philosophers, indeed, would be inclined to jib at the statement that truth is a value in any sense at all. They would admit, perhaps, that knowledge is power and that there is joy in the exercise of power, as well as many other consequential benefits. They would also admit, perhaps, that the joy is a value, but they would maintain, nevertheless, that the knowledge itself is but a means to this or to some other value and is not itself a value. Other philosophers hold, however, that insight *per se* is something fine and supremely high, a noble and exalted thing quite apart from its power in the vulgar sense (that is, its power to build, and to bake, and to destroy) and also apart from its power in a sense that may not be quite so vulgar (that is, its government of wide domains of apparently recalcitrant facts, its conquest of lesser and more untidy principles). Such values, it is clear, attach to knowing and not to numbers and propositions and whatever else may be known. Unless everything is a spirit or at least a mentity, it is simply false to assert that everything is true or has the "value" of being true.

(*b*) *Omne ens est pulchrum.* This statement, to be plausible at all, must refer to beauty-or-ugliness and include æsthetic dis-values as well as positive æsthetic values. This being assumed, it is clear that we do sometimes speak of beauty—for instance, the

natural beauty of a lunar rainbow or of hedgerows in spring—
without appearing to imply any reference to possible minds.
Hence it is not obviously absurd to suggest that everything
whatever must be beautiful-or-ugly. Thus if beauty, as some
æstheticians maintain, applies only to the sensible shows of
things, it would be possible to hold (and many realistic philosophers believe) that the beauty that is manifested in sense is
an actual property of things, discovered and not produced by
sensitive minds. If so, the *things* would have these properties if
there were no minds to notice them; and some philosophers
further maintain that everything that exists must have sensible
properties. Again the truth of the matter might be that beauty-
or-ugliness is not confined to sensory shows, and that there may
be beauty, say, in a mathematical demonstration or in an act of
self-sacrifice. Therefore things that are not *sensibilia* might still
be beautiful-or-ugly. Similarly it might be said that beauty is
"significant form", that everything has some form, and so is
either ugly if the form is unsignificant or is beautiful if the form
is "significant"—whatever that may signify.

As we have seen in an earlier lecture,[1] however, it is very
generally held that "beauty-or-ugliness" even more obviously
than "truth" is a term that covertly connotes the presence and
the relevance of a mind. Beauty, it is said, is a species of the
admirable or of the charming or of the enjoyable, ugliness a
species of what is hateful, repellent or revolting. If so the term
would be only superficially non-mental. There is no sense in
talking about charms if there is not a mind to charm.

I need not, I think, pursue the point now, or recall sterile
controversies about the possible beauties in a frozen world when
life had perished and the angels hid their faces, or about the
sense, if any, in which the statues recently recovered from the
Gulf of Lepanto, to the glory of the Museum at Athens, could
be said to have been beautiful during all the years of their im-
mersion. As on a former occasion it should suffice here to say
that beauty may not be independent of possible admiration, and

[1] Lecture IX of the First Series.

that ugliness may not be independent of possible distaste. If so the term "beauty", like the term "truth", would indicate an extrinsic determination and not a proper feature of whatever is said to be beautiful. Even if there were *some* characteristic of non-mental things that was fitted to evoke admiration or repugnance in some mind (or is it in some *expert's* mind?) that characteristic need not itself be beautiful or ugly. An instance might be the proportions of the golden section, or, again, the mathematics of counterpoint. Without a beholder or without an auditor these, by hypothesis, would not be beautiful.

I do not know whether the people who hold such views (that is to say the great majority of writers on æsthetics) further maintain, on analogy with what I have just said about truth, that the axiological *value* of beauty is wholly in the beholder's mind. They seem to me to speak with a divided voice; but many of them would say that the *value* of beauty is entirely in the fine and high experience of beauty although that experience implies a relation of the admiring mind to the thing that is admired. Others, when they say that the value is relative, may mean that it *is* a relation between mind and thing.

(c) *Omne ens est bonum*. In this proposition there is apt to be cloudiness regarding the relations between maintenance-values and axiological values, between fulness or strength of being on the one hand, and excellence or fineness of being on the other. "Perfection", in a large assemblage of traditional arguments, was equated with fulness, development with aggrandizement, reality with opulence of characteristics. That was characteristic of the Ontological Proof in nearly all its forms. Thus according to Spinoza, perfection, reality and power were identical and were also identical with goodness in one (and, as he thought, in the most accurate) of its meanings. Thus also Descartes (and Kant too) regarded man's reason as his strongest medicament. Their "reason", they thought, was literally the principle of their lives, their rational conceptions caused the continuance of their existence. Queen Christina's comment is very well known. "His oracles have let him down", she said when Descartes died of pneumonia at Stockholm at the age of fifty-three. In Kant's case the oracles were rather more careful. The tiny desiccated frame of that philosopher defied dissolution up to its eightieth year. But four score years is a brief space, and Kant's powers had waned before the end.

To speak with brutal brevity, excellence, if high, may be short. It does not seem to be the toughest thing in nature, still less the very principle of natural toughness. There are the strongest possible objections to the assimilation of axiological with maintenance-values, and it is the former and not the latter with which we are now concerned.

If, however, goodness just means excellence its connotation is still very wide. On that interpretation, it means axiological value in general, and in that sense *bonum* should not be contrasted with *verum* and with *pulchrum*.

To obtain the contrast it is usual to interpret *bonum* moralistically, but even on that interpretation there may be much dispute concerning the boundaries of morality. Deontologists in ethics regard the conception of right conduct as the citadel of ethics. "Right" in this sense means "morally right", not "right" in the general sense in which there is a "right" answer to a problem in arithmetic. Such deontologists oppose "right" to "good" and some of them hold that although our motives are moral they are irrelevant to right conduct (which, according to them, must be right irrespective of motive). Teleologists in ethics, on the other hand, base ethics upon the conception of the doing of good. In the tumult at Lystra Paul illustrated what he meant by God's moral providence by saying: "He left not himself without witness, in that he did good, and gave us rain from heaven, and fruitful seasons, filling our hearts with food and gladness."[1] This conception would apply to all well-doing, even when unintended; it would include generous motives and would still be very

---

[1] Acts xiv. 17. Consider also Cicero's *De Natura Deorum*, iii, ch. 36: "All men are agreed on this, that we get from the gods external goods, like vineyards, cornfields, olive groves, rich crops and vintages, in fine all the good things of life; but no one ever reckoned virtue as obtained from a god."

general if the emphasis were as much upon what God meant to do as upon what he did. Perhaps we might say that such beneficence would be moral, in a stricter sense, if it were not merely intended but was *also* intended to be better than anything else. It may be doubted, however, whether even that rather narrow definition would not be wider than what we commonly understand by moral as opposed to non-moral well-doing. In short, moralists are not agreed about the precise boundaries of morality.

However great the difficulty of defining the boundaries of morality may be, we may nevertheless be confident that there is such a thing as moral goodness and righteousness, moral virtue and moral duty. We accept the fact that there are right actions, even if we are not always prepared to say precisely where morality ceases and why. We can also conceive of a state of affairs in which the aphorism *omne ens est bonum* might be true in a moralistic sense. That would happen if God were a moral being who had designed everything, with complete. success, for wholly moral purposes. It would happen if God were always and essentially a moral being and if all else emanated from him in such a way as to retain this moral essence. It would happen if pantheism were true provided that it has the stamp of morality everywhere, if some moral effluence or Dharma brooded over and sustained all that there is.

On the other hand, the direct application of moral predicates to all that exists would seem to be forbidden by the very evidence on which we rely for asserting that there is such a thing as morality. We distinguish between moral and sub- or non-moral beings, between responsible men and women, on the one hand, and imbeciles, the lower animals and inanimate beings on the other hand. Responsible beings, we say, are moral agents. Therefore there is moral agency. But that particular piece of evidence shows equally that there are non-moral agents; for there are irresponsible beings. We hold, in short, that moral beings are beings of a very high grade, privileged existents among existents not so privileged. In that sense we cannot significantly say that existence, as such, has moral properties, or that every being must be a moral being.

It may be argued, indeed, that all existence is somehow someone's moral opportunity and also (as we have seen and shall later consider more fully) that there may be certain nomic tendencies, either moral or congruent with righteousness, that pervade all existence or at any rate predominate in it. In a direct and literal sense, however, we have to say that even if truth and beauty were universally applicable in *some* intelligible sense, moral goodness is *not* universally applicable. Truth-values and æsthetic values would not reside in everything, if the *value* of truth were held to reside in a penetrating mind and in nothing else, and if the *value* of beauty were held to reside in the experience of the beholder and there alone. But even if the axiological values of truth and of beauty were supposed to have a more spacious abode than in minds or in mentities, it would be much more difficult to take a similar view about moral values. These would seem, quite plainly, to be the exclusive possession of a high-grade order of conscious beings and of no others.

There is a further point to be noted about all axiological values. What is usually maintained by those who refuse to "divorce" value from existence is that because value and existence are inseparable, it is reasonable to infer that what counts for most in the way of value also counts for most in the general order of existence. "We are to put the central things in the centre", Bosanquet said, "to take for our standard what man recognizes as value when his life is fullest and his soul at its highest stretch."[1] On this view, what is central in *us* must be held to be central in our world, and what is central in *our* world must be held to be central in *the* world. Therefore if our aspirations are more instructive than anything else for giving us the clue to what *we* are, these same aspirations must be the most significant clues to the nature of all reality.

Such an inference, if just, contains a concealed premiss. We should accept the conclusion if, for instance, we knew in advance

[1] *The Principle of Individuality and Value*, p. 3.

or were able to divine that man is truly the microcosm, reality the macrocosm, and that the microcosm mirrors the macrocosm in all relevant respects. Without some such premiss the inference is vain. With it the conclusion is already asserted and not genuinely inferred. I have illustrated the fallacy on more than one occasion from the manuals on formal logic. Let us recall what the manuals say. If we argue, to use Dr. Keynes's illustration, "A negro is a fellow creature; therefore a suffering negro is a suffering fellow creature"[1] we are prepared to accept the conclusion (whatever we may think about the "therefore" in the alleged "argument") because we know in advance that pigmentation is irrelevant to most human suffering. If we did not have that piece of knowledge the whole argument would float in Limbo. In that case we might as well argue that because a Jew is a fellow creature, therefore an Aryan Jew is an Aryan fellow creature.

With these reflections in our minds we may return to Lotze's *credo* quoted earlier in this lecture. The passage, more in the long, runs as follows: "The true beginning of metaphysics lies in ethics. I admit that the expression is not exact, but I still feel certain of being on the right track when I seek in that which *should be* the ground of that which *is*."

What is the track that Lotze indicated?

Up to the present I have spoken of value either as a substantive or as an adjective of goods or of their property of being good. The suggestion now is that *validity* is what is all-important, a derivative of the verb. After Lotze's death Windelband, Rickert and many other philosophers explored this track very confidently. We, on our part, may therefore enquire whether its footing is secure. Does "value" mean "validity"? Is validity the assured basis of a metaphysics of existence?

The most usual and the most obvious application of the term "validity" is to logical inference. An inference is valid when we ought to draw it, when, in the language of the Latin grammars, it is "deserving or requiring to be drawn". Lotze also used such

[1] *Formal Logic*, p. 149.

expressions. "God", he said, "has ordered all things by measure and number, but what he ordered was not measures and numbers themselves, but that which deserved or required to possess them."[1]

Valid inference, in short, is true inference, and validity, more generally, is the truth of true apprehension. Our problem at this point therefore is, as often before, the problem of truth, and of the relation of idea-ism to existence. We have seen that in all inference and in all truth there is an implied reference to an apprehending mind, but "existence" (as we have also seen) implies no such thing. Consequently the omens are not favourable to any attempt to show that reality is the child of validity.

The same thing may be shown in the convenient vocabulary of the German language. German philosophers speak about *Sein, Dasein, Sosein* and *Mitsein*, i.e. of being, of being that is *there* in front of us, of being such-and-such, and of the togetherness of beings. In all this terminology, however, *Sein* is what is fundamental. Even if all *Sein* be *Sosein* and *Mitsein, Sosein* and *Mitsein* could not reasonably be supposed to generate *Sein*.

In other words, it is quite illegitimate to make *existence* subordinate to logical validity. Existence itself is ingenerable. If an existent is generated it cannot be sired by a non-existent parent, even if the putative father be logical validity.

That fundamental criticism would apply to all validity. It is not restricted to logical validity. The topic, however, may be profitably pursued even granting that the end is certain. In particular there is interest and importance in the attempt to make truth and logic subordinate to ethics and so to put idea-ism under the ægis of axiological idealism. Lotze's *credo* would be shelved and not discussed if this aspect of the affair were forgotten.

A possible line of argument would be the following: A valid inference, we may be told, is one that we *ought to* draw. A valid belief is one that we ought to hold. What "*should be*" or what "*ought to be*" in these instances, therefore, may turn out to be

[1] *Metaphysics*, penultimate page.

something that *we* ought to do. The obligation is *our* obligation, and it would seem to be a moral obligation in a very definite sense, conditional in certain cases and unconditional in other cases. It is conditional in so far as the meaning is: "*If* your true intent is to find out what X is, *then* you ought to sharpen the cutting edge of all your logical instruments." It is unconditional, or appears to be so, if the meaning be: "As a thinking being you are in duty bound to be a most scrupulous logician." That, in Kantian language, would be a particular form of the categorical imperative. Another name for it, in the present context, is the scientific conscience. A man's scientific conscience, as we all know, may be very highly developed although the rest of his conscientiousness is not equally scrupulous. Similarly, however, a man may be scrupulous about paying debts of honour but not about paying tailors' bills. Conscience, in a word, may be a wayward faculty; but a "scientific conscience" is an authentic department of conscience and would seem to be moral in the simple and plain sense in which any other department of conscience is a moral thing.

That, as I have said, would not so much as suggest that the beginnings of *ontology* or of *metaphysics* are to be found in ethics. If we say that things "deserve or require" the obligations that are binding upon a sensitive scientific conscience, our language is plainly metaphorical. As the Chinese philosopher Chuang Tzŭ said long before Bishop Butler: "Everything is what it is and does what it can do."[1] If we are bent upon discovering what things are, we ought to think correctly about them. That is all that the obligation means and entails. It cannot determine what the things are. All that results is the much more modest contention that the beginnings of logical inference and of truth-searching lie in ethics. We may say, quite generally, I think, that "ought to be" always means, in strictness, "ought to do", that inferring is a kind of doing, and that "doing" in the relevant sense always means, in strictness, morally responsible conduct.

[1] Fung Yu-Lan: *A History of Chinese Philosophy* p. 240.

Value and Existence

The validity of inference and of cognitive apprehension, however, does not exhaust our present topic. According to many philosophers there is also validity of appreciation and of approval, a right way of loving and of being loyal. In short, we are told that an idealism of appreciation should replace the lesser theories of idea-ism or of ideatism. Validity of taste and of admiration, we are told, is the very heart of æsthetics. Validity of desire and enjoyment is the breath of a liberal ethics. Goodness, as Brentano, Kraus and others have thought, is rightness of loving.

To be sure, this analysis is frequently rejected outright. A great many philosophers assert quite dogmatically that our satisfactions and our desires are wholly incapable of the rightness or correctness of which our beliefs and our inferences are capable, or of anything analogous to such rightness or correctness. These very philosophers, however, might be compelled to admit that there are certain analogies between what is morally and what is intellectually right, that there may be moral rightness of character, aspiration and motive as well as of intention, resolution and volition, and that our feelings and desires may be fitting or becoming or appropriate. If so, these philosophers need not differ profoundly from the theorists whose darling conception is validity in varied forms.

Admittedly certain philosophers hold that worth or good is just worth or good and that there's an end on't. If so, goodness and worth would not be constituted by, or dependent on, or inseparably connected with anyone's appreciation of any kind whatever. The doctrine would be that certain things (which might always, perhaps, be certain experiences) are axiologically good, and that certain other things are axiologically bad. True, we may call a man good if he wills and desires what is good, that is, we may apply the term in a secondary sense to his volitions and to his desires. In the same secondary sense we might call a man better than any of his fellow animals if he desires and chooses better things than they. But that would be the whole of the story. If anyone asks why a man should choose and pursue what is good, the answer is simply that he wouldn't be a good man if he didn't.

I think that this simple-minded theory may very well be true, but it is not very often held, and there would be more bluster than philosophy in simply assuming its truth. Suppose, then, that it is doubtful. In that case the opinion that axiological value is simply a name for validity or rightness of desire, volition or satisfaction deserves close attention. According to this theory, that would be good which yields valid satisfaction and is the object of right desiring or of right loving. I cannot see any insuperable objection to such a view unless desire and satisfaction and their kind are incapable of any sort of rightness. Dogma apart, I cannot see that they are so incapable.

It would follow from such a view that there was a natural affinity between right desires and right performance. Desire prompts to action. Therefore valid desire might be expected to prompt to valid action. Between the statement: "This would be splendid if it occurred", and the rejoinder: "Let it be so. What is that to us" there would be, if not a solid bridge, at any rate, some encouragement for pontifical enterprise. True, it would still be possible for a man to say, "I admit the validity of such and such a desire. I admit even that it makes a certain appeal. But I prefer some other". All desires move us, but only some of our desires are valid. It would still be possible for a man's deeds to give the lie to his protestations. Nobility of speech is in general a cheaper commodity than nobility of deeds. Therefore the contrast, for the most part, is to the detriment of action although the converse case may and does occur. Nevertheless, there would be a natural and obvious connection between desiring *de facto* and the hegemony, *de jure*, of valid desire.

Again the restriction of axiological value to *valid* desires and satisfactions, or to what Meinong called the "dignitatives" of desire and of satisfaction, frees the analysis from a strong *prima facie* objection. Satisfactions may be evil or may be taken in what we call evil things. Unless the human species is axiologically superior to all else on the earth it could have no just title of any kind to lord it over the earth. I do not say that it *must* have such a title because it *is* axiologically superior. I am only saying that it could not have any just title at all if it were not superior. The fact, if it be a fact, that man is the only logical or the only religious animal does not of itself confer upon mankind the unlimited right to consume, destroy or enslave all other terrene beings, but it might begin to justify such exploitation, if the exploitation were inevitable for human existence.

In any case, even if there be *something* good in all satisfaction, it is quite impossible to identify "good" with *de facto* desire or agreeable feeling, and also to maintain, without simple effrontery, that the word "good" has retained its proper or its usual meaning. No such objection, however, brings disaster to the view that goodness is *validity* of satisfaction or of desire. According to this view, it may also be maintained without inconsistency that man is the only animal who is capable of *valid* satisfactions and of *valid* desires. He may be (although it need not be supposed that he *is*) the only animal that can validly approve just as he may be the only animal that can validly infer.

Let me pass to a related point. In English we have here a rather odd divergence of word-terminations. We mean by "desirable" that which should be desired, by "admirable" that which ought to be admired, by commendable that which is praise*worthy*. By "enjoyable", on the other hand, we often mean, quite simply, that which *can* be enjoyed, and by pleasurable that in which pleasure *can* be taken. Terms like "loveable" and "likeable" seem to hover between the two interpretations, with a slight preponderance, perhaps, towards the former.

This divergence in current English and in some other European languages may be an oddity with no recondite philosophical significance. On the other hand it may tend to show that the sort of attitude that is relevant to axiological valuation has a *nisus* towards validity in some quite special way. We never, I think, use the term "desirable" if we mean only that such and such a thing *could* be desired by somebody.

This reflection has some bearing upon our general problem.

Can we translate the statement that existence cannot be divorced from value, or that actuality is merged in ideality, or that ideality is merged in actuality, into the statement that all existence must be somehow desirable because it must be the object of right or of valid desire?

Plainly we should have no business to say so if the meaning were that nothing that exists could be undesirable, the object of valid aversion. If earth be crammed with heaven it may also be chock-a-block with hell. The statement might be defensible, however, if the meaning were that all that exists must be an appropriate object either of valid desire or of valid aversion. Moreover, an attempt might be made to link value with existence in the following way: Whatever is desirable, it is said (i.e. whatever ought to be desired), must at least be such that it *can* be desired. Therefore valid appreciation must always refer to possible existence.

Here the argument seems to be loose. Desires occur, but that which is desired may never occur. Indeed the term "desirable" is usually connected so negligently with actual desiring that all such inferences are very precarious indeed. Desire, in the strict sense, always refers to the future. We no longer desire what we already have even if we like it very much. At most we desire its continuance. On the other hand we do not usually impose any such restriction upon the term "desirable", not even the hypothetical restriction that someone *could* have desired it before it occurred. Again, it is possible to desire impossibilities, as the moth has been said to desire the star, and nothing is more usual than to say that something or other, although desirable, is impracticable. The fact is ominous regarding any reputedly indissoluble connection between the desirable and the actual. The desirable would be the object of a valid desire if anyone did desire it; but even this condition need not be fulfilled. Much may be desirable that, as yet, has never entered into the heart of any man to conceive.

In the last of these respects, the relation between valid satisfaction and the enjoyable has similar implications, although it is exempt from some of the considerations that are pertinent to desire. I shall not discuss the point separately, but would like to say something about rightness of willing in moral matters, the more especially because, as we have seen, it is possible that *every* "ought" is a moral "ought".

It is common for moralists to hold that "ought" implies "can", i.e. that an impossible moral obligation is a contradiction in terms. Therefore, some of them argue, value and existence cannot be separated in morals.

There may be senses in which it is undeniable and even tautologous to say that "ought implies can". In that case, however, it may not be equally clear that "*right* implies can", although Kant believed that this also was true.[1] The meaning of this statement would be that nobody is ever too weak to do what is right, or perhaps, that nobody in his right mind is too weak to do so. Such a proposition, in the ordinary sense of language, surely arouses misgivings, but even if it were defensible on certain interpretations, it would be twisted out of all semblance of certitude and, indeed, of verisimilitude, if the meaning were that every one of us could become a saint if he chose, and that no moral ideals are too high for anyone. If such a maxim were true the pace of morals would be set by the pace of the weakest runner. It is incredible that this should be the truth.

Summing up, then, we have to say three things about the supposed indissoluble consortium between value and existence. In the first place there can be neither connection nor disconnection between the property of existence and the property of value, for existence is not a "property" (i.e. a property of any existent) in the sense required. If it be argued, nevertheless, that all existents are and must be valuable, we have to say, secondly, that this proposition is plainly false unless it means that all existents have in fact either value or disvalue, and that it is not evident (and probably isn't true) that every existent either has axiological value or axiological disvalue. In the third place we have to say that validity covertly or expressly implies mental or

[1] *Critique of Practical Reason*, Book I, chap. i, sect. vi, remark.

mind-like attributes. Therefore unless everything that exists is either a mind or a mentity, *something* exists of which validity cannot be predicated.

To speak more generally, it appears to me that all attempts to subordinate existence to validity are instances of a pan-idealism similar in principle to pan-idea-ism and to pan-ideatism. They substitute "appreciation" for mere cognitive ideation, but are committed in all relevant ways to the same sort of topsy-turvy-dom in metaphysics—the attempt to generate existence itself from some sort of mentality. Hence their affinities with the Ontological Proof, and with a phenomenalism of validity.

This leads me to certain concluding observations about Lotze's dictum. He sought in that which "should be" the ground of "that which is". I submit that the phrase "that which should be" is an incomplete expression. When completed, it means that which should be inferred, that which should be willed, that which should be desired and the like. Desires, inferences, states of admiration, states of aspiration are matters of fact that occur. If they are not illusory they also refer transcendently to real existence. But they presuppose real existence and do not generate it.

Similar comments must be passed upon all attempts to discover a reason for existence itself. It is senseless to ask why being is made. There can be no reason *for* existence. There can only be rational connections *within* existence. Such connections may indeed pervade all existence, but they do not and cannot explain why existence came about or why it continues in being. Existence is not a characteristic from which rationality or righteousness can be deduced, and, by the same logic, rationality and validity are not characteristics that can be deduced from the characteristic of existence. It is dreamer's work to suppose so, the dream of outsoaring the ultimate.

The error is due to a very natural oversight. It is reasonable to ask a man why he did this rather than that. If he is able to show that he chose the better course, we would allow that he had given a proper answer although we might argue interminably about the correct analysis of his reply. The same would hold, *simpliciter*, if the man did something because it was good to do it. By an easy but fatal transition we proceed to abolish all the limitations that are presupposed in such questions and also in the answers to them. We attribute to all existence the sort of effect that some existent (e.g. the thought of value) can excite in some other existent (e.g. a man), and so profess to speak about a reason for existence itself. A little brief reflection, not too strenuous, should be sufficient to dispel all such dreams.

I should also like to make some further remarks about validity in particular.

Valid mental processes occur, and existence may be inferred from correctly apprehended existence. More generally it is futile to argue that the ideal can never be actual, or that the actual can never be ideal. What a man should do he may actually do. The validity or rightness of his practice need not be compared to the cup that forever eluded the lips of Tantalus, or to the legendary pot of gold at the rainbow's end. If, in fact, there is always a flaw in any extended piece of human practice, some further thing that is needful, the reason does not lie in the metaphysical impossibility of ideal things, but only in the prevalent weakness of actual humanity.

Nevertheless it is the *difference* between the attribute of validity and all other attributes that is most striking in this affair. The validity of our thoughts and of our appreciations is wholly *sui generis*. The rightness of right thinking, right willing, right desiring is something that cannot be translated into other terms. This can be seen in a host of ways. It may be the case, for instance, that a logical transition follows a different brain-track from an illogical association. If so, what would we not give for a drug that would block all the side lines and keep the logical track in smooth running order? But if we discovered that logical track—although there is no reason for believing that we ever could find it—what probable reason could be assigned for the *validity* of this track and for the *invalidity* of all the others? There could be no reason except the unintelligible empirical fact that the traffic along this particular track was always "valid" traffic. Critical standards have to be self-critical. There is no other court to which appeal could conceivably be made, and there is no need for any other court.

There is a moral here for the theory of mind and body. Because the property of validity is unique it is argued that it must be the property of a unique kind of substance, i.e. a mind. I would not suggest that anything except a mind or what is mind-like is capable of valid actions. We do not apply the term "validity" to anything except inferences, desires, aspirations and their kindred. If we did attempt to apply the term more widely there would only be sound, I think, and not sense in the attempt. It seems to me to be altogether doubtful, however, whether cause or substance or any other such metaphysical principle can be validly employed to explain validity itself. Validity is not inferable from existential categories of that kind any more than they are inferable from it.

VIII

The Moral Proofs of Theism

IN the present lecture I intend to examine what seem to me to be the most important of the arguments which profess to show that morality reveals something on the basis of which a metaphysician, if he knows his business, is bound to erect a theistic conclusion. Since the hinterland of morality, as opposed to its central provinces, is of debateable extent, I shall try, so far as I can, to argue from what is indisputably moral. Again, I should like to give notice that I shall not try, in the present lecture, to revise (still less to unsay) what was concluded in the last. I shall assume now, that value and existence cannot be shown, in the abstract, to be inseparable. That type of axiological metaphysics is renounced. I shall also assume that validity is ultimate and *sui generis*, not derivative from general metaphysics or from anything else. With regard to ethics this last assertion means that all appeals in matters of ethical standards must be made to ethics itself. That is not to say that ethical ideas are infallible, or that they approach infallibility more closely than other ideas. It is simply to say that if these standards falter or fail, no other standards have the right to supplant them. If ethics boggles there is either no remedy or the remedy lies in a better ethics.

I

A famous argument in the history of this subject, and an argument that is still sometimes used, is the proof of theism from the implications of moral law. A law, it is said, implies a lawgiver. Nature issues no commands. Governments and dictators do issue commands, but they themselves are morally subject to moral law unless international morality is a meaningless term, and the actions of sovereign states are neither right nor wrong. Again it is sometimes argued that since moral law forms a unity, it must have a single source. Hence it may be maintained that *monotheism* is established by this proof. He who is not ungodly must be One-godly.

In the Stoic, mediæval and post-mediæval tradition of our Western philosophy, this debate turned upon a particular interpretation of the "laws of nature". It is convenient for us now to interrogate that tradition.

It is usual at the present time, and it has been usual for some centuries, to speak of the "laws of nature" in one context only, and to regard them as patterns of structure or of behaviour, uniformities of co-existence or of sequence. That is a violent departure from the older tradition where the significance of the phrase "the law of nature" was primarily juristic or ethical. The "law of nature" in this traditional sense was essentially the law of justice or of right, the *ius naturale*. The sum of it was to treat equals equally, and to prevent passion and prejudice from presuming a relevant moral inequality where there was none. Some light upon the *ius naturale*, so understood (it was said), was thrown by the *ius gentium*, that is to say, by international practice in the contacts of the nationals of different political communities on trading and other occasions. It was clearly perceived, however, that the common practice of semi-civilized trading communities, even when interpreted on general principles of equity, and the sort of principle that a *praetor peregrinus* applied when dealing with the established customs of alien conquered peoples, were often but a makeshift sort of justice. The *ius gentium*, consequently, was a very imperfect image of the *ius naturale*. For instance, according to the ancient jurists, it accepted slavery although the *ius naturale* could not justify that practice.

The natural comment of a modern philosopher upon this piece of history would be to say that these two senses of the "law of nature", the uniformitarian and the juristic, had nothing in common. The modern mind, it would be said, has emancipated itself from at least one gross confusion. It declines to consider the "laws of nature" except when they are interpreted in the uniformitarian sense.

That, we are told, may be seen in several different connections. Consider, for instance, what is meant by "obeying" a law. There is no sense in maintaining that a falling apple or a revolving satellite "obeys" the law of gravitation. The law has instances, but all talk about obedience or disobedience to the law is antiquated metaphor. A moral or juristic law, on the other hand, may be obeyed or disobeyed. Its field is voluntary action; and voluntary action is not uniformly law-abiding; men sometimes conform to laws and sometimes break them.

This explanation, however, although it seems to be so very clear, contains the seeds of perplexity.

Consider, firstly, the ethical side of it. What is obeyed or disobeyed in any given instance is a command. Juridical laws are commands or prohibitions of a sovereign. Such commands may be obeyed or disobeyed. It is not apparent, however (and in my opinion it is falsely averred) that the *rightness* or *equity* of any juridical law is just what the sovereign commands, and so that if there were no commander there could be no such thing as justice or equity. Consequently the supposed theistic demonstration vanishes. It was based upon the principle that moral rightness and equity are or depend upon some command. Therefore there must be a commander. Therefore since neither monarch nor governors are the ultimate moral commanders, there must ultimately be a super-human commander, that is, a God. Therefore a clear-headed atheist must be a moral outlaw. Whether or not earthly sovereigns rule by right divine, there must be a king of kings who does so rule. Without him there could be no morality.

That is the argument. I suggest that it depends upon an initial mistake in analysis. The laws of the land are the commands of an actual commander. Rightness or wrongness (I submit) are not commands and do not imply a commander. True, they apply to voluntary actions, and the agent in such actions may choose the right or choose the wrong; but the language of command applies to government and does not determine rightness of government or of anything else.

Consider, secondly, the uniformitarian interpretation of the "laws of nature". Certainly there is no contradiction in maintaining that nature is patterned in uniform ways and is likely to continue so. If that is all that we mean by saying that nature is "nomic" or that it exhibits "law", we are saying what may be true, and what, if it were true, would be very important. On the other hand we have to be very careful indeed lest the juristic associations of the word "law" return to mock us.

Some such error suffused many theistic arguments at least as recently as the late nineteenth century. The uniformitarianism of nature, it was said, was a mere brute uniformity, wholly destitute of inner coherence. Therefore the uniformitarianism of nature is *arbitrary*, and arbitrariness bespeaks volition. Consequently the uniformity of nature was said to be imposed upon nature from the outside, for reasons that, in respect of nature, were arbitrary. Therefore, in the last analysis, the stars were said to keep their courses because God commanded them to do so. They could not disobey celestial orders, but they were orderly because commanded. In ultimate metaphysics (it was said) the juristic and the uniformitarian senses of the "laws of nature" effectively coalesced.

All this is perverse. If "arbitrary" means "non-principled", there is no logic in the inference that because non-principled willing is arbitrary willing, therefore everything unprincipled is somehow volitional. It is equally illegitimate to argue that because nature is non-principled, it must be the work of a God of principle. If your premiss is that nature, even when it is coherent, has no "inner" coherence, you should stick to it. It implies no absurdity.

If it be asked whether there is *nothing* common to these different senses of "law", the answer, I believe, is very simple indeed. The common meaning, I suggest, is adequately expressed by the word "principle". Principles are general and they hold either of other principles that are less general or of particular instances. That is one of the senses in which we speak of a "law". We also say that principles "govern" their instances, and that in a principled hierarchy, the superordinate principles "govern" the subordinate principles. We never mean, however, that any principle issues commands to its instances, or makes its commands effective by means of punishment or of some other sanction. Our minds, when they think in a principled way, may indeed be said to arrange their thoughts and to bring order into them; but they do not *command* their thoughts. We ought to think in a principled way, but we do not literally command ourselves or obey ourselves in such thinking. If we did so, the theistic proof would fall, for the commander would be ourselves. Command, however, is an interpersonal relation, requiring at least two parties, one who commands and another who obeys, or at any rate is told to obey. So we cannot command *ourselves*.

If it be complained that this "nomic" approach to theism, although traditionally prominent, is now abandoned and should therefore be passed over in silence, I have several answers to give. In the first place I do not think that the nomic argument is dead or even moribund. Dr. Webb, for instance, has revived it in its monarchical form, knowing very well indeed what he was doing.[1] Theism, he says, is theonomy, and theonomy is an implication of a nomic universe, intimated to us not only by our sense of reverence but also by the strength of juristic analogies. In the second place, even if the nomic argument were dead, its ghost continues to haunt us. I think I can discern the spectre, for instance, very clearly in Bowman's pages. No moral obligation, Bowman said, would be binding unless it is grounded upon "a person commensurate with the universality of the demand. Men are obliged to men because of one comprehensive obligation which accrues to them in their relation to a divine being".[2] Such an assertion, as it stands, seems to me to be entirely arbitrary. Certainly, if, firstly, moral obligation is ultimate and

---

[1] *Divine Personality*, pp. 132 ff.
[2] *Studies in the Philosophy of Religion*, II, 103.

unconditional, and if, secondly, "God" be simply a name for whatever is ultimate and unconditional, it follows that anyone who accepts the ultimacy of moral obligation accepts "God". But why should atheists be forbidden to believe in ultimates? Why should it be more difficult for atheists than for other people to accept self-evident propositions or self-justifying duties? I do not believe that Bowman's assertion would ever have been made if it were not, in fact, the lingering ghost of the nomic argument. In the third place I should say, and shall try to show, that the nomic argument is implicit in a type of metaphysics that seems to me to deserve very close attention whether or not it is now in the fashion. I mean the alleged primacy of the practical over the speculative reason.

To that I now proceed and I intend to make it the central, the longest and the most substantial part of the discussion in this lecture. I do not claim that the nomic argument together with the argument from the primacy of the practical reason exhaust between them all that can be put forward as a moral proof of theism. As a matter of history, the moral proofs have been more resourceful; but I think that these two proofs, and especially the second of them, are the greatest, the most exciting to a philosopher, in a word the most serious. While I have to explain my plan in this lecture I do not think I need offer any apologies for it.

II

The metaphysical argument with which we are now concerned is the thesis that ethics is synonymous with the "practical reason" and that the practical (or operative) reason is that which energizes all reality.

If that were the truth, Lotze's dictum, which was the text of our last lecture, would be both simple and palmary. The true beginning of metaphysics, of all that could abide the assaults of ultimate criticism, would lie in ethics. The practical reason would be, not only the overlord that a man should follow, but also the producer as well as the governor of all that there is. It would be the *fons totius entis*, very God (or very Godhead) if God (or Godhead) could be ascertained by metaphysics at all. There could not be a more determined, a bolder or a more explicit effort to reach a metaphysical proof of a metaphysical theism.

One form of this metaphysical thesis is the application of the nomic argument from moral law to a moral legislator. Kant argued so when he summoned his intellectual forces for a final rally before the night fell, and set about the enterprise whose fragments are known as his *Opus Posthumum*. Among the excerpts from these fragments that have been arranged by Adickes we read (for instance): "Reason goes to work according to the categorical imperative; and God is the law-giver. There is a God because there is a categorical imperative."[1] "The being whose will is practical law for all rational beings is the supreme moral being (*ens summum*), the highest intelligence, which, distinct from all worldly things, is legislative under a single principle, that is to say, is God. Therefore there is a God, distinct from the world-soul or creative demiurge."[2] "A universally and morally legislative being, which by implication is all-powerful, is God. So God exists, that is to say, exists as a principle which, as substance, is morally law-giving."[3]

These statements, as we shall see, are subject to important reservations and explanations both in the *Opus Posthumum* and in the greater finished work of Kant's maturity. We shall also see, however, that they conform to a metaphysical standpoint of whose general truth Kant, throughout his maturity, was sceptical but convinced. I shall proceed, then, to a wider consideration of the metaphysical theory that reason lays the foundation of all reality, and that it is morality that reveals the essentials of the practical office of reason.

The theory is old enough, and may take many forms, but I intend to keep Kant's form of it very firmly before us. His genius had a breadth and a fertility both in axiological and in metaphysical questions that seem to me to be unrivalled among

[1] *Kant-Studien*, Ergänzungsheft 50, p. 778.   [2] *Ibid.*, p. 779.   [3] *Ibid.*

the rationalists; and it is rationalism that we are discussing now. On the other hand I have neither the space nor the knowledge that would be requisite for assessing Kant's axiological metaphysics, his cosmic moralism, in its entirety. The more I read of Kant and the more I read about him, the less inclination I feel for making confident pronouncements upon what his theory essentially was. In other words, I want to discuss certain leading ideas that were prominent in Kant's philosophy. I am not claiming that I can reveal the secret of Kant, if he had just one such secret.

In approaching this subject it seems expedient to make two preliminary remarks, the first concerning the place of rationality in ethics, the second concerning the possible identity of moral with operative rationality.

As regards the first point, there are grave objections to the theory that morality is exclusively an affair of *mere* reason. Kant himself held that all reason was formal, but that all forms had a "matter". This "matter" in ethics consisted of sensory inclinations that the forms of reason did not directly create. He further maintained, however, that our inclinations, in morally justifiable conduct, had to be wholly subordinated to the moral reason and could not collaborate with the moral "reason" except to the detriment of morals. Reason *gave* the law to our inclinations. Similarly, contemporary deontologists in Oxford hold that duty or obligation is exclusively an affair of "moral logic" but that our motives and much else that belongs to the moral part of us are non-rational. In general there are very few who would maintain that generous, loving and loyal actions may not deserve high moral commendation *although* they are not exclusively or principally rational. Moreover, Kant himself held that the righteous man should "summon all the means in his power" and he frequently denied that mere reason could tell us what these means were.

Nevertheless it seems indisputable that there is *principle* in all conduct that is morally right, whether or not the agent is thinking about the principle at the time of action. It seems also to be clear that beings wholly incapable of understanding such principles are at the best sub-moral. Therefore morality, whatever its ultimate nature may be, is a reflective and even an intellectual thing. Morality, in short, *is* rational even if there be more than *mere* reason in it. It may therefore be capable of giving us peculiarly important information concerning the power of reason both in ourselves and in the world.

The second preliminary question is whether we are at liberty to assume that the "moral" and the "practical" reason are precisely the same thing. Such a statement might be taken to mean that wherever reason operates it does so simply and altogether as a moral duty. That would be very hard to believe, say, in the case of a burglar who correctly infers that his jemmy is adequate for his burglarious job. It may be true that no human employment to which a man gives his mind is exempt from morality, and also that morality is, in some sense, supreme *de jure* in all human reflecting conduct. Despite that, it is surely incredible that the operative and the moral reason are simply identical. If we were to speak empirically of the "practical" or of the "operative" reason there is only one thing we could mean. Our meaning would be that reflective thoughts are operative, that men who reflect act differently from men who don't reflect. Plainly that is true. Cities and battleships and ration-cards are evidence. Nevertheless town-planning and ration-cards are not, on that account alone, a sub-department of ethics.

But let us abandon these preliminaries.

In his *Opus Posthumum* Kant, in many passages, seemed to rest his case upon the reality and divinity of the practical reason in men. God, according to these passages, was *our* Idea (or Ideal) if we sedulously reminded ourselves that "Ideas are not mere notions, but laws of thought that the thinking subject prescribes to himself".[1] Kant's language, here, was bold. He called God "the ideal of a substance that we ourselves fashion."[2] "Est deus in nobis",[3] he said, meaning, as he stated in another passage, that "God can only be sought in ourselves".[4] One of

[1] Adickes, *op. cit*, p. 794.   [2] *Ibid.*, p. 793.   [3] *Ibid.*, p. 814.   [4] *Ibid.*, p. 819.

237

his strongest statements was the following: "God is not a being outside me, but only a thought within me. God is the practical moral reason giving the law to itself. Therefore there is but one God in me, around me and above me."[1]

In such statements the transcendental philosophy seems to withdraw itself both from earth and from heaven with a violent shuddering contraction. It becomes a metaphysics about ourselves. I think that this contracted metaphysics was seldom absent from Kant's mind in its prime. For the most part, however, Kant was much more ambitious or seemed to be so. He believed that freedom was evidenced in morality and nowhere else, but that moral freedom proved incontestably, and with a cosmic significance, that things are not what they seem, that natural science (which, according to Kant, was unfree because invincibly deterministic) is not everything, and that a thinking man, because he knows he is free, must be prepared for a revolution in his entire conception of reality. Success might elude us if we tried to accomplish the revolution in detail, but we would not be philosophers at all if we did not make the attempt.

If the invincible determinism of natural events be granted, these are very bold claims, but I do not think they are overbold. If men are free, their freedom should appear more clearly in their moral action than elsewhere; for morality seems to be the supreme instance of such freedom. Again, if men are free, and if determinism reigns in physics, there would be chaos in the heart of things unless a revolution could be accomplished. The illusion of moral freedom, some philosophers say, is the most egregious instance of human conceit. When they claim to be free, men arrogate to themselves an altogether unique status in nature. But what if the claim were valid? In that case the reproach of eccentricity would recoil upon the critic. According to Kant, the claim *was* valid, and therefore it was necessary to

[1] Adickes, *op. cit.*, p. 819. Such ideas may be pressed into the service of a Folk-theology. Thus Rosenberg writes: "The God we honour would not exist if our soul and our blood did not exist. So would the confession of a Meister Eckhart run in our day." *Mythus der XX Jahrhundert*, p. 101. On p. 201 of the same work Rosenberg quotes Eckhart: "If I did not exist, neither would God."

revise our whole conception of the status of what we call "natural events". That was Kant's problem, that determined his attempts to solve it. I do not think that any other philosopher has grappled so strenuously with the metaphysical problem of freedom as Kant did. Therefore I submit that his views compel our closest attention.

Kant persistently and strenuously denied that we could have scientific knowledge of metaphysics, theistic or atheistic, but he also maintained that morality revealed *something* in the nature of reality that natural philosophy was never entitled to affirm. What ethics revealed was a *fact* of pure reason, its actuality as an operative principle. In natural philosophy reason was not a datum but only the interpreter of sensory evidence. In moral philosophy reason gave the law to sensibility, and the fact that it did so was a datum. This fact of pure reason, Kant further maintained, did not enlarge our speculative knowledge. We could not do more than hazard guesses, as reasonable as might be, concerning the way in which the fact might be conceived to occur. Nevertheless we knew for certain that there *was* this operative determination.

This way of stating the case implies that there are absolute data, and that the distinction between data and what are not data is also absolute. Both of these assertions may be challenged, and, as we have seen, it is, to say the least, very doubtful whether rational self-determination (or operative reason) coincides with the morality of conduct.

According to Kant the *factum* of pure reason that is evidenced in morality is the positive aspect of what, in its negative aspect, is freedom. Here another comment seems appropriate. When I spoke above of the immense importance of Kant's problem, and of freedom as, in a unique sense, the meeting-point of spirit and nature, my remarks might have been challenged on the ground that indeterminism was a possible creed in natural science and so that Kant's statement of the contrast between spirit and nature was misconstrued. If freedom and indeterminism were simply identical this objection might be sound. Kant may have erred with others in his age in accepting the unqualified determinism of natural science. But it is the positive side of freedom, it is rational self-determination that is the crux of a metaphysics developed on Kantian lines, and his argument might readily be amended in such a way as to avoid all dogmatism regarding the invincible determinism of natural science.

Nevertheless the free self-determination of the actions of a reasonable being would seem to imply the possibility of emancipation from *something*, that is to say, to imply "freedom" in its negative sense. According to Kant, rational self-determination implies an emancipation from mere sensory determination, and that is what is so important and so striking in ethics. It is a man's freedom to control and even to extirpate passion, and lusts and the enticement of fleshly desires. It is the conflict between moral principle and passionate inclination. Kant may have exaggerated the conflict, and may even have slipped into the error of holding that a man can never act from duty unless he acts in the teeth of his desires, but the conflict, when it occurs (as sometimes it must) may be the best *evidence* that we have of operative rationality.

The metaphysical construction that Kant believed to be convincing although indemonstrable took its cue from the *fact* of this freedom. If we were realists regarding the order of rational determination, he said, and were also realists regarding the order of sensory determination, then, if the two differed, there would be an insoluble contradiction at the heart of reality; and that is impossible. If, on the other hand, it could be maintained that the sensory order was only "empirically" and not "transcendentally" real, if it were only a working policy of the natural sciences, inevitable from their standpoint and incorrigible there, yet ultimately unreal, the contradiction would disappear. The *ultimate* order everywhere might be the order of supersensible rational determination. The *provisional* order of sensory determination might be only its imperfect image.

Such in general was the solution that Kant suggested in the *Critique of Practical Reason*. The substance of it is conveniently indicated in the following quotations from the *Opus Posthumum*. "God and the world. The whole supersensible and the whole sensory object represented together in their logical and real connection." "God, the world (both outside me) and the rational subject that joins the two through its freedom." "God, the world, and the consciousness of my existence in the world. The first is noümenon, the second is phenomenon, the third is the causality of the self-determination of the subject in and through the consciousness of its personality."[1]

We may begin our discussion of this famous metaphysical argument by considering the form of the contrast that Kant drew between natural determination (which he took to be the necessitation of sensory representations) and the supersensible determination that (he said) gives the law to our inclinations and curbs their arrogance.

Kant's way of stating the contrast invites several criticisms. On the side of sensory representation it may be enquired whether sensations are (or are *only*) representatives of fact, whether their necessitation is imposed upon them or elicited from them, whether, if it be imposed, the rational faculties do not lay down the law, whether, if it be elicited, a genuine connection of real existence is *not* what is elicited. On the side of moral determination there are the difficulties we have already noticed—the inaccuracy of speaking of moral imperatives, laws or commands, the snares that lurk in the idea that morality is an affair of *pure* reason. Indeed one might ask whether the office of reason in morals is not to elicit what is fine and pure in our passions and other inclinations rather than to dominate and repress them.

Despite such criticisms we may agree that there is a genuine contrast. We may state it in a way that was not Kant's. The understanding, we may say, does not make nature. It makes natural *science*; and natural science, for the most part if not entirely, should be based upon sense-observation. On the other hand, the moral reason does contribute to the making of actual moral conduct. It does not merely make moral *philosophy*. It is

[1] All three passages printed together by Adickes, *op. cit.*, p. 781.

not true that what a moral man ought to do is simply to interpret the implications of his passionate and impulsive nature. Brief as this statement of the contrast is, it describes something of major importance.

Let us turn next to Kant's identification of free with rational conduct.

There has been a long and a very powerful tradition to the effect that reason connotes self-mastery, and that passion is a kind of slavery. This traditional story, it may be presumed, corresponds to something that is likely to be substantially true, but it need not describe the facts with precision if it is taken to mean that "reason" is a homogeneous entity that operates as a specific cause-factor either in us or in the cosmos. What we find in experience, as I have said, is primarily the fact that reflective conduct is different from unreflective conduct. This fact may be interpreted in various ways. Kant's is one of them, namely that "reason" in man (and perhaps also in God) is a spring of action, and that rightness of conduct implies and is wholly dependent upon, that spring. Some other philosophers would hold that reflection *per se* is a myth, and that its presumed operation is equally mythical. What moves us in a rational action, they would say, is reflective and deliberate desire, reasoned appetition, clear-headed instinct and impulse.

I do not intend to discuss this intricate psychological question here. I do not share the confidence with which so many in the schools profess to be able to isolate the relevant cause-factors. In a general way, however, I think that our conclusion should resemble Kant's. I held in the last lecture that validity or rightness is *sui generis*, quite different from everything else. If this be admitted, I see no more reason for doubting that a man's recognition of moral rightness may influence his conduct than for doubting that his recognition of a green light may influence the way in which he drives his car. I don't profess to be able to isolate all the relevant cause-factors, but I can point to a plain empirical difference. The recognition of moral rightness does seem to play an important part in moral conduct. It need not be the sole cause of any action, or exhaust the morality of every moral action, or even be indispensable in every moral action, but it seems to be central when morality is truly serious.

To say, however, that the freedom and rationality of moral conduct are the same thing is to depart abruptly from common notions. It would imply that no one is free to go wrong, for "rationality" in this sense means right reflection, right deliberation and right choice. The phrase might describe God's freedom, but it would not describe what we mean when we speak about a man's freedom. Nevertheless Kant asserted the reality of human freedom in its ordinary sense. He held that men have an elective will. They can choose the right or they can let passion have its way.

Kant's metaphysical argument, on the other hand, depends upon the identity of freedom with rationality. We might paraphrase it as follows: There seem to be two distinct orders in human behaviour, the order of validity and the order of patterned consecution of a sensori-motor type. Action in conformity with the order of validity is rational, free and divine, action in conformity with the other order is non-rational, unfree and merely "natural". Man, who is half a beast and half divine, might appear to belong to both orders, and would really belong to both of them if metaphysics did not have a revolutionary suggestion to offer. The revolutionary suggestion is that the order of validity alone is real and that the apparent order of sensori-motor consecution is but a shadow. That is because reason alone is real and because sense, everywhere and always, is an incomplete and imperfect shadow of its rational archetype.

Such a theory would hold in effect that sense was illusory and that reason was the reality scurvily reflected in the illusion that we call the natural world. Whether true or not the theory would not be self-contradictory and it would be consistent with the opinion that some (but only *some*) of our actions may reveal a rift in the mists, a gleam that peculiarly transforms although it never completely dissipates the shadows of sense. The theory, however, is quite inconsistent with Kant's belief in an *elective* will. In terms of the latter belief, moral struggle actually occurs, and is a genuine struggle between the two orders in the same being, both orders, consequently, being regarded as real. What is more, the struggle occurs, according to Kant, in the natural world. The man who conquers his lusts and the man who gives way to them act differently in the natural world. Therefore, however different the two orders may be, there is contact between them; and both the adversaries are equally real. If it could be consistently maintained that the natural order is shadowy and only "empirically" real, it would still be illegitimate to confound two different views. The first would imply that there could be no conflict between the unreal shadows and the shining reality that they mirror so imperfectly, because the shadows are unreal and cannot fight. The second would apply to shadow-land itself, and would describe a disturbance among the shadows and the way in which the shadows may appear to be struggling with the mere reflection of the light. But the plain implication of Kant's statement is that it is not shadows but realities that struggle.

I submit, therefore, that Kant's theory of freedom oscillates between two senses of freedom, in one of which the order of space and time is an illusory appearance, in the other of which the temporal order of moral struggle and temptation is not illusory at all but refers to a "reason" that operates complete with dates. It might be suggested, it is true, that both orders are genuine and that men and women (who are rational beings and also are parts of nature) belong sometimes to the one order and sometimes to the other. They would be like an electron according to the quantum theory. It is always in some orbit and it changes its orbit; but we are forbidden to ask how it gets from one orbit to the other. At one moment it is in the train for Birmingham, and at another moment it is in the train for Crewe, but it does not change at Rugby, or at Nuneaton, or anywhere else. Such a theory, however, would not explain the choice that Kant presupposes in his account of the elective will, and it would not conform with his revolution in metaphysics. The axis of that revolution was moral freedom. It was essential to the revolutionary theory that noümena alone should be real and that phenomena should be unreal shadows.

Let us examine the relation between phenomena and noümena.

To be a phenomenon is just to appear. Something appears to a mind when a mind is aware of it by sensation, by intellection or in any other way. So there may be sensory or intellectual phenomenalizing or a combination of these. The most natural interpretation of the process of phenomenalizing is to say that minds perform it. It is they that are aware.

Kant, like many other philosophers, regarded phenomena as *sensory* representations. *My* phenomena were *my* sensory representations. An "objective" phenomenon was mixed with intellection. It was a permanent necessitation of sense representations. There was no reason why he should deny that such necessitation always occurs in someone's mind. Sometimes he said so. Thus in the *Opus Posthumum* we read: "God is only thought (*ens rationis*)."[1] In the same context he said that all the three great metaphysical Ideas or Ideals, including "God", are "only thought-things".

Let us consider the matter. When Kant said that the senses and the sensible world were, after all, only appearances, his logic may have been without reproach. Sense data need not be the reality to which they are commonly supposed to testify. The same is true of mixed sensori-intellectual evidence, and of the chains of valid implication that may hang on sense-evidence. Again, such a necessitated rule of interpretation may be *only* a rule, that is, only an endless series of implications, and not a determinate thing.

That, in substance, is what the logistical positivists say to-day when they repudiate metaphysics but cling to science. They are concerned with the sort of fact, whatever it may be, that can be verified in a certain way. They do not claim that the potentiality of verification constitutes a definite whole. Their theory may be taken to mean that there are true natural propositions, but that there is no such thing as "nature".

[1] *Op. cit.*, p. 799.

Mind and Deity

Of course the logistical positivists would deny that there are any true propositions about existing reals except the sense-verifiable propositions of "natural knowledge". There they may be wrong. Suppose, then, that there could also be pure rational apprehension, perhaps in the experience of righteous freedom. In that case the likely conclusion would be that if sense-evidence should not be confused with the reality to which it testifies, intellectual or noümenal evidence should also not be confused with the reality to which *it* testifies. If there is much that escapes the senses there may also be much that escapes the intellect. Neither sense nor intellect can exhaust the inexhaustible, viz. reality itself. There may be excellent reasons for believing, in fine, that sense-representations and the implications that may be linked with them do not form a world, and that natural implications are neither nature nor God. "Nature", so-called, may instead be a rule for interpreting sense, and a rule that only minds can follow. It may be a policy and not a thing. In the last analysis, however, there may be the same reasons for making similar assertions about noümena. They also may be rules of inference that only a mind can follow. Such a mind may just be ours, and the metaphysics of the theory may apply to minds, indeed to *our* minds, not at all to a supersensible world or to a supersensible God.

What could a world of noümena be? Kant called it a *corpus mysticum* whose members were all compact of reason, *entia rationis*. Again, he spoke of it as a realm of purely rational ends whose monarch, God, was also an *ens rationis*. But what could a being *be* who was *nothing* but "reason"? We can understand what is meant by a being whose reflective processes are always valid, that is, we can conceive, readily enough, of an infallible reasoner. We might be able to persuade ourselves that we could conceive of an infallible mind whose psychical processes were all compact of rational insight and of rational inference. We might say that such a being either sublimated all that is sense-knowledge in us into *his* non-sensory rational apprehension or in some other way was free from all traces of sense-knowledge

246

yet ignorant of nothing. But how could we so much as conceive of a being who *was* mere reason, who was made up of pure validity? Parodying a parodist we might say of such a fancied being: "No root, no trunk, no sap, no twig, noümenon."

All attempts to prove the primacy of the practical reason in the macrocosm take their rise from its supposed primacy in us. That may be legitimate if reason be the mainspring of our being, if it makes us what we are, and if we are, so to say, fair samples of everything that there is. In Kant's theory (and, I think, in all similar theories) there is an illegitimate transition from the valid inferences and rational insight of reflective beings to a reified and deified "reason" regarded as a homogeneous entity that fashions, produces, restrains and acts. In this sense "reason" is but an idol, none the better for being supersensible. I have examined Kant's views because his appears to me to have been by far the most powerful intellect that adopted this way of arguing in modern times, and I have selected it in preference to his other "moral proofs"[1] because the others seem to be much weaker and also much more commonplace.

Let me add an observation. In Kant's philosophy the argument from the implications of freedom could not be more than a speculative construction, and the theism in it was (shall we say?) not at all pietistic. It was a speculative construction designed to show how we might accept "nature" and still believe that the supersensible alone was real. To call the supersensible "God" may be more misleading than helpful. The difficulties that I find, however, refer to the very meaning of the suggestion. Even if reality could be supersensibly known, and if the senses and all sense-implication were in the end only "empirically real", it would still be unintelligible that anything could *be* mere reason, mere validity. Kant's speculative hypothesis, therefore, appears to me to have led to the void. Still, I should like to say something more about it.

When it is counted for arrogance in a philosopher or in any other man that he takes himself to be something singular in all

---

[1] Especially in the Dialectic of the *Critique of Practical Reason*.

existence, crediting himself with moral and logical powers that are quite unique, it should surely be remembered that there *is* this order of validity in human minds, and that the fact *may* be unique. We do sometimes recognize rightness and validity for what they are. We do sometimes act in accordance with our recognition. On the other hand, we have no good reason to suppose that everything in nature is capable of such recognition.

This has to do with our "freedom" in one of the senses of that many-sensed word. There are many ways in which philosophers have tried to show that psychical actions are "free" actions. Some of their arguments seem to me to be strong. I have much sympathy, for instance, with the view that anyone who says that the "strongest motive" must prevail in psychological as in all other natural action is the dupe of a fairy story. He is assuming, quite illegitimately, that all psychical motives must be regarded as units of constant energy, the same before and after a decision is made. On the other hand it would be equally illegitimate to infer that "freedom" in the sense of indeterminism could be established in this way. What would be shown might be only that there was a different *kind* of determination in minds and in other things.

On the whole the plain statement that human beings are capable of insight into rightness, and of action in accordance with such insight, is one of the best ways of indicating the primary difference between human beings and all other natural beings that we know of. Human beings are not, of course, infallible. There is much bad reasoning, much hollow and merely ostentatious moralizing among men. That, however, is not an objection. The insight is often quite genuine, and so is its influence. When mistakes are made, they really are *mistakes* and they would be wholly impossible in a being that neither saw nor erred.

Nevertheless it seems perfectly clear that validity or rightness is not in itself an operative thing, a *causa causans*. To show this, it may be sufficient to revert to a simple instance previously mentioned. It is true in fact that car-drivers commonly stop

when they see a red signal and go on when the red signal changes
through amber to green. It would be senseless to say, however,
that the redness of the red signal is a cause-factor in the stoppage
of the car. So of rightness. It is senseless to hold that the rightness of a right action *does* anything.

What does seem to be a cause-factor in such instances is the
driver's *recognition* of the green signal and the moral man's
recognition of his duty for what it is. This may be proved, if
proof were wanted, by the fact that if either of them makes a
mistake, his action will vary in accordance with his mistaken
notions, and not in accordance with the greenness of the green
light, or with the rightness of right conduct.

Validity or rightness, then, is something of which we can
take account, and I have tried to show and am here assuming
that it is *sui generis*. On the other hand, the truth remains that
causal action belongs to the order of patterned consecution and
to no other. Whatever "freedom" we possess cannot disturb
this verity. There is no arrogance, there is only simple truth in
saying that, often, we are able to respond to rightness when we
see it, and so are significantly different from many other beings
by the mere fact of being responsible agents. If the quality of
rightness is discerned in a supersensible way and in that way
only, the inference is that we may respond to that of which we
have supersensible cognizance, but not that we can ever be
translated clean out of the order of temporal consecution. There
is no elective will that can switch us from temporality to eternity
and back again.

Personally I would go further and hold that there is no intelligible sense of moral freedom except the sense that is seldom
disputed and should never be disputed, the truism, namely, that
in a certain limited class of actions we are able to decide in
accordance with what we believe (and sometimes *see*) to be
right, and to act accordingly. *Such* freedom does not imply that
our minds are exempt from temporal causes at any time. On the
contrary we usually believe that there is no such exemption. A
man, we say, is not responsible, that is, cannot decide and act in

the relevant moral way, if he is drugged or starved or in a fever. His lack of freedom in that case has temporal causes. Is it reasonable to account for his *lack* of freedom in this way, but to renounce that type of explanation altogether when the drug wears off, or when the man is fed or bled?

This last remark, however, is an interpolation of my own. Let it be forgotten if it proves to be too perplexing.

The supersensible is the rationalist's heaven, for he assumes that "reason" and the supersensible coincide. When he says that the natural and the sensible are but the shadows, ultimately unreal, of the glory of the supersensible, he is saying that there is nothing, in the end, *except* heaven and that the earthly order is only a persistent and obsessive dream. When he holds that the natural and the sensible, although real, are fragments of the supersensible, he is holding that heaven is ubiquitous in space and time. It is always here in the world and can be shown to be so to anyone whose intellectual eyes are not holden. Thus in his own rationalistic way the metaphysical rationalist achieves a rationalistic interpretation of God's supernatural grace. He reaches divine justification by a kind of all-penetrating faith. Kant's moralistic emphasis upon the "practical reason" was the counterpart, in rationalistic axiological metaphysics, of the emphasis upon deliverance from sin in the glad tidings of the Christian apocalyptic. Such freedom is the rationalist's goal. His account of its relation to the so-called *liberum arbitrium* of puzzled and stumbling men is a colder version of the burning theme that Augustine debated with Pelagius, that Luther thundered and that Calvin legalized. And the rationalist, too, in his own rationalistic way, can pass into glory. As Spinoza said: "We clearly perceive in what our blessedness or liberty consists, namely in constant and eternal love towards God, or in God's love towards man. And this love of blessedness is rightly called glory in the sacred Scriptures. For whether this love refers to God or to the mind, it may rightly be called acquiescence of the spirit which cannot truly be distinguished from glory."[1]

[1] *Ethics*, V, xxxvi. Schol.

The Moral Proofs of Theism

Totalitarian idealists, especially in our country, would say that experience as a whole is rational but is not mere reason. According to some of them, the totality of experience is healthied o'er by the warm cast of reason; according to others, reason, like all else that is not the Absolute, is transfigured in the Absolute. Both parties attempt to retain reason without making an idol of it. Both, in consequence, conceive themselves to be free to accept the life, the light, the gladness, the glory and the beauty that Christian theology, despite the vein of asceticism in it, finds in its story of reality, and has enshrined, notwithstanding all the pain and darkness of ecclesiastical history, in the music, the altars and the liturgy of the ecclesia. And all with a seriousness without which gladness would be a passing enchantment, beauty mere ornament, and glory but fading pomp.

III

During the remainder of this lecture I mean to touch upon the relations between moral philosophy and natural theology, but again without unsaying anything that was said in the last lecture. It seems to me to be plain that the validity of moral standards has to be judged by moral philosophy and by nothing else. I should say the same about logic or about æsthetics. If anyone were to tell me that pagan logic must be bad logic because it is unchristian, I would not believe him. If he were to tell me that pagan art must be bad art because it is unchristian I would not believe him either. In ethics, it would seem, the great majority of apologists say things like that about ethics, and say them strongly. I don't believe them. Ethics, it is true, affects a man's whole life in a way that logic and æsthetics, superficially at least, may not seem to do, and "art for art's sake" may be a pernicious maxim if part of its meaning be "sin for art's sake".[1] Religion, like ethics, lays claim to a man's whole life, although salvation is not everything, any more than all disease, all suffering and all misfortune are due to someone's

[1] What of the maxim, "Be a vandal for righteousness' sake"?

wrongdoing. That, however, is irrelevant here. It is ethics that is the sole judge of moral standards, whether these standards are or are not incorporated in some religion.

The criteria of right conduct, then, cannot be governed or modified by existential metaphysics or theology. If anyone asserts, for example, that what theism stands for is the doctrine that reality is essentially good and that nothing but the good is real, I should say two things in reply. The first is that the doctrine is unintelligible unless it also asserts, quite falsely, that there is no evil. The second is that even if the statement were true it would be unintelligible unless it could discriminate between what goodness and badness respectively mean.

Consequently I shall not discuss what seems to me to be a plain absurdity, namely the doctrine that it is the deiformity of existence that determines what righteousness means. It does not follow, however, that ethics must repudiate divine guidance, divine succour and divine grace, or that it is indifferent to the metaphysical and theological problems that cluster round the destiny of man and the glory or triviality of his estate.

As we saw when we discussed the problems of the theodicies, there is no clear and completely satisfying way of drawing the boundaries between God's common and his special grace. The same difficulty, as we have seen all the time, affects natural theology in general. "Nature" is ill-defined; but we may speak with some confidence about much that is "natural" even if we do not know precisely where, if anywhere, "nature" ends.

Accordingly if we attempt to discriminate between what a man can learn for himself and what he has to be told, between what a man himself can do and what he can do with God to help him, between human goodness[1] and grace that is infused from above, we dare not pretend to more than a reasonable conjecture (if so much) regarding these boundaries. If we knew

---

[1] One remembers what Henderland the catechist said to David Balfour in *Kidnapped* when he spoke of the patient and heroic loyalty of the clans in the Appin country, "There's something fine about it, no perhaps Christian, but *humanly* fine."

what a man's "own" powers were, how corrupt they were, how sane they were, how long they could last and how far they could reach, we might then attack the problem with a high confidence. As things are, natural theologians should be reticent where non-natural theologians may have to expound some dogma. It is no part of the business of any Gifford lecturer to ask whether a man must take the initiative if God is to save him, whether some only are elected unto life, and why and how; whether if a man be once in grace he is always in grace; and the like.

The argument from dubiety of frontiers, however, is double-edged. If the boundaries are wholly unknown, nothing intelligible could be said. If, on the other hand, we have a fairly accurate knowledge of the ordinary powers of human nature, two opposing views may be held. The first is that secularism suffices for secular morality. The second is that our moral standards are altogether too high for common (if not even for uncommon) humanity and so require the support of a religion and of a God.

So it may be said (and, very often, it *is* said) that the moral man needs a religion (1) because he needs to be *shown* what is good, (2) because he must be strengthened if he is do what is right, and (3) because he must have rational assurance that he is not living his life in vain. If any of these three opinions were true, the *meaning* of morality and of its standards would not depend upon theology, but ethics, all the same, would have to take much account of much that theology has to say.

(1) As regards the first point, there is no special reason for holding that moral knowledge is essentially different from other knowledge, and either more or less "natural". What secularists usually say about it is that none of us could be expected to achieve any considerable proficiency in mathematics, in philosophy or in the ordinary gumption that we call common sense if he were not shown and taught many things in his youth and afterwards. Their point is that what is shown and taught may come to be seen, the capacity for seeing what is shown being "natural", and the power implied in acquisition and in progress

being fundamentally of the same order. If nothing like this could be said, there would be nothing to discuss. The prophets and the great moral teachers have a message. So have all leaders. They all discover new ideas or make old ones vivid and fresh. Without them, most men would never come to see what, with them, they both see and believe. The general presumption is that anything that can be shown is something that could be discovered, although very few of us individually could discover much for ourselves, without the help of our teachers and forebears.

I do not myself believe that a man's duty is always a simple thing to know, and that peasants, savages, bourgeois and intelligentsia must always be presumed to know it. It may be very hard to discern, requiring the nicest spiritual powers as well as ages of earnest and meditative tradition. On the other hand, the power of discriminating between true and false ideas of duty does not of itself imply any special theory about the way in which these ideas come into men's minds. The roots of moral notions seem to be eminently "natural". In the main they are sympathy and fairness. Sympathy involves a certain insight, partly imaginative and never wholly unemotional, into the health and the gladness as well as into the sickness and the sadness of all companionable beings. Equity or fairness is reflective as well as imaginative. In it we have to see the other fellow's point of view, and put ourselves imaginatively in his place. It is only the finer and most expert development of these powers that is uncommon in the course of nature.

(2) As regards the second point, it is often said that unless morality is made vital by an emotion that is more than merely moral it is far too feeble to fulfil its own obligations. The most hardened secularist (we are told) must have a religion, as secularists have often admitted. "Candid persons of all creeds", said J. S. Mill, defending the legitimacy (not necessarily the sufficiency) of Comte's Religion of Humanity, "may be willing to admit that if a person has an ideal object, his attachment and sense of duty towards which are able to control and discipline

all his other sentiments and propensities, and prescribe to him a rule of life, that person has a religion."[1]

In other words, unless a man is *possessed* by his moral ideas, he is not a good man, and such possession (it is said) is religion and not mere ethics. To decide upon the point, therefore, we should have to know what emotional and other motives could so possess a man, and whether these might not be secular. May not patriotism or vengeance have that effect, and are these motives not secular? If it be said that the only moral motives worth considering in this connection are a tepid humanitarianism or a frigid sense of duty, one may dispute the limitation of the list, and may also ask whether humanitarianism must be so very lukewarm, and the sense of duty so very cold. A passion, indeed a possessing passion for righteousness is not unknown, and the brotherhood of man, although it may begin with one's neighbour, need not stop with him. In the Book of Leviticus[2] the command to love one's neighbour as oneself was confined at the first to fellow tribesmen and resident aliens. May it not spread over all the earth?

In the main these debates beat the air. To solve the problem we should have to know how great a part passion plays in human affairs, what passions are capable of becoming master-passions, after what fashion such passions can transcend selfishness, parochialism and mere planetariness. Then, but not before, we might be able to determine how far our knowledge of our duty could generate and sustain the resolute will to do our duty.

(3) The third question seems to me to be of vastly greater moment. It must be conceded, indeed, that an ethics of duty for duty's sake, regardless of consequences, would seem, by its very constitution, to be indifferent to cosmic questions, and to the difference between planning for earth only and planning for heaven too. For such an ethics the only relevant question would be whether a man has over-worldly duties as well as this-worldly duties. But if consequences matter it would be *vital* to ask whether the relevant consequences were but worldly and

---

[1] *Auguste Comte and Positivism*, ed. 1907, p. 134. [2] xix. 18.

ephemeral, or were also cosmic and sempiternal. A moral agent has to adapt himself to his environment. He should not be indifferent to the question whether his environment is vast or petty, cosmic or planetary.

I shall try to illustrate by referring, very briefly, to the time-perspective in the case, and chiefly to the difference between planning for a mere human lifetime, on the one hand, and planning for an everlasting future on the other.

There is always a close and a necessary relation between what we should try to do and what, in fact, we are able to do. If we can properly plan for eternity then we should plan for eternity. If it is theology that is our tutor in this matter, to that extent ethics is theology's pupil, just as ethics is medicine's pupil if health be a worthy moral end. For better measure I may refer to what is called other-worldliness in ethics, beginning with egoistic other-worldliness and proceeding to a less selfish view.

Some people say that a man's action is morally justified if and in proportion as it is directed towards *his own* good. If so his action might vary very much according as he was or was not entitled to reckon on his own other-worldly status and prospects.

There is the same sort of difference if it be held (as surely it should) that it is a man's duty to seek and ensue what is good whether he or others are to reap the harvest. In this case as in the former the greatness of the opportunity would affect the nature of one's duty; and the difference between a this-worldly perspective and a this-and-other-worldly perspective might be very great indeed. In both cases the greatest good on the whole, whether puny or majestic, should be chosen and ensued. The *meaning* of good would not be affected. Its scope might be affected very much.

"Ut puto, deus fio"

I SHOULD like to say something about immortality, and shall take the ironical remark of the dying Roman emperor as my text.

He meant the remark (I suppose) as a gibe at the quaint superstition of imperial apotheosis, but he might have referred to a serious philosophical belief. For many philosophers have held that immortality is a species of deification, being the attainment of a status similar to the status of the deathless gods. God's existence, it is assumed, connotes immortality; and human deathlessness is due to the fact that man is God or angel as well as brute. One may ask, it is true, whether the possibility of attaining this status is wider or narrower than mankind, whether, say, it extends to all living things or is confined, among men, to heroes or emperors or saints or the elect who are in grace. The answer to this special question would not affect the general idea.

It may seem to be absurdly over-curious even to raise the question whether God must be immortal. Mortality may seem to be the most signal proof of weakness that there is. It is the weakness of utter extinction, and, as we have seen, serious theists never believe that God is weak. But the speculative question may be tackled, perhaps with profit.

If God were timeless, and if timelessness had nothing to do with temporal process, permitting of no inference to what we call time and incapable of being inferred from any temporal marks, God's immortality, in that sense, would have little bearing upon anything that we normally believe about it, and I shall not argue the matter. I have tried to show (in the first series of lectures) that if God exists he must be temporal, and most of the theologians who assert God's timelessness further maintain that God, in some sense, includes what we call or take to be time, although he also transcends it. In other words, they believe that certain temporal statements better express his nature than others do, that his timeless existence is manifested *sub specie temporis* in one way and not in another way. So I shall here consider the appearance that God's immortality may be held to show forth *sub specie temporis*.

I think that nearly everyone would say that God's immortality must appear, *sub specie temporis*, as his everlasting pre- and post-existence. If having existed from all eternity, he ceased to exist, either of his own volition or without it, he would, if his cessation were permanent, be just what we call mortal. There remain, therefore, the two possibilities (*a*) that he did not exist from all eternity but came into being and endures for ever after; (*b*) that his existence is intermittent in time. Neither of these views is at all usual, but each would be consistent with a certain kind of immortality.

(*a*) If the first were true, God would be immortal in a sense that we often ascribe to men. We seldom hold that any human spirit has been pre-existent from all eternity, but often believe that a human spirit survives death and persists to all eternity (or does so "naturally" unless God annihilates it by a special act). The idea of a growing God who is born but never dies is not inconceivable.

(*b*) God's intermittent existence *sub specie temporis* has been asserted in the East. It has been held, for instance, that great and divine cosmic cycles come out of a being who is beyond existence and non-existence alike and that the godhead in such cycles of manifestation, materialization or the like has a rhythm of existence similar to a man's waking, sleeping and waking again.

Such assertions probably identify "existence" with visible or material existence (say) and so do not really assert that Brahman ever ceases to *be*; but they might be put forward without any *arrière pensée* of that sort. It might even be said that we have an analogy in our own lives. We wake up the same persons as we were when we went to sleep, and it is possible that *we* are nothing at all when we are asleep. If so, intermittence in time would be quite different from death, and God's life might resemble ours in this respect. He would be a temporally limited God, but still a God and deathless.

Very few philosophers, I think, would be willing to lay so little stress upon temporal continuity. Nearly all of them would hold that if our "selves" are intermittent in this way, the fact is proof that "selves" are weak and subordinate beings, the sort of beings that, like many other things, could not be divine.

Let us now turn to various questions regarding human immortality, bearing in mind the possible connection between human immortality and human deification.

A view sometimes held is that man's immortality consists of a certain kind or splendour of life, and has nothing to do with persistence or survival of bodily dissolution. A living man may attain heaven *now*, and put on a garment of light. That is his immortality.

That, I submit, is quite consistent with man's deification but not with his immortality in any sense that even approaches the usual sense. It might very well be temporary deification. He who puts on the garment of deity in this way may also put it off. There is no reason why he should not cease to exist altogether, and become incapable of a divine kind of life because incapable of any kind of life. Man need not be like a beast, but he may perish as a beast perishes. If the theory be that time is illusory, the most persuasive inference would appear to be that neither man nor beast perishes. Nothing would perish, although, also, nothing would last.

A second view is that immortality means sempiternity of existence, appearing *sub specie temporis* as endless endurance.

It is true, I suppose, that if a substance is indestructible it is immortal; but it is very difficult indeed to *identify* the substances that are said to be indestructible by any satisfactory mark. What is the substance of a man, and what reason have we for concluding that *his* substance is indestructible? Waiving much that is relevant to such a question I propose to say roundly that the chief problems regarding a living man refer either (*a*) to the empirical continuity of his body-mind, or (*b*) to the empirical continuity of what we call "conscious personality".

(*a*) Some sort of physical continuant may possibly survive the dissolution of the gross body. This continuant might be "the same substance" as the body that once was alive in the ordinary gross recognizable way. If so its "minding" (if "minded") would be the minding of "the same substance".

(*b*) We might admit the possibility that our conscious personality (supposed to be attested by self-acquaintance) may be the same substance *although intermittent*. That, as we have seen in the fifth lecture, is a possible account of our substantiality during life. If, in the same way, we awoke from the sleep of "death", however long that sleep might last, we would be immortal in one of the usual senses of that word provided that we never fell on sleep for the last time.

All these things are possible, but how could anyone even begin to show that they *must* be true?

Each of the alternatives that I have labelled (*a*) and (*b*) is consistent with deathless post-existence without pre-existence. I may say something more about that.

(1) I think we may say that we have no evidence at all that favours human pre-existence, although some men would say that we have. Certainly the present body of each of us may be the continuation of a single specific substance that may also survive it; but we have no evidence that this has occurred in the past. In so far as our self-identity (perhaps intermittent) is attested by our self-acquaintance and personal memory, we do not have that kind of evidence of our pre-existence. The absence of such evidence is a very strong reason for denying that the fact occurs.

That, as Locke saw,[1] is very important for those who hold that identity of substance is the essential consideration in this affair. Suppose that the substance of each of us had pre-existed from all eternity, but never revealed itself to our memory. How

[1] E.g., *Essay*, II, i.

could we then identify this substance? What would we mean by saying that lo! it was ourself? If our post-existence were of the same order, so that we survived death but could never recall any previous existence, how much satisfaction would any hater of the idea of death derive from the circumstance? I would not say that such an one should not derive *some* satisfaction. If his deeds and attainments had some permanent effect upon the substance of him, that effect, *ex hypothesi*, would necessarily persist for good or for evil as the case might be. The metaphysical necessity might be of major importance. Provided, however, that the man's influence persisted, I do not see how it would matter to anyone whether *his* or some other persisting substance received the influence. Our concern for ourselves is too closely interknit with our memory and self-acquaintance to give place readily to a "substance" with which we are *not* so acquainted. If it be said that there might be a *chance* that we would "wake and remember and understand", the answer is that such "memories" (at any rate if they were but seeming memories) might arise although there was *not* the identity of substance.

(2) It might be held that an immortality that is both pre- and post-existent is stronger than one that is only post-existent. If so, God, if he himself has the stronger type of immortality, might not have given more than the weaker type to his creatures.

(3) If the theory were that men become immortal by being deified, the question would arise how, if some but not all men are deified, it is possible to distinguish between those who are and those who are not. In particular, we should encounter the problem that used to be known in theological circles as "falling from grace". Perhaps God alone knows who is truly in grace. If, however, the high achievement of any man is any sort of indication that he is deified, it is a sobering reflection that *all* a man's gifts and powers appear to deteriorate when he grows very old or very ill. The presumption would therefore appear to be that anyone who, by reason of excellence, appears to come near to being divine, appears later to recede from divinity, to "fall from grace". That is what Tennyson thought about

Tithonus and what Swift thought about the Struldbrugs. In other words, if deification is a *kind* of life we have *some* empirical evidence that that kind of life is very far from being persistent in living men.

I have now briefly discussed two of the ways in which men have been said to be immortal, namely the view that immortality is a *kind* (perhaps a divine kind) of life, and the view that it consists of the indestructibility of human substance. Let me now say something more about the main subject of this appendix, the connection between human immortality and either human deification, or man's attainment of a Godlike status.

Many theologians hold that God (who is immortal) *requires* man as truly as (although, perhaps, not so much as) man requires God. This statement might be interpreted as applying to each particular man, and the strongest form of the statement would be to say that God, to be himself, must be deified in *each* man that there is (or at least in *each* of the elect).

God is immortal. Does it follow that every man who is thus required for God's existence (or, in the extreme case, is deified) must therefore be held to be immortal too?

It doesn't seem to me to follow at all. God's need to become each of the elect might be fulfilled by the temporary deification of the elect that he needed at any given time.

Let us take an empirical analogy. Of each of us it might be said that he would not be what he is (in some very important sense of that statement) if he had not, let us say, served in the forces, or if he had not had a university education. Surely it does not follow that each such man is always a soldier or always *in statu pupillari*. That would not be true of terrestrial biographies to say nothing of pre- and post-existence.

The point seems to me to be quite fundamental, and has a distinct bearing upon the common assertion that unless we are immortal in some sense that includes the persistence of our individual personality after death we ought to be atheists, and, what is more, irreligious atheists.

In my opinion, no such consequence follows, and it seems to

me to be of the utmost moment to recognize clearly that it doesn't follow. Many of us find it very hard to believe that a man's personal identity, in any sense that is not a travesty of what we commonly mean by that term, does in fact continue after death. I think that nobody should be intimidated by the illogical threat that he must renounce all genuine theism and all genuine religion unless he believes in personal survival without end.

So far as arguments of this type have any force at all, they derive their force (I believe) not from the impossibility, or even from the improbability, that God's genuine (and indeed metaphysical) need for John Doe or for Richard Roe is temporary, but from other associated ideas. Setting revelation aside, it is argued in a general philosophical way that Doe and Roe would be cheated if their natural thirst for continuance after death were never assuaged, if all the intimations of their immortality were spurious. That is quite a different argument. It would be met (if it could be met) by questioning the alleged intimations or by disputing the fact alleged, viz. that every normal man is not merely reluctant to die when he is well and strong, but also has a strong positive desire for endless continuance. Again it might be held that even if the intimations of immortality were strong, and the thirst for it universal and undeniable, it would still be precarious to infer that, taking a wide survey, men would really be cheated if such hopes were vain. I shall not argue many of these questions now, but I should like to point out that the hypothesis of God's *essential* need for the *temporary* existence, in himself, of Doe and of Roe is not at all inconsistent. Its acceptance, therefore, cannot imply atheism.

Indeed I would go further. I resent the inference, very frequently drawn, that human existence is just a bad joke unless each human soul is immortal (post-existently) in a sense that appears in time as endless persistence. Such a view, I believe, depends upon a hasty and even upon a superficial misreading of certain common human hopes, and not upon the necessary implications of what are often called God's purposes. I should like to support this statement by a short further argument.

The strongest objection I have to meet, I think, is to the following effect: Unless individual men and women are immortal, it is said, there can be no ultimate conservation of the values they labour for, either in themselves or in others. To be sure, even if individual men and women *were* immortal, the conservation would not be secure. They might progressively deteriorate. Nevertheless, it is claimed, there is a chance of conservation of values if men and women are individually immortal, and no chance at all, or as good as none, if they are not.

This follows, we are told, from the fact that if men are ephemeral, so are nations and civilizations and eventually the human race itself. It is admitted that an immortality of influence might be the genuine conservation of specific values. Such influence would be conserved by successive living men, and it might be very great. Let us now praise famous men and our fathers that begat us, even if they were not more famous than we. England may really need John Doe, although he dies, and John Doe's influence, for good or for evil, may be very considerable after John Doe is dead. That, it is said, must be conceded and should be conceded frankly. But we are told that it is not enough. It would permit a certain diffused influence to John Doe and his works so long as England and its civilization had any influence. But if that passed away too, all John Doe's influence would cease. Civilizations *have* passed away, and although most of them, since the earth is now a single connected region, have had (or may have had) some small effect upon mankind everywhere, there is no absurdity in the idea that some contemporary civilizations may have as little effect upon the future civilization of the world as Aurignacian civilization had upon the Australian aborigines before the Dutch and the English sailed the seas. Eventually the human race itself will disappear. Its influence, it is true, *might* be continued in some other planet; but that is steep conjecture. In short, to a long view, the existence of the human race is very nearly as precarious as the existence of individual men and women upon the earth. Therefore the immortality of a man's influence upon other living men is no sort of substitute for a genuine immortality.

I think it must be allowed that such an argument is strong. If human values disappear altogether, we should be robbed of clear evidence of the persistence of *any* high values. The existence of any other high values is at best conjectural. Certainly we may suppose, if we choose, that other high values may exist in connection with beings that are not at all like men. There may be flint-souls in Jupiter (or is it Sirius?). Again, the truth might be that the universe has a nisus towards the emergence of something of high excellence, some Dante, some Beethoven, some St. Francis. If so, it would be not unreasonable to suppose that even if the human race perished, something of the same sort would blossom again, either on the rubble of the earth or somewhere else. Such ideas, I think, are not disheartening to mankind. They may even suggest a cosmic status for the human type of excellence, but they could not be described as the conservation of *human* values, unless this nisus, having taken form in the human race, influenced and was conserved in some other instance of its blossoming; and for that there is no evidence.

I therefore agree that individual human immortality would provide a much more plausible basis for indestructibility of the values (or disvalues) humanly achieved than, so far as I can see, any alternative theory. But it is not true that there could be no conservation of human values if a human soul never survived the death of its body.

In particular I would say that, if God needs *me*, then, although I am ephemeral, my existence would *eo ipso* be justified. There is neither impiety nor despair in such a view. Again, if, as some think, it is a man's fate (or the best men's) to be absorbed into deity, such a fate would be exalted even if a consequence of the absorption were that the individuality of each individual psyche were wholly impermanent.

IX

Pantheism

OUR discussion of the relations between mind and deity in this second series of lectures went from idea-ism to idealism, and the subject of pantheism has never been absent from the enquiry. Pan-idea-ism usually tends to be pantheistic unless it overleaps theism altogether; and any idea-ism that is not pan-idea-ism tends to be weak and halting. The tendency of idealism may often take the contrary direction. In the form of it that is moral theism it is, for the most part, strongly opposed to pantheism. What is commonly asserted in such a theism is the dominance of a personal God who is not the All. On the other hand, our enquiry has led us to question this prevalent personalistic tendency of moral theism. An impersonal moral theism does not seem to be at all impossible and the fact may even be encouraging to theists.

Again, as we saw at the close of the first series of these lectures, cosmological theism tends to be dia-cosmic rather than hypercosmic, to believe in an immanent and ubiquitous deity rather than in a supra-mundane deity ἐπέκεινα τῆς οὐσίας. In other words, it tends towards some form of pantheism.

For reasons such as these, it seems advisable to discuss the general theory, and the wider forms of pantheism, in a more deliberate and in a less incidental way than hitherto. That is the more necessary because, as it seems to me, so many Western philosophers, and so many Western theologians have been very unfair to pantheism. Instead of attempting to explore its logical potentialities, these philosophers and theologians seem usually to be content to define it in some limited and perfunctory way and to proceed forthwith to caustic criticism. Pantheism is nature-worship, they say, and they make fun of degraded and primitive forms of nature-worship. It is Spinozism; therefore it is monistic and deterministic; therefore it deserves the drubbing that Parmenides and Spinoza so fully earned. It is said (by Hegel[1]) to degrade the Godhead to mere empty being, to forget the principle of individuality, to forget that spirit is higher than substance. It is said to be "intellectual idolatry" by the critics who regard Hegel as a pantheist despite all his disclaimers, and Flint added (thinking of Schopenhauer) that since Hegel's time it had "decidedly gone from bad to worse"[2] and that he would "proceed to consider the historical fatalism, the glorification of war, the hero-worship and the contempt for weakness, poverty and suffering virtue which pantheism generates"[3] if he had not already considered them in another book. According to Bowman (thinking of the East), "a universe which is all God is as incompatible with religion as a universe in which God is altogether wanting. To be completely lost in God is to lose God completely".[4] According to Dr. Oman, "A genuine individual frontier would be the denial of any scheme of scientific pantheism".[5] According to Pringle Pattison, the "lower pantheism" is empty verbiage. "If every event, every feature of the world, in its isolation as a particular fact just as it occurs, is referred directly to the operation of the supreme principle, that principle becomes simply the pell-mell of empirical occurrence over again";[6] and this author did not have a much better opinion of the "higher pantheism".

This way of arguing seems to me to be thoroughly unsatisfactory. There is no more reason for repudiating every form of pantheism on account of the shortcomings of some particular pantheist than for repudiating all theology because some particular theologian has failed rather signally. What is required is a wide and dispassionate assessment of the resources of all

---

[1] *Philosophy of Religion*, e.g. English translation, I, 420.
[2] *Anti-theistic Theories*, p. 429. [3] *Ibid.*, p. 403.
[4] *Studies in the Philosophy of Religion*, I, 421.
[5] *The Natural and the Supernatural*, p. 162. [6] *The Idea of God*, p. 219.

species of pantheism. There may be insuperable objections to the theory, but the methods I have described above are quite unsuitable for showing that pantheism is negligible and indefensible.

These reflections have the greater importance because it is plain that many theologians, and a great many Christian theologians, are pantheists. Anyone is a pantheist who, being a theist, denies that God is limited in any extrinsic way. Anyone who denies that there is anything outside God, anything beyond or beside him, is a pantheist; for he is saying that God is all and that all is God. To say these things, to say them passionately, and yet to belittle pantheism is very odd indeed.

What such theologians commonly say is that although, in a sense, they are pantheists, they are not *mere* pantheists. In that case they can hardly expect their own nests to be clean if they spatter pantheism with mud, and they are bound to show in some detail what is missing from "mere" pantheism. That is an onerous obligation. It needs much more than a few smooth phrases or than a few vituperative explosions for its fulfilment. If it be said that pantheism is justified in what it asserts but mistaken in what it denies, the question at once arises, "What, then, does it deny?" So far as I can see there is just one thing that pantheism denies, namely that there is anything that is not God; and most Christian theologians are very anxious indeed *not* to make that denial. Instead they attempt to draw distinctions, and for the most part take refuge in the most labile and most nebulous *distinguo* in all theology, the distinction between God's immanence and his transcendence. It is quite intelligible, I allow, that God should be in all natural things and also that his divine amplitude should encompass them all. It is also quite intelligible that God's presence and his encompassing amplitude should be interpreted figuratively rather than literally. It is not intelligible, however, that God should be everything and also should *not* be everything, and neither piety nor wit can transform an unintelligible contrast into an intelligible pair of complements.

Consider some of the things that are said. God, we are told, creates a world other than himself but he could annihilate it at his pleasure, and he retains complete control over it so long as he permits it to exist. What is that except to say that the world is *as* nothing although it is not nothing—a plain subterfuge? It is said that the world has a relative, non-ultimate mode of being, but that God, and he alone, has an absolute and ultimate mode of being. What is that except to say that in the last analysis pantheism is the truth and all the truth, although, in a superficial analysis, it should be resisted? It is said that although to-day there is much that is not divine, the world is advancing towards complete divinity, or has lapsed from the complete divinity of its origin in a Golden Age, or has repeatedly attained divinity in a cyclical process as often as the tide of things is at its flood. What is that except to say that reality is about to become a pantheism, or has lapsed from pantheism, or is intermittently pantheistic as often as the *Saturnia regna* recur. In any of these cases is it at all surprising that so many theologians should strongly deny that deity is a quality in the future but not in the present, that it is an intermittent quality, that it is a quality that used to exist but has now faded away—in short, that they should assert that pantheism, which is the ideal, is always actual?

I repeat therefore that we should take pantheism seriously and examine its logical scope.

The principal varieties of pantheism are the distributive and the totalitarian. These need not be irreconcilable but they are *prima facie* very different. I shall therefore deal with each of them separately.

By distributive pantheism I mean the doctrine that each several thing that there is, is divine. Strictly, I think, such a theology would also have to maintain that each several thing that there is, is *wholly* divine. If all that was held was that there was *something* divine in each several thing it might also be consistently held that there was something, perhaps much, in everything that was not divine. That would be a theory of a limited pantheism or, as we might say, of a mitigated distributive pantheism. It may be doubted whether the phrase "a mitigated pantheism" makes better sense than the parallel phrase "a mitigated scepticism" in Hume's philosophy. We are here in the region of all or nothing. For the sake of convenience, however, I shall speak of "a mitigated pantheism" when I mean to speak about the theory that there is *something* divine in each several thing that exists. That, for instance, is one of the ways in which Erigena's statement "every visible and invisible creature is a theophany" might be interpreted.

As we saw, the Hegelian critics of pantheism, thinking very often of distributive pantheism although their argument would also apply to totalitarian pantheism, regard pantheism as a simple-minded attempt to equate "being" with divinity. Their complaint against it is that "being" is the poorest of all the qualities. Therefore, they say, pantheism impoverishes the quality of deity with such ruthless and devastating thoroughness as to make it completely empty.

That is strange criticism. It translates the statement "All is God" into the statement "God is mere is-ness" and then it executes a victory roll. The criticism, however, has an even more slender justification than might appear on the surface since, as we have seen so often, there is no such characterizing property as "is-ness". To put the point in another way, no clear-headed pantheist asserts that "being" and "divinity" mean the same thing. When a pantheist says that all beings are divine, he is asserting, not a veiled tautology, but a proposition that would be momentous if it were true, and a proposition in which he discerns a profound significance. The logic of his position is similar to the logic of those who would say with Leibniz that whatever is, is some sort of mind, having the rudiments at least of perception and appetition, or of those who would say with Professor Dixon and some others among the moderns that whatever is, is somehow alive. Pantheists are no more likely to assert that "being" and "divinity" mean the same thing than pan-psychists are likely to assert that "being" and "soulfulness" mean the same thing. On the contrary, it is just because being and divinity are *not* synonymous that the assertion "Whatever is, is divine" demands philosophical investigation.

Again the critics complain that pantheism is indistinguishable from naturalism. It is a magniloquent and fluffy naturalism, they say, but naturalism all the same. It is naturalism that is laureated *honoris causa tantum*. There, however, we have another instance of stealing the answer. The question is whether the honorary degree is or is not earned, whether nature is or is not divine in all its constituents. That question cannot be answered by the simple assertion that nature, after all, *is* nature. If the common view of nature be inadequate, if "nature" must be transfigured in order to be true, the question whether it be divine in all its parts is the very reverse of an empty enquiry. Few questions could be more considerable. The pantheist's question may be speculative and rather wide. It may be too wide for many scientific purposes and for many of the affairs of daily life. But in many of its aspects it is not at all negligible.

On the other hand, some such criticism would be justified in the case of any pantheism that did not make a serious attempt to show why and how the common interpretation of natural things needs to be divinized. The mere assertion that "whatever is, is divine" is of little avail unless there is pith and substance in the conception of divinity that is so widely applied. That is clear in itself, and it may be abundantly illustrated from the history of ideas.

Let us return to a point I mentioned in the first series of these lectures and consider Greek science, particularly in the medical schools. These Greeks denied that anything, and more especially any disease, was "sacred" in the sense that it was something quite apart, too numinous to be treated by patient scientific methods. They saw in general what some of us are just coming to see about mental disorders, namely that madmen should not be regarded as "God's fools", divinely afflicted in a way that makes therapeutic alienism a sort of blasphemy. Their general view was wholly consistent with universal reverence and ubiquitous natural piety, and the Greek medical professors said so when they affirmed that all things were divine. Theirs was a divine art within a divine field. Nevertheless, equality of sanctity, like any other equality, may be obtained by a process of levelling down as well as by a process of levelling up, and there is no occasion for surprise if the difference between the two methods should frequently be forgotten.

Consider, again, the mischief that was done to the science of physics by the Aristotelian doctrine, not very generally shared in the classical Greek tradition, of the perfection of stellar matter as opposed to the imperfection of matter beneath the moon. Galileo and his friends had to explode that dogma in order to vindicate the legitimacy of their methods. The result in the general view was the secularization of astronomy and not the sanctification of mundane events.

In short, "natural" and "divine", in the common use of these adjectives, are *contrasted* terms. Therefore if one of them be applied to the whole field in which the contrast used to be drawn, it is necessary to show that what used to be called "natural" is liker what used to be called "divine" than it is like what used to be called "natural". If nothing of the kind is shown the result resembles atheism at least as closely as it resembles theism.

Here again the resemblance to pan-psychism in philosophy is very close indeed. So it ought to be. For pan-psychism is a sort of secularized pantheism, profoundly "mitigated", in which the empirical terms "psychical" or even "vital" are substituted for the more magnificent but less interrogable name of divinity. As we saw in our discussion of pan-psychism, if the nett result of pan-psychism in metaphysics is a vague suggestion or a merely official assurance that neutrons and positrons, cups and saucers, planets and suns have some sort of rudimentary mental or vital properties (which are quite unspecified) there may be so little difference between what is and what is not pan-psychism that the most bellicose philosopher cannot expect more than the airy shadow of a battle. So with pantheism. The name may be understood in such a sense that it confers only a shadowy honour. On the other hand, the name may be understood to have serious import. In the former case it is trivial. In the latter case it has to show what its substantial contentions are.

According to many of its critics, distributive pantheism reduces everything to bare equality, an equality of superlatives, no doubt, but a featureless equality just because there is nothing but superlatives. It is theism in monochrome, these critics say, without even a variety of tint. Its home is in the effulgent shallows of Pope's *Essay on Man*:

> As full, as perfect, in a hair as heart:
> As full, as perfect, in vile man that mourns,
> As the rapt Seraph that adores and burns:
> To Him, no high, no low, no great, no small;
> He fills, He bounds, connects and equals all.[1]

In other words these critics accept the concluding couplet in these verses of Pope's. They deny all distinctions in and of glory. There, however, they may have erred with Pope, and they certainly should not accept such a conclusion without interrogating the inference. Why should there not be one glory of the sun and another glory of the moon, even if sun and moon are both divine? What opposes the theory of a diversified pantheism? The traditional counter-argument to any such inference as Pope's was debated in terms of perfection or fulness and illustrated by the case of the pitchers. All the pitchers may be quite full, although some of the pitchers are big pitchers, and other pitchers are quite tiny. That undoubtedly is a possibility, and it may be applied to a diversified excellence as well as to a diversified fulness. "God," said Richard Hooker, "by being everywhere, yet doth not give unto all places one and the same degree of holiness."

Nevertheless there is something exhausting about this idea of

[1] Cf. a Sufi ode:

> "I am the theft of rogues, I am the pain of the sick,
> I am both cloud and rain; I have rained on the meadows,"

quoted by Nicholson, *The Idea of Personality in Sufism*, p. 52.

a universe that is all superlatives, all peaks with no valleys. Besides, there are stronger objections than exhaustion or a faulty metaphor. Consider pan-psychism yet again. That theory, in its usual Leibnizian form, asserts that everything that is, is some sort of soul. It also asserts that most of the souls are very low-grade souls whose appetition and perception are enormously more primitive than the appetites and perceptions even of *very* sleepy men. It may be quite intelligible that souls should show these differences, but how could there be just these differences among divine beings? Are we to suppose that the universe contains billions of humble godlings, ignorant godlings, stupid godlings, sleepy godlings, forgetful godlings, depraved godlings? Would it not seem that divinity is far too high a term to permit of *such* distinctions? And if all distinctions of that order are abolished, is it at all clear *what* distinctions can be retained among the superlatives that alone are applicable to deity?

Such an objection, however, need not reduce distributive pantheism to silence. Its contention is that each several thing that exists is divine; but it is not committed to any particular theory regarding the *severalty* of each several thing. If the ultimate units of existence were not what they are commonly supposed to be, the theory might be much more plausible. Without denying that the distinctions that we commonly draw within nature have a genuine basis, it is surely not unreasonable to deny that the supposed independence of electrons, cups and suns is necessarily and metaphysically indiscerptible. We can challenge the *aseity* of such supposed units without challenging the utility or the provisional and approximate accuracy of the language that refers to them.

In that case the possibility of another line of argument emerges. If nature is made up of electrons, cups and suns, it is hard to take the alleged transfiguration of *these* entities very seriously. Their nature seems to be quite sufficiently described in the usual accounts of them. It is not a defensible piece of metaphysical economics to attribute vast concealed riches to *them*. Suppose, however, that these divisions and distinctions, although legitimate for many purposes, come nowhere near to ultimacy, but that, none the less, there is an ultimate pluralism in the sum of things. In that case it would be quite reasonable to maintain that although it would be very shoddy metaphysics to label each gnat, and each cell, and each atom in nature "divine", there need be nothing shoddy in holding that the *ultimate* constituents of nature are each and all divine. *These* units might be big enough and fine enough to be the bearers of divinity.

If what pan-psychism asserts is in substance that every grain of sugar or of sand, every drop of cod-liver oil, every follicle of every hair is a stupid sleepy little soul, pan-psychism would not seem to be one of the stronger branches of the metaphysical forces. If, on the other hand, the theory be that reality consists of selves and of their representations, and that insentient "nature" (as we call it) is a name for certain sets of these representations, it may be much more credibly theistic. I do not say that it would be a very good theory. It would be Berkeley's theory with Berkeley's God left out, and Berkeley's theory without Berkeley's God may be even more difficult to accept than Berkeley's theory *with* Berkeley's God. The theory, however, might be developed rather more persuasively. It is rather like McTaggart's metaphysics, although McTaggart himself, it would seem, was rather more of a Leibnizian than of a Berkeleyan.

Some philosophers hold that the only natural units that we know for certain to be indiscerptible units are human selves, and perhaps, the selves of the higher animals. While it may be disputed that we do know anything of the kind *for certain*, the opinion is not one of philosophy's weaklings. Let us consider, therefore, whether it could be a first step towards a distributive pantheism, and whether such a pantheism would be wholly incredible.

It is fantastic (I think) to believe that reality at any given time is composed exclusively of the men and the higher animals that exist at that time, being wholly made up of these spirits and of their experiences. But that is not the only possibility.

Mind and Deity

Let us construct a story, a mild philosophical romance, to the following effect: Every human being and every higher animal, we may suggest, has an inner life (as it is called) that includes sense-experiences. Some of these sense-experiences represent without resembling the inner lives of others. Such are the sounds that we interpret as a cry of pain. Let it be granted, then, that these sounds represent the condition of a self other than the hearer's. If so it is merely perverse to maintain with confidence that all the rest of a man's sense-experience is either non-representative or represents other possible experiences *of the man's own*. Let us further admit that we have no reason for believing that the sense-experiences which do not, like an animal cry, represent or seem to represent the inner life of another self, really do represent some other self that is clearly similar to ours. In that case we should not hold that what appears to be the inexpressive "choir of heaven" and the inexpressive "furniture of earth" are, in reality, expressive of other spirits *like our own*. Indeed, I do not think that we are entitled to affirm that they are expressive of other *spirits* of any kind at all. Nevertheless they might be expressive of a type of being in some respects akin to spirits, and in any case of beings of a very high order of integration—shall we say of gods and of angels that are not at all like men but are never lower than men?

I can discern no absurdity in such a theory. It depends on the strong empirical ground that the sense-experiences of our own that we take to represent the inner lives of our fellows do not *resemble* that inner life. The more usual forms of pan-psychism hold that the visible shape and size of this or the other existent entity do not merely represent but *are* its shape and size. If that view be abandoned, conjecture has its freest scope. It is indeed too free to be positive. But if the freedom be well grounded we cannot reasonably complain that it is very wide.

Such a philosophical romance, of course, need not be pantheistic. It would be interpreted most naturally as meaning that what we call the outside appearance of men and of animals evidenced the reality of human and animal souls, while the

276

outside appearance of what we call physical nature evidenced the reality of the high gods and the angels. If the animals, the men and the angels were not gods, there would not be pantheism. If they were there would be pantheism.

The pantheism in the pantheistic forms of this romance would be principally concerned with two themes, the first whether *we* are divine, the second whether every ultimate constituent of reality that is neither an animal self of a high order nor a human self is also divine.

Regarding the first point I may recall the passages from Kant's *Opus Posthumum* that I quoted in the last lecture. The substance of them was that the only God we know is in ourselves, and that the God we know in this inner throne is very God. But we all know that few theistic assertions are more usual than the statement that there is *something* divine in every human being. Indeed this piece of mitigated distributive pantheism is almost a theistic commonplace. Man is said to be a God as well as a beast because he is spiritual as well as fleshly, because he is rational as well as sensuous, because he is free to obey the categorical imperative, because he can aspire so nobly. The Incarnation of the Word is said to occur whenever human beings exist. The inference that without man, indeed that without *me* there would be no God, is also very frequently drawn, not by fervent philosophers only, but also by some Christian mystics. According to "Angelus Silesius" (i.e. Johann Scheffler in his *Cherubinic Wanderer*) God could not exist for a moment without me. "Were I naught, he must cease."

> Ich weiss dass ohne mich Gott nicht ein Ny kann leben,
> Wird ich zunicht, er muss von Not den Geist aufgeben.

And many of the Sufis have said the same thing again and again, as Mr. Nicholson shows.[1]

The other part of the theory I have sketched, the part of it that refers to the testimony of our senses to something that is

[1] See his *The Mystics of Islam, The Idea of Personality in Sufism,* and *Studies in Islamic Mysticism, passim.*

not a human or an animal spirit, that may not be a spirit or a
society of spirits at all, but that may, nevertheless, be akin to
our spirits, and higher, or at any rate, not lower than they would,
if it were theistic, be a theism of a less familiar sort. But I do not
think it is the worse for that. Indeed it is consonant with one of
the major trends of theistic speculation, with the view, namely,
that we should avoid, not merely the humanizing of deity in
some gross and obvious way, but also that we should avoid all
the more obvious ways of personalizing or of spiritualizing his
nature. While some may think that nothing but atheism can
result from such a policy in theological speculation, others are of
a different mind. However that may be, the arguments cannot
be disowned simply because they may seem to be dangerous.

So much in our recent enquiries has been on these very lines
that it should be unnecessary to revert to them here. I shall
therefore merely refer to one of the less familiar ways in which a
kinship between our spirits and what need not be a spirit may
be asserted. In Kant's æsthetic theory,[1] beauty attested the
general conformity between things, or some things, and human
faculty, but only the *general* conformity. It was not a matter of
specific assignable knowledge. Instead it sounded the universal
note in a diffused response. That is a more abstract and may
seem to be a thinner note than, let us say, St. Bernard's "*Experto
crede*, you shall find a fuller satisfaction in the woods than in
books. Trees and rocks shall teach you what you cannot learn
from masters. Surely honey can be drawn from stone and oil
from the hardest flint. Do not our mountains drop sweetness,
the hills flow with milk and honey, and the valleys stand thick
with corn?"[2] Nevertheless St. Bernard's symbolism suggests a
general and diffused pantheism. To choose a clearer instance,
when it is said in the *Hermetica*, "This is God's goodness, this
his clemency, that he manifests himself in all things",[3] the thought
is the thought of distributive pantheism, and it is not absurd

[1] *The Critique of Judgment.*
[2] Cp. 106. Quoted by Kirk, *The Vision of God*, p. 311.
[3] Quoted *op. cit.*, p. 49.

even if the consequence be that divinity is often very unlike a human spirit, and is better represented as being merely (and vaguely) akin to our spirits than as being, in the strict sense, spiritual or mental at all.

Let us next consider totalitarian pantheism.

According to this theory it is the whole of reality that is divine. God is that whole. The theory does not necessarily exclude distributive pantheism, for it is logically possible that the divinity of the whole should permeate every part of it. On the other hand, the whole may have properties that the parts do not possess, as a horse may gallop but not his mane. Again, the most interesting form of totalitarian pantheism is the form which asserts that the whole is God but that the parts are not. That is the form of the theory we should now consider.

In several respects this theory seems markedly preferable to distributive pantheism. It admits and asserts that everything real is a part of deity but is no more compelled to say that *each* such part is a God than it is compelled to say that every cell in a man's body is itself a little man. Again it need not hold that every part is equally divine, for the excellence of the whole is quite consistent with the most pronounced differences in the value of the several parts. Therefore the theory has its private solution of "the problem of evil". The whole may be altogether good although the parts may have qualities which would be bad if they were qualities, not of some part, but of the whole. This seems to be a logical possibility regarding most if not all kinds of evil.

The theory, however, is strenuously disputed upon at least three grounds, for it is attacked by logistical positivists, by metaphysical pluralists and by many moralists.

I shall say very little here about the first set of critics. Their criticism turns up everywhere. If they were consistent finitists they would deny that it is ever legitimate to talk about "all that there is". That would mean that all general statements are illegitimate. Yet that statement is itself general as well as arbitrary. A less intransigent form of the criticism is that "whatever there is" need not constitute a whole. That is sound criticism if the meaning be simply that if reality is said to be a "whole" of such and such a type (let us say of some highly integrated type) the statement would have to be proved and cannot simply be assumed. The phrase "whatever there is", however, describes what it does not enumerate and in that sense defines a proper subject for philosophical investigation.

The point introduces the critics of the second type. Pluralists are partisans of the many, and monists are partisans of the one. The two parties, however, need not come to blows. For every plurality is some sort of unity and the unity of the All is diversified however highly integrated the All may be. Nevertheless the two parties very frequently come into conflict, and conduct a lively action regarding the interpretation of the unity or of the plurality in all that there is.

Here there is very definite contact with totalitarian pantheism. Those who ascribe deity to the Whole usually maintain that the Whole is very highly integrated and has properties, the divine properties, that could not belong to a ramshackle, helter-skelter congeries. Aesthetic analogies are pressed, and the Whole is said to possess "significant form" in an elaborate pattern, even when full allowance is made for the romantic dimension of beauty, and for all the gracious disorder that may be found in nature. The Whole, it is said again, cannot be less integrated than a human mind.

As we have seen, however, an ultimate metaphysical pluralism is often defended on the ground that selves or persons are indiscerptible natural units and resist every attempt at totalitarian synthesis since they cannot be combined into a larger self. They are *for* themselves, it is said, not merely *in* themselves. They are *responsible* beings or substances, not merely "beings" or "substances".

This argument, so far as it is ethical, will be examined in due course. We may now examine it in so far as it is metaphysical without being specifically ethical.

As I argued in a former lecture,[1] it does not seem to me to be

---

[1] Lecture V of this series.

wholly impossible that the Whole should be a Self in which all finite selves are included. I do not think, however, that we have any appreciable empirical evidence that favours such a conjecture, either from multiple personality (as it is called) or from societies of selves. From our point of view, therefore, the idea may be quite sterile.

That, however, is not a fatal objection to totalitarian metaphysics. Totalitarian philosophers need not maintain that the Whole, which they believe to be so very highly integrated, must be a *self*. They need not say so even if they believe that human selves are the most highly integrated entities that are known to us empirically. They may quite easily hold (as, in fact, they often hold) that the Whole is a totality that contains all finite selves, but is more highly integrated than any self could be. In saying so they may even claim support from empirical experience. Suppose that deity resembles a church rather than a man, a spiritual community rather than a single self. In that case it would be fantastic to infer that individual men must necessarily be higher than God. It is, to say the least, intelligible to maintain that individual selves are *not* the highest things that we know, but that communities (which comprise selves but are *not* selves) may, as Aristotle thought,[1] be higher still. In other words, those who attempt to follow the clues of experience and are accustomed to browse freely in imaginative pastures that are analogical rather than strictly logical are not compelled to abjure totalitarian pantheism on the mere ground that the Whole, even if it *might* be the self of all selves, is not at all likely to be so.

In the third place there are the moralistic arguments against totalitarian pantheism. A morally responsible agent, it is said, is aware of the unity of his own personality and of his own free efficacy in his moral acts. The moral man is self-determining and by that very fact is a living refutation of totalitarian pantheism. Indeed moralists commonly go further. Sin, they say, is rebellion against the right, and it is impossible to believe that

[1] *Nic. Eth.*, 1094b 8.

a righteous and holy totality could contain and could ever be the better for containing obstinate rebels against itself.

Here the argument seems to include much that is curious. Its talk about "rebellion", for instance, seems to be fruity with metaphor. There have been rebellious devil-worshippers, but they were poor deluded creatures, committed to a dirty kindergarten rebellion. There are atheists and there are agnostics, but it is ludicrous to regard such people as engaged in sedition against the right and the just. If it be literally true that God is a monarch, the talk about "rebellion" may have a certain justification, but even in that case it would not seem to differ substantially from the less picturesque statement that much wickedness is voluntary.

Again it would seem that most canonical and most Protestant moralists exaggerate the importance of volition in wrong-doing. After all, mistakes are often voluntary, and moralists are usually lenient to mere mistakes. The most serious objection, however, is opposite and complementary to that one. Is it really so certain that vice, depravity and turpitude should be condemned simply or chiefly because they are voluntary? Would they be less revolting, less thoroughly nasty, if there were as little of express volition about them as frequently there seems to be? Is it easier to reconcile corruption with a healthy totality than to reconcile voluntary transgression with a righteous totality? Surely it is a mistake to be preoccupied with volition in these matters.

In general, however, the moralistic objections to totalitarian pantheism seem to be well grounded. If the Whole were just a drama (or just a melodrama) it may be granted that its æsthetic splendour might be enhanced and not diminished by the spectacle of the vice and folly and meanness even of its most heroic figures. Is it likely, however, that there is any analogy *except* an æsthetic analogy for such a state of affairs? Is it credible that the Whole could be perfect in knowledge and in wisdom if its parts were ignorant; sound and healthy if its parts were weak and diseased; righteous altogether if its parts were vicious, misguided and corrupt? It seems to me to be improbable in the highest degree that things could happen so.

Consequently, if totalitarian pantheism be true, it is much easier to believe that the Whole is beyond morality than that it is moral in the ordinary sense of that word. Again, the view that the Whole, although surmoral, is still moral in a higher unknown way has rightly earned emphatic condemnation from a strong body of moralists. McTaggart said that Mill's well-known criticism of Mansel was "one of the great turning-points in the religious development of the world". I do not think that the world had to wait so long, but Mill's words were a turning-point in the religious development of McTaggart and of very many of his contemporaries. So I shall quote them, even if they seem now to be stale.

Here is what Mill said:[1]

If, instead of the "glad tidings" that there exists a Being in whom all excellences which the highest human mind can conceive, exist in a degree inconceivable to us, I am informed that the world is ruled by a being whose attributes are infinite, but that what they are we cannot learn, nor what are the principles of his government, except that "the highest human morality which we are capable of conceiving" does not sanction them: convince me of it, and I will bear my fate as I may. But when I am told that I must believe this, and at the same time call this being by the names which express and affirm the highest human morality, I say in plain terms that I will not. Whatever power such a being may have over me, there is one thing which he shall not do; he shall not compel me to worship him. I will call no being good, who is not what I mean when I apply that epithet to my fellow-creatures; and if such a being can sentence me to hell for not so calling him, to hell I will go.

On the other hand, the implications of the "freedom" that is said to be an inevitable aspect of "action for self" or of responsible self-determination are much more disputable. So far as I can see there is *no* sense of freedom that is inconsistent with *distributive* pantheism. In that respect the critics of pantheism are usually

1 *Examination of Hamilton*, pp. 128-9.

very wrong indeed. *Per contra* "freedom" in any sense that involves action genuinely independent of the Whole is inconsistent with *totalitarian* pantheism. It may be held, however, that the most important sense of "freedom", and the only sense that is clearly entailed in moral responsibility, is the fact of self-determination itself, and particularly the determination of action by the apprehension of principle, right and validity. The *fact* of self-determination, it may be said, is not inconsistent with the view that the determining self is part of a wider whole that acts in and through it.

That seems to me to be true. Monists like Spinoza deny that man is an *imperium in imperio*; but if man were an *imperium in imperio* his authority, although delegated, might be perfectly genuine authority. Again, if he did not know that his authority was delegated but could perceive that it was genuine, he would assert his freedom on empirical grounds. That, as a recent author has said, "accords generally with the very moderate degree of freedom which experience of human nature would lead us to conjecture as a fact".[1] As the same author says, freedom "of a more metaphysical kind" could not be reached by such arguments, and it was the more metaphysical kind of freedom that Spinoza denied. But self-regulation in the responsible moral way need not imply anything more metaphysical than itself.

We have now considered distributive and totalitarian pantheism, and have noted that they were not always and in all respects irreconcilable. Let us next proceed to examine a view that many theists hold, namely, that it is consistent to believe that God is the supreme being and *also* that he is the whole. That is the usual creed of the theologians who say that if, in a sense, they are pantheists, they are not *mere* pantheists. With some apologies for the name I shall call it "monarchical pantheism".

There is no opposition between monarchical and distributive pantheism, for it is consistent to hold that everything is wholly

[1] J. L. Stocks, *Time, Cause and Eternity*, p. 152.

divine and yet that some one of these all-divine beings lords it over the others. On the other hand, *prima facie* at least, it seems incredible that totalitarian pantheism could be reconciled with God's supremacy and sovereignty. That, however, is precisely what is held by the philosophical theologians who maintain that God is All but is also above all. If these theologians are right their opponents must have overlooked a logical possibility, perhaps a subtle possibility, but still a possibility. Let us enquire, therefore, whether there is such a possibility.

I have used the term "monarchical pantheism" because it has been so very common for Western theologians to speak about the "kingdom of God" and because these words appeal so very strongly to nearly all of us. The political associations of the phrase, however, seem to be rather unfortunate. Yet even today it is sometimes held that monarchical analogies are illuminating. Therefore I should like to say that I do not think they are helpful at all. Many have argued, like Hobbes,[1] that there is a sense in which the political sovereign *is* his people as well as their ruler, and some have tried to show, in a way rather similar to Hobbes's way, that anyone who accepts the status of a subject thereby surrenders or donates his sovereignty over himself to the political sovereign. If the political sovereign were a single man, a monarch or a dictator, this donation of self-sovereignty might be taken to mean that the dictator bore the *personae* of all his subjects, although he himself was an individual person, and even, in some sense, subject to himself.

It does not seem to me that any such views can bear close scrutiny. They are all fictions summarily describing a complicated hierarchy that, given patience, can be adequately interpreted without asserting what seems to be so absurd, namely, that a part can be a whole and also remain a part. We have to ask, however, much more generally, whether the category of whole and of part may not itself be capable of revision in a sense that is favourable to the theology of monarchical pantheism.

[1] E.g. *Leviathan*, chaps. xvii and xviii.

It may be argued that when we speak of the parts of a whole we habitually employ two different conceptions. In the one case we think of the parts as entities which, in any given instance, participate in some whole, but are also capable of being dissociated from that whole and of participating in some other whole. In this sense, spare parts may replace the original parts without appreciable alteration in the whole. In the other case we think simply of a part as something that actually functions in the actual whole of which it constitutes one of the parts. In that case, that and that only is a part which actually functions as a part. Classical observations to the effect that a severed hand is no longer a *hand* may be quoted effectively.

In terms of this distinction we might speak of dissociable and of participating parts respectively. Some wholes might be composed entirely of dissociable parts. Every single brick in a building might be replaced by another similar brick. Every single cell in a living body might be regenerated from other material. Each of us and, for that matter, the entire human race might (some would say) be dissociable parts in a spiritual whole that does not need any of us severally or all of us collectively in order (if we were replaced) to be just the spiritual whole that it is. On the other hand, there might be wholes none of whose parts were dissociable parts. There may, for instance, be some artistic masterpieces that cannot be "restored" even in the smallest way without visible loss. Again, there might be wholes some of whose parts are dissociable while other parts are not dissociable, a possibility that seems to come nearer the truth regarding many of the masterpieces that are said to be "restored".

Again, there may just conceivably be an intelligible use of language in which it makes sense to say, not merely that certain wholes are composed entirely of dissociable parts, but also that such wholes are *more* than their dissociable parts, more, that is, than these dissociable parts in a certain interconnection, and, *a fortiori*, more than the sum, or mere aggregate, of such dissociable parts. Even in that case, however, it would be absurd to suggest that a whole could be either a dissociable or a participating part *of itself*, and the absurdity would not be diminished if, instead of a "whole", we spoke of a Form or of an informing spirit of totality. Again, it is monstrous to suggest that if a whole can dispense with this or the other dissociable part, it can therefore dispense altogether with *all* its parts or even with all its dissociable parts. It may not need *this* dissociable part, or *that* dissociable part, but it needs *some* parts of the kind.

The distinction between dissociable and participating parts, therefore, would not go any way at all towards suggesting the possibility of monarchical-totalitarian pantheism, that is to say of a Whole that both was and was not a part of itself, *totum in toto ac totum in qualibet parte*, a part in so far as it was supreme over the rest, not a part just because it *was* the Whole. There is a sturdy and a lively faith in any pantheist who maintains that he is *not* a dissociable part of deity, any more than Newton or Demosthenes, Savonarola or Genghis Khan. There is a similar but more austere faith in any pantheist who maintains that the human race or his Nordic tribe, or his church, or some saving fragment of culture that survived the lost continent of Atlantis is not a dissociable part of the Godhead. There is no such faith in the empty assertion that a man or his country both *are* and *are not* participating parts of deity.

Indeed, monarchical pantheism should be treated even more curtly than this. In the last analysis *every* part must be a participating part. What is meant by a "dissociable" part is an entity which, without renouncing its identity, is capable of being a participating part, now in one whole, and anon in another whole. If and when it is a part at all it must be a participating part. Conversely, the particular whole in which it is a participating part needs that particular participating part and no other.

This reflection (I submit) is decisive, but if I were wrong about that I could clinch the point in another way. Suppose that there were an absolute metaphysical distinction between participating and dissociable parts. Suppose that we could speak intelligibly of a whole that was more than and could govern its dissociable parts although it also included them. I do not believe that the supposition makes sense, but suppose that it did. Then the alleged possibility could occur only in the case of parts that *were* dissociable. But pantheism refers to the All, and nothing can be dissociated from the All. Even if a monarchical totalitarianism could be just conceivable in the case of finite totalities that were not the All, it would be wholly inconceivable in the case of *pantheism*. For pantheism is concerned with the entirety of *everything* and with nothing smaller.

Consequently we should conclude that a monarchical theory of reality, however freely the term "monarchical" may be construed, is not consistent with totalitarian pantheism. The Absolute, in the usual sense of that term, is beyond God, as well as beyond good, beyond beauty and beyond truth. It is fortunate if it stops short of the great inane.

I shall now return to a point that I mentioned briefly at an earlier stage in this lecture. As we then saw, it has been very usual for men to believe that there is *something* divine in everything that exists. I call this theory a "mitigated" form of pantheism of the distributive type. If it is conjoined, as it usually is, with the belief that there is something *un*divine (perhaps much) in everything, a "mitigated" pantheism is a form of the doctrine of a limited deity.

Strictly interpreted, as we saw, the expression "a mitigated pantheism" comes near to self-contradiction. As precisians we have the right to dislike it. But it may serve, and it may clumsily designate a form of theism that is not self-contradictory. For theism may be a limited theism. Indeed if it be not pantheism in the fullest sense, theism *must* be limited.

It must be confessed that the statement that everything is in some degree divine might describe a theism so washy and so tepid as to be barely discriminable from simple forthright atheism. The doctrine that it describes, however, may also be very different from a mere theistic cup of tea. Suppose, then, that what was asserted was the dominance of divinity in everything that exists. Would such a theism be unlikely to be true? Must it be a slick and flashy sort of theory in its mere conception?

Again, if the mitigated pantheism were of the totalitarian kind, asserting that divinity pervades and transfigures the universe, although never in the sense that denies the non-divinity in much that occurs, would such a theory be an improbable or a puerile sort of theism?

As it seems to me, some such view as this is what many people very actively believe, without caring very much whether, technically speaking, they are to be accounted atheists or not. It is, I daresay, a very pedestrian theory, even if "theory" be not too high a name for it. It may not attract the poets and the prose of it may be drab. Still, it may be sincerely held and be a hypothesis that strengthens the life of many a man and soothes many a death. Indeed we may ask what else a man should believe if he is a theist and if he also accepts certain premisses which, if not wholly irrefragable, are very hard to discredit. These premisses are, firstly, that there is just one reality (which we commonly call the universe); secondly, that *this* world is, or is a part of, the universe; thirdly, that, on the whole, we ought to believe that the properties we seem to find and the distinctions we appear to be forced to draw in this our world are not, in the main, deceptive; fourthly, that evil is not an illusion; and fifthly, that our comprehension of axiological values is not a fancy or caprice on our part. Conjoin these premisses with theism. The conclusion, I suggest, must be rather similar to the pedestrian theory I have indicated above.

I propose to discuss certain of the implications of such a "pantheism" for the rest of the present lecture.

The trend of the theory is not doubtful. Like any other or fuller form of pantheism it is a theory of divine immanence as opposed to divine transcendence, and of the sufficiency of divine immanence without any divine transcendence. Deity is held to be dia-cosmic, not hyper-cosmic, and the cosmos is taken to mean the world, astronomical, biological and human. The theory is a theory of *Natura sive Deus*, but not of a Godless nature; for it holds that nature is deiform although it also holds (being but a mitigated pantheism) that nature contains much evil and much else that cannot, obviously and directly, be called divine.

It would be generally agreed, and I think it is clear, that the idea of the pervasive deiformity of nature is quite empty unless it connotes a pervasive worth or excellence in and of nature. Indeed it seems to be plain that the principal difficulty that any form of pantheism has to meet is wrapped up in the general problem whether, if deity be not a hyper-cosmic spirit but only the greatest dia-cosmic principle, it would be intelligible to attribute axiological value to the Godhead in an eminent degree.

The difficulty is formidable for the following reasons. There is a wide although not a universal consensus of opinion in favour of the view that the great axiological values are only to be found empirically in the appreciations, the volitions and the contemplative insight of men, in human minds that are finely touched and nowhere else. Hence the inference is drawn that all such values must have their home in men, or at any rate in individual spirits and societies of spirits. A dia-cosmic principle of deiformity, on the other hand, would seem to be impersonal, or at any rate most probably to be so.

When we discussed axiology we found ourselves, in the main, on the side of the prevalent opinion. It seemed to us to be true, or at any rate to be probable, that the axiological value of knowledge lies in actual spiritual insight; and similarly of the axiological values of beauty, felicity and moral character. The mere conformity of non-mental existence to the nomic intellect, to æsthetic appreciation or to the moral conscience did not seem to be an intrinsic axiological value. There may be an empirical exception in the case of spiritual communities which are not themselves spirits yet often appear, empirically, to be the bearers of greater values than pertain to any individual man.

It would follow from this, and I do not see any adequate reason for believing, that all the higher values in the universe must be values that pertain to personal conscious beings. On the other hand it might be said, very reasonably, that any other high value is for us a mere abstract possibility, and that if the smell of Paradise cannot be discerned in true insight, in beauty and in moral character there can be no savour of divinity for us any-where. If, then, all the high values that we know are personal values, the conclusion might seem to be that if deity be not personal, deity does not have any of the axiological attributes that we are accustomed to ascribe to it. An impersonal dia-cosmic theism, it might be said, would have less value than many men have—so far, at any rate, as the savour of divinity has any empirical meaning.

That is a question to which we have addressed ourselves more than once during the last few lectures. I shall now say something more about it when stated in this form.

Some people may think that the difference between a personal and an impersonal form of theism is only verbal, and many statements about axiology in theology appear to use personal and impersonal language indifferently. In the concluding chapter of Mr. Bevan's *Symbolism and Belief*, for instance, we find the two modes of expression side by side. To say, as he does in that chapter, that "the universe surrounding us should in some way *care* for values" is a personalistic statement. To say, as he also says, that it "subserves the purposes of spirit", that it "should be such that Spirit, for which values exist, should be eternal and triumphant" is entirely consistent with an impersonal theory. If either statement suffices, it would not seem to matter very much which form of expression is used, and Mr. Bevan in the context seems to use both of them indiscriminately.

Such a translation from personalistic to impersonalistic terms is, in general, neither impracticable nor unsatisfying. Instead of saying that nature is God's science, the translation asserts that it is logically consistent, and has a principled pattern with a rela-tively simple groundwork of principle. Instead of saying that nature is the poem of a divine creative artist the translation says that it is lovely and gracious. Instead of saying that nature is God's plan or scheme or policy, the translation says that it is patterned in a functional hierarchy.

Such a translation, however, is much more than a trick or a dodge. It involves a profound alteration of fundamental conceptions. For the most part, the God of Western theology, logically regarded, is a hypothesis to explain how certain patterns in nature and in human nature have come to pass. To accept the result without the hypothesis, and studiously to avoid the hypothesis in all the language we use, is to reject altogether the familiar and (as many would say) the inspired and inspiring conceptions of what most men mean by theism, as well as the penumbrae of its moving associations. It is, in general, to assert deiformity without a God—θειότης instead of ὁ θεός. The translation into impersonal terms may still be theistic. It may (and I have argued that it often does) retain the substance of what theism stands for. But the altered words have an altered meaning, and that explains the importance of asking how the translation of personalistic into impersonalistic theism would run.

I have tried to make the translation on several occasions during the last few of these lectures. My only regret is that I have not translated very well. An impersonalistic theory of theism, if it be a likely theory, has need of all the persuasiveness that an adequate expression of it can give. I submit, however, that my account of it should not be condemned as unlikely simply because I have expressed it badly.

In these fundamental matters of axiology, the language of personalistic theism may seem to be much more adequate, and much more straightforward, than the language of impersonalistic theism. In the former it is explained that God unites in his person such personal values as insight, and the joy of beauty, and moral solicitude. An impersonalist would have to say, instead, that deity was, as the scholastics put it, only *virtually* and not *formally* good. Deity would be the source and the guardian of goodness but not itself good. I do not myself see that much is lost in the latter form of statement, especially if, in the former statement, it is further explained that the difference between divine and human is so very great that the adequacy and straightforwardness of the personalistic theory has to be very seriously modified. But having stated the point I must leave it to the reader.

Pantheism

Many people think that the greatest difficulties in the way of an impersonal theism are of a moral kind, partly because ethics may seem to be so much more human than cosmic, partly because an impersonal moral principle seems to be frigid and aloof. There may therefore be some importance in returning to the argument of some previous lectures, and pointing out that many of these difficulties can be overcome rather easily.

There is no serious difficulty in the conception of a bountiful impersonal nature whose trend and pattern make for the banishment of wretchedness and despair. There is no logical necessity that such natural bounty should be indiscriminate. In so far as ethics is concerned with good and ill desert, there is no need to assume that an impersonal nemesis must be a clumsy nemesis. Again, if the dominance of righteousness in the universe stands for certain laws of the human spirit, or is chiefly evidenced there, an impersonal form of theism is not at all incredible. If victory over temptation makes further victories the easier, if fineness of moral character brings the sweet fruits of spiritual peace, if the good man's reward be neither prosperity nor freedom from disease but a catholic sympathy with all men and the affectionate esteem of the best men, it could not be said that such natural laws were of little account to a moralist or were impossible on an impersonalistic theory of theism.

Arguments such as these would count for nothing to a man who knew from his own personal experience that God was his father and his friend, but I think they should count for something to those who make no such claim yet are convinced that a theistic view of the world is more probable than any other. The arguments are often consistent with theologies that are not pantheistic, and they are not absolutely required by pantheism, since pantheists may hold that God is the Self of all nature, and also of all the selves within nature. On the other hand, an immanent theory of deity is the more credible if it be both dia-cosmic and pantheistic, and would have a strong motive to credence if it could be interpreted as an impersonal deiformity, stable and dominant in the cosmos.

X

Concluding Reflections

I SHALL divide this lecture into three parts. In the first part I shall try to give a sketch of the argument in the second series. In the second part I shall examine the relations between the discussion in the first series and the discussion in the second series. In the third part I shall offer certain general observations.

I

The discussion in the second series may be generally described as an ennead in three triads. Except as regards its arithmetic, this general description is rather loose and rather too ambitious. There is no magic in the nine of the ennead or in the three of the triads, no miracle of construction in which the structure of the triads reflects the triad of triads that makes the nine. Still, the groups tend to cling together and I shall now consider them in respect of that tendency.

The first triad dealt with the philosophy of mind, and more particularly with the metaphysical ontology of mind. Its general problem was whether reality could be proved to be mind-constituted, and, if so, in what sense. It began with a discussion of the traditional Ontological Proof, proceeded to an account of the nature of mind, and ended with a discussion of pan-idea-ism, pan-ideatism and pan-psychism.

The traditional Ontological Proof, we maintained, was invalid, and we tried to see where and why it was invalid—a much more difficult task. We also saw, however, that its more recent supporters, following Hegel's lead, trans-essentiate it into something that is not a *proof*, but is rather the Grand Ontological

Concluding Reflections

Assertion of Absolute Idealism. In this trans-essentiated form the so-called "proof" is the most ambitious of all philosophical attempts to show that thought and reality are metaphysically indissoluble and that what is central in a thinking mind must also be central in all reality. Such an assertion seemed obviously to require an investigation into the nature of mind, and into the meaning of the contention that reality must be "mind"-constituted.

Peering into the nature of mind, we took our cue, as seemed legitimate and indeed inevitable, from the conscious quality of waking experience. This conscious quality, we concluded, had a transcendent and also a reflexive dimension, neither of which could be surrendered or reduced to the other. That is true of human minds and would seem to be true of any mind as such. We further concluded that there was no sufficient reason for believing that everything that exists must possess the conscious quality. Not everything need be a knower, and that which is known transcendently need not have any community of nature with its knower. To say that everything must be "conformable to knowledge" is not to say that everything is somehow a kind of knowing, but only to say that there is nothing that cannot be known.

I hope that the conclusion thus summarily indicated was defended with equity and with some patience in its proper place, the twelfth lecture. For it was accepted, expressly or by implication, throughout the remainder of the discussion.

Its relevance to the assertion that all is mind or mind-constituted is very plain, and was the subject of the last lecture in this first triad. As we there saw, pan-psychism, i.e. the doctrine that all that exists is spirit, is sometimes defended on epistemological grounds. It is then a doctrine of pan-idea-ism or of pan-ideatism. The first is metaphysical phenomenalism, sensory, noëtic or mixed sensory-noëtic, and we maintained that no doctrine of phenomenalism can do justice to the transcendent dimension of cognition. Phenomenalism in all its forms is incapable of becoming an adequate ontology. Pan-ideatism, ostensibly more modest in its assertions, has ultimately to make the same claims, and so falls under the same condemnation. Since minds or spirits, if they exist, are not mere phenomena or ideas, the proof of pan-idea-ism, if it could be effective, would destroy instead of establishing pan-psychism. Pan-psychism, however, may be defended upon quite different grounds, and we tried to examine the chief among them. We concluded that it was not a plausible theory upon any directly ontological grounds, although it was not impossible.

So ended the first triad.

The second triad was concerned generally with divine personality both in its intellectual and in its moral aspects. We began with the intellectual aspects (and their kindred) asking first whether we *must* and secondly whether we *could* legitimately believe in the existence of an all-knowing mind. Our conclusion was that it was impossible to demonstrate the existence of such a mind, either as an implication of the validity of human knowledge or otherwise, but that it was not incredible that there should be such a mind if "omniscience" were interpreted in a reasonable and not in a fantastic or irresponsible way.

Here we tried to take the conception of omniscience seriously. The term was not regarded as a magniloquent gesture vaguely asserting that the all-knower knows in a way that is quite unlike our ways of knowing, being exempt from sense-acquaintance, from sympathy and from empathy, exempt also from the sharp distinctions that characterize the clear intellectual notions of mankind. One of the most significant questions of this kind concerns human self-acquaintance and the reflexiveness of the conscious quality in human experience. If such reflexiveness in each man were immitigably private, even God would be a stranger to the hearts of private men. He would know human hearts from the outside only, although he would know *himself* reflexively. We concluded, however, that the reflexiveness of human self-acquaintance did not absolutely prohibit the inclusion of such knowledge in a wider knower who was also reflexively acquainted with himself.

Concluding Reflections

That is one of the persistent problems that beset the conception of divine personality, the subject of the second lecture in this triad. In the first part of that lecture it was argued that the objections, admittedly strong, that are commonly brought against the very idea that God could literally be a person, are not absolutely conclusive. We are accustomed to think of persons as embodied beings whose bodies require a bodily environment, as selves whose selfhood requires an environing not-self, as forensically responsible beings who have to live in a world of claims and counter-claims. If these requirements were absolute, God could not *be* a person. It did not appear to us, however, that these requirements *were* absolute.

Nevertheless the notion of a God who is impersonal rather than personal might seem to be firmer and more easily credible than the notion of a personal deity. God, for instance, might resemble a church rather than a man. The Christian conception of the Holy Spirit would not seem to be wholly unfriendly towards such an interpretation. Again, if, as many think, the philosophy of theism points towards the divinity of fact rather than towards the outpouring of divinity upon the facts of existence from some over-worldly chalice, the impersonality of the quality of deity would be very strongly suggested. The implications of an impersonal theism (or pantheism) should therefore be explored.

The second part of the lecture upon divine personality examined these implications, more especially in their moral aspects. Our question was whether it would or would not be atheistic to believe that divine beneficence, divine justice, divine mercy and even divine tenderness (as they are called) were names for an impersonal principle of bounty and of righteousness, and should be regarded as inherent in the facts of nature (especially of human nature) instead of being regarded as the influence of a personal being behind and above the natural facts. We concluded that the moral resources of an impersonal theism were very much greater than its critics usually suppose.

The third lecture in this triad reverted, so to say, to the

vulgate of theism. Its theme was providence; and providentia or πρόνοια are the common terms for the benevolent and moral purposes of an over-worldly divine person. We also discussed, however, whether it was possible to make a translation from the vulgate into another and (some might think) into a less metaphorical theology, speaking about functions instead of about purposes, and about patterns instead of about plans. Here again the feasibility of an impersonal theory of "providence" had to be examined. It had further to be examined in connection with God's special grace as well as in connection with his common grace. That distinction, in a measure, had to be arbitrary since it depends upon the shifting boundaries that may be drawn between "nature" and "super-nature", and upon special assumptions regarding the former, such as its corruption, its "wounded" character or its merely unsanctified condition. Both in general and in special, however, the graciousness of God may well appear to be a more adequate as well as a more delectable expression for describing divinity than the language of bounty and reward and punishment. It also, we concluded, might be interpreted in impersonal terms.

In this lecture certain suggestions were made regarding optimism, pessimism and the "problem of evil". Granting that the existence of *some* evil need not be inconsistent with the supreme goodness of a deiform reality, granting also that the sort of moral accountancy that would be required for arguments based upon the *amount* of evil in the world is almost if not quite indeterminate, it seemed hard to believe that the sins in the world, medicable or immedicable, are consistent with a reality that is righteous *altogether*, and difficult to hold that either their redemption or the need for it is consistent with such a belief.

The third triad in our ennead returned to a more abstract type of metaphysical argument. Indeed the theme with which it began, namely, the alleged impossibility of dissociating value from existence, has close affinities with the Ontological Proof and may be described, generally, as metaphysical idealism in the sense in which an ontology of *ideals* takes the place of an ontology of *ideas*, and valid appreciation takes the place of valid ideation.

In our discussion of this question we concluded that since the meaning of *esse* was, quite simply, *esse* it was illegitimate to maintain that *esse* connoted *valere*. If the Ontological Proof be thrown to the winds, so must this form of it. On the other hand, it could be suggested that although "to be" does not *mean* "to be valuable", nevertheless we might be entitled to say that nothing exists (or, so far as we can see, is likely to exist) without being of some value. Since evil exists, the doctrine would have to be that what exists must be either good or bad, and not that whatever exists must be good. Since much that exists seems to have only instrumental value, that is to say to be a means to value without necessarily *being* itself valuable at all, it might be doubted whether the supposedly indissoluble connection between existence and value came to more than the washy generality that everything that exists is somehow connected with something that is either of value or of disvalue.

More significantly still, if in our reference to "value" we were really thinking of the higher axiological values that we find in experience to be high (and, in the main, were thinking of truth and joy and beauty and moral virtue), it seems clear that the only beings that, to our knowledge, possess these excellences are men and women and (perhaps) some of the higher animals. Consequently, unless we could show that these beings, or beings very like them, were the only beings that could exist, our theory would be (shall we say?) outrageously speculative. I do not believe that we can prove anything of the kind, or produce well-grounded conjectures that, although inconclusive, should strongly incline us towards such a conclusion.

In the second lecture in this triad we discussed the moral proofs of theism, beginning with the argument, recurring in many forms, that moral principles are not merely descriptive but are also obligatory and so that they are commands. A command, it is averred, implies a commander. Therefore, according to many theists, there must be a God. For the metaphorical sense in which we are said to command *ourselves* to do our duty, and the juristic sense in which the political sovereign commands its subjects, are held by these theists to be quite insufficient for an adequate theory of moral obligation.

That (sometimes) was one of Kant's arguments. As he said succinctly in the *Opus Posthumum*: "There is a God because there is a categorical imperative." We concluded that moral principles are not, strictly speaking, commands, and therefore that the argument falls.

Among the other arguments that are employed in a moralistic metaphysics of this kind, the most considerable, in some form or other, is that to which Kant gave so much of his speculative genius. The trend of it is roughly as follows. In moral experience we have either the only or by far the clearest evidence of a type of determination that, without such experience, would be only a speculative dream. This occurs when a man acts rightly, and is free to act rightly, in accordance with his rational apprehension of what is right. It gives evidence of the operative power of the practical reason, and it may be developed into a metaphysics that, although problematical as regard its *modus operandi*, is neither baseless nor impossible. The metaphysics in question asserts that the supersensible alone is real. It is a supernaturalism of rationalistic grace. What we call "nature", it maintains, is only the necessitation of sense, and sense, although "empirically real", is ultimately illusory, a defective image of the supersensible that alone is real.

In discussing this view we allowed that belief in rightness or validity is an independent motive to human action and that rightness is *sui generis*. We also allowed that there need be nothing surprising in the view that even if moral experience seemed peculiar to mankind among empirical beings it should, nevertheless, give us a clue that demanded a most thoroughgoing revolution in our common notions. This revolution may imply that most of what we are accustomed to regard as assured is not at all what it seems. Setting aside lesser objections to the theory, however (such as the difficulty of believing that nature is really illusory, and the equivocation in Kant's account of "freedom" which was a name both for a man's elective will to do right *or* wrong, and for the *rightness* of his rational self-determination *as such*), there seemed to be insuperable difficulty in the conception of a reality that was composed entirely of entities of mere reason, or, in Kant's language, of noümena. It is the *apprehension* of validity, or of seeming validity, that is a motive to human action, not mere validity in itself. We can conceive of an infallible being, that is to say of a mind all of whose mental processes are valid; but it is inconceivable that a being could exist who was entirely made up of mere validity.

The last lecture in this triad dealt with pantheism. There were many reasons why it should. To say that God is all is to assert a kind of pantheism. A dia-cosmic theory of divinity tends to be pantheistic. An impersonalistic theory of divinity is congruent with many forms of pantheism. In short, much in our discussion converged towards some form of pantheism and it seemed necessary to discuss the logical potentialities of such a theory in a systematic way. We therefore discussed the relation of distributive to totalitarian pantheism, the possibility of combining these in some form of monarchical pantheism and other such questions.

I concluded that an unqualified distributive pantheism was an improbable theory, that is to say, I thought it improbable that everything that exists is *wholly* divine, at any rate if our account of the things that exist, and of their boundaries and constitution, has a close resemblance to what science and common sense tells us about them. For deity is a name that we *contrast* with the names of common things. The totalitarian doctrine that All is divine need not be subject to that difficulty. We may reasonably contrast the infinite with the finite. It would seem to be frankly incredible, however, that the whole should be healthy if many of the parts are diseased.

Objections of that kind cannot upset and need not seriously disturb the chastened and pedestrian belief that there is *something* divine in everything that exists and something divine in the Whole. Such a theory, however, might be so feeble in its theism as not to be worth considering. God might be just a *something* that is extolled but not defined. No one is seriously a theist who cannot say *Magna est deitas et praevalet*. The "problem of evil", however, and the consequent limitations of deity (if deity be wholly good) need not be more tormenting to a pantheist than to any other theist; and pantheism, I thought, was a much more serious and a much more defensible form of theism than many writers supposed.

II

That is a short summary of the second series of these lectures. And so we come to the second major division of the present lecture, the relation between the second series and the first series.

In the first series we discussed cosmological theism, with two important reservations, the first of which was that we should adopt a provisional realism during the first series, and the second that we should postpone consideration of the moral and axiological aspects of theism to the second series. There was a connection between these two reservations, for it is frequently maintained that the moral and more generally the gracious arguments for theism are shorn of much of their force if it is not remembered, or if it is denied, that reality can be shown, by metaphysical and valid arguments, to be spiritual through and through.

These questions and these arguments were the theme of the first triad of lectures in the second series. The conclusion was that the provisional realism of the first series might be final as well as provisional. It could not be overthrown by pan-idea-ism or by pan-ideatism. On the contrary, these philosophies were themselves untenable. We did not, it is true, directly attempt to establish the truth of a realistic view of nature, or of supernature. Realism may not be the only alternative to pan-idea-ism and/or pan-ideatism. If anyone knows of a better alternative, let him suggest it.

Concluding Reflections

Certainly it may reasonably be said that what theism welcomes is not pan-idea-ism or pan-ideatism in all their philosophical strictness, but something wider and more genial, viz. a spiritual view of the constitution of reality. If such a view of reality were a spiritual realism, theists would rejoice, if for no other reason, because Absolute Pan-idea-ism threatens to absorb and transmute deity as well as all else. It is also clear that one celebrated theory of spiritual realism (I mean pan-psychism) may be supported on grounds that are quite independent of pan-idea-ism or of pan-ideatism. On investigation, however, it did not seem to us that these grounds were very strong.

The denial of pan-psychism, of course, does not imply the denial of theism. Many (indeed most) theists have believed, like most other people, that the world contains a number of quite unspiritual things, and have constructed their theologies on the basis of that belief. Logic did not stand in their way. Again, as we saw in some detail in our discussion of pan-psychism, a pan-psychist need not be a theist, and need not find that either the more superficial or the graver difficulties that stand in the way of theism were removed by pan-psychism. He need not be a theist because the spirits that, according to him, are the only existents need not be gods or friendly towards what we call divine things; and if the cast of his theism be trust in God as his saviour from perils and distress, it is obvious that calamities would not be less calamitous or distresses less poignant if they were caused by other spirits, than if they were caused by unspiritual beings. Even if man's inhumanity were the greatest evil that men have to endure its consequences would not be the less terrible on that account. Remember war, and torture, and man's ingratitude and his injustice to man.

What I think most theists would say about these matters is that although pan-psychism is not essential to theism and may even be something of an embarrassment to it, nevertheless a cosmological theism is much easier to defend if everything be akin to spirit than if the stars in their courses are quite unspiritual in their proper nature. That contention, I think, is true. The disproportion between what appears to be non-spiritual or sub-spiritual, on the one hand, and what we know to be spiritual, on the other hand, is so great, and the power of spirit is so small in appearance, that the dominance of spiritual values in all reality for all time seems to be a very hazardous assertion unless the stronger dia-cosmic forces work for good and tend to produce beings rather like men, just because there is a fundamental affinity between their nature and a spiritual nature. It is possible, to be sure (and indeed it is not unlikely), that God's goodness is very unlike the goodness of any finite spirit, perhaps because God is not a spirit but greater and finer than any spirit. If so he may often be present where no spirits could be discerned (because they would not *be* present). On the other hand, if the best in spirit and in mind as we know it has no savour of divinity, we are altogether at a loss to conjecture what divinity could be; and if the stronger cosmological forces were definitely non-spiritual, theism would have a harder task than on most other cosmological theories.

I have to confess that this part of my argument does not do much to facilitate theism. Empirically I cannot find high spiritual properties except in human minds or in societies of human minds. Human minds do not seem to me to constitute a large part of the world, or to be the strongest part of the world. Such appearances, no doubt, may be very deceptive; but they *are* the appearances, and on that account they yield a certain degree of presumptive evidence. It may be true that everything is akin to our spirits, but the kinship seems to be vague, and it is the difference between our spirits and what seems to be non-spiritual that impresses most of us most persistently when we think of these matters. That has been obvious from the course of this entire discussion. I should not be sorry to be wrong, but I cannot see that I am wrong. So I have to say so.

That, in curt summary, is what I am bound to say, generally, about the relation between the first series of these lectures and the first triad of the second series. We have now to consider the relation between the cosmology of the first series and the providence and axiology discussed in the remainder of the second series.

In a poem entitled *Riding Westward*, and dated Good Friday, 1613, John Donne wrote:

> Could I behold those hands which span the Poles
> And turn all spheres at once, pierced with those holes?
> Could I behold that endless height which is
> Zenith to us and our Antipodes
> Humbled below us? Or that blood which is
> The seat of all our souls if not of his,
> Made dirt of dust, or that flesh which was worn
> By God for his apparel, rag'd and torn?

The paradox of the Incarnation, and its climax in the Crucifixion, oppressed Donne's spirit as he rode towards the west on that sacred anniversary.

These mysteries remain incomprehensible to many Christians today, although Dean Inge, the late Professor Creed and others of our age and country speak resolutely about "the cosmic Christ". I cannot think that the phrase was happily coined. The union of the divine and of the human natures in Christ is, as all Christian theology allows, a coincidence of opposites, an incomprehensible concord of apparently irreconcilable contrasts. Why then assert one side of the contrast without asserting the other? Why attempt such an assertion in a single phrase? The term "the cosmic Christ" is precisely similar to the terms "the pre-mundane Christ", "the omniscient Christ", "the omnipotent Christ". The man Jesus of Nazareth was born of Mary and not pre-mundane; he was not omniscient; he was not omnipotent. Similarly he was not cosmic. If it be said that even in his humanity Jesus of Nazareth gathered into himself the entire essence of God's tenderness and love and so was, very imprecisely, its "microcosm", the same could not be said without absurdity of dia-cosmic attributes. Jesus of Nazareth was not the universe and it is rare to find anyone who thinks so, although George Borrow, describing a painting of Murillo's, says something of

U

the kind. "The form", he said,[1] "is that of an infant about five years of age, and the expression of the countenance is quite infantine, but the tread—it is the tread of a conqueror, of a God, of the creator of the universe."

I know that the doctrine of a cosmic Christ is asserted in the Scriptures. In the Epistle to the Colossians[2] it is written very explicitly: "By him were all things created that are in heaven and that are in earth, visible and invisible, whether they be thrones or dominions, or principalities or powers; all things were created by him and for him." I do not, however, feel inclined to retract what I have said.

The mystery of the Incarnation, it must seem to all of us, unites two quite different strains in our Western theology. Of the one part, God is regarded as the supreme cosmic principle, or, if the physical cosmos be taken to be a subordinate department of reality, God is said to be the supreme hyper-cosmic principle. These are the "hands which span the Poles, and turn all spheres at once". They are not at all like human hands. Of the other part, our thoughts go out to God's love and pity and tenderness for broken beings such as men, and to the possibility of a man's communion with his God. Then we think of the hands that were pierced. In the first case the natural analogies are astronomical. It is the stars (as so many of the Greeks thought) that are made in the image of God. In the second case the natural analogies are human. It is man who bears the divine image.

Certainly the contrast, for all its apparent violence, may be less than it seems to be. Astronomy may be the realm of star-souls as Plato thought. The appearance of it, if we think long enough and hard enough about it, may be trans-essentiated into an actuality that is divine. In that divine actuality the finer possibilities that seem peculiar to the human spirit may be incorporated without being obliterated. That may be the truth: but if it is more than a genial supposition, it is not a truth that we could expect to acquire easily. For the contrary indications to all appearances, are very stubborn indeed.

[1] *The Bible in Spain*, chap. 48. Col. i. 16.

Concluding Reflections

Such a contrast, I think, is even more stubborn to the modern than to the ancient mind. Plato's proof of God and of his Providence in the *Laws*[1] depended on the premiss that it was soul that originated motion. He therefore inferred that what we knew to pertain to soul, viz. "judgement and foresight, wisdom, art and law" must be prior in nature to the four elements or to the other soulless entities of vain but natural philosophy. Few at the present time could endorse such a proof. Even if a modern were satisfied that conscious beings do originate *some* motions and do so consciously, not sub-consciously—and not all of the moderns are satisfied under this head—they would not dream of inferring, at any rate without the interposition of a whole philosophy, that *all* motion, and particularly all astronomical motion, must be similarly initiated.

Indeed many Christian and some other theologians are tempted to turn their backs upon cosmology. The Christians have warrant in the Fathers of the Church. "Deum et animam scire cupio", said Augustine. "Nihilne plus? Nihil omnino." Augustine, in other words, was concerned with that Truth which was the Way and the Life and with nothing else. In comparison with *such* a Truth, natural science was a very little thing. Such an attitude towards natural science is comparatively rare today, and although the modern attitude may not be entirely to our credit—for we may be all too prone to worship science because its name is so often praised and so seldom flouted—it is not all to our discredit. To most[2] of us, I think, Coventry Patmore's lines are simply puerile:

> The best that's known
> Of the heavenly bodies does them credit small . . .
> The Universe, outside our living Earth,
>   Was all conceived in the Creator's mirth,
>   Forecasting at the time Man's spirit deep,
> To make dirt cheap.

Yet many would doubt whether Meredith's clean contrary opinion was more convincing:

[1] *Laws* x, 892.   [2] *Pace* Dr. Bevan, *op. cit.*, p. 383.

*

So may we read, and little find them cold:
  Not frosty lamps illumining dead space,
Not distant aliens, not senseless Powers.
  The fire is in them whereof they are born;
  The music of their nature may be ours.
Spirit shall deem them beckoning Earth, and voiced
  Sisterly to her, in her beams rejoiced.

If and so far as theism is regarded primarily as a theory of the perfectibility, of the deification or of the redemption of mankind, of the conservation of human values and of the dissipation of human disvalues despite the vicissitudes of mindless things, and the like, it need not be cosmological at all. If tortured and weary men do not readily find succour for their souls when they put their trust in other men, they might still find a rock of refuge in something much smaller than the cosmos, or perhaps in something afar from that scene of our sorrow. If less than the cosmos sufficed it might be enough if there were reasonable assurance of a "divinity" a little greater than any human empire, a little more lasting than the history of any known and powerful people. That is why men's thoughts recur so often to the conception of a nation-God, a race-God, a culture-God, a God in or of humanity. In the eyes of many modern writers the wheel has turned full cycle. The revolution began with a tribal deity. It has returned to something very like a tribal deity. During the turn of the wheel it brushed against many things, including cosmology; but it shook them off. (And if the immortal unearthly existence of terrestrial conscious beings were all that counted, it would not matter whether dirt were cheap or dear. It would be irrelevant.)

The trouble is, of course, that men have far too pronounced a metaphysical bent to be satisfied with any such views. Let God be a rock of refuge strong enough to withstand any probable earthquake or tempest or thunderbolt. Let a man have all the conviction that Cromwell had that God at all times had visibly protected his saints. Let one of ourselves, despite all that has happened in the present century, believe in man's unconquerable goodness, and in the future impotence of human brutality and greed. *Such* security, after all, would be highly precarious, and might be very temporary. What is sought is absolute security, an ultimately invincible power on the side of the good. Therefore, it is said, all must be God, and all sidereal nature must be his footstool. If it were not so we should have two alternatives. One would be to escape into a discarnate and other-worldly realm of being so different from anything that we know that all our evidence for its existence is obtained by denying any evidence that we have. The other would be to regard deity as a sort of spiritual enclave in a universe that might be godless in principle, and so to put our trust in something far too fragile for anything but superficial comfort.

That is why so many theologians believe, and believe so rightly, that a theism (so-called) that is less than cosmological is not theism at all. That is why philosophical idealism seems comforting to so many theists, despite the fact that it does not tally with many of their theistic beliefs and despite the fact that, if it were true, the burden of human sorrow would not be lessened by a single spiritual ounce. If the firmament were man's work, and if man were *not* nature's work, man's existence, even if it were precarious, could not be *more* precarious than the existence of "the indifferent sky". If man's aspirations were ultimately impotent they need not be feebler than anything else that there was. There is not much comfort about that conclusion; but there may be some.

Theism may be what many people say it is—a "hypothesis to live by"; but it is not *any* sort of hypothesis to live by, like family honour, or patriotism, or the belief that art and science are worth a man's while without any other spiritual fee or any other kind of reward. If a hypothesis, theism is an *ultimate* hypothesis, and that is the only reason why it is metaphysical, why it is part of a philosopher's business to discuss it whether he likes it or not. Again, theism cannot be less than cosmological although it may be more than cosmological. The whole discussion in these lectures has been planned upon that assumption, and I see no occasion for revising it now. I shall therefore go on with it.

A theist, in short, must believe that deity is evinced on a cosmic scale—that it is at least dia-cosmic. That would have to be true whether God was everything or was not everything, whether or not one's creed was a limited theism. That being admitted, a further and very vital question at once arises. Must deity be hyper-cosmic as well as dia-cosmic?

Those who believe that deity is hyper-cosmic would say, if they argued from the facts of the world, as in the traditional Cosmological Proof, that the self-insufficiency of the world demands an over-worldly complement. They might even say that God is dia-cosmic *because* he is hyper-cosmic. *Per contra*, those who attempt to prove God's existence without any reference to the world or to any empirical facts, would seem to have a free choice in this matter. They would have proved God's existence from premisses that need have nothing to do with the world. If they also admit that the world exists they might consistently hold that the God whose existence they had proved was identical with that very world whose existence could be proved in some other way. They could also consistently hold that deity was hyper-cosmic but pervaded that minor thing, the world, as he must pervade all else.

Neither the hyper-cosmic nor the merely dia-cosmic alternative can be conclusively proved. That is not surprising; for theism itself cannot be conclusively proved. It might, however, be possible to show that if theism were true one of these alternatives, and not the other, is either by far the firmer or vastly the more probable.

Our discussion of cosmological theism in the first series of these lectures did not achieve so definite a result. It inclined, however, on all relevant occasions, towards an immanent and away from a transcendent cosmological theism. It seemed to us that there was no sufficient reason for believing that deity must be hyper-cosmic as well as dia-cosmic, that the substance of cosmological theism is consistent with a purely immanentist view, and that it is never permissible to forget or to neglect the substance in order to escape into the shadows. In general, time is better spent on exploring the possibilities of an immanentist or merely dia-cosmic theism than in pursuing hyper-cosmic speculations, although the latter, of course, should not be neglected. Too often hyper-cosmic theories seem to be based upon the anti-theistic appearances in the empirical world. If these are really repugnant to theism, it is folly to try to evade them by what, in effect, is a philosophy of escape. There is no science, no philosophy and no courage in such a course.

It is true that any attempt to explore the deiformity of the cosmos may be rating "dirt" too highly both "outside our living earth" and inside it. On that issue we argued that temporal process seemed inexpugnable from all existence however over-worldly such an existence might be held to be. We were less confident regarding space. It is conceivable that God and his heaven are literally nowhere, yet greater and stronger than all that is anywhere. On the other hand, although we cannot ignore that logical possibility, we are not compelled and need not be inclined to accept it. Deity has dia-cosmic influence if deity there be. The executive order of the world of bodies is God's order, if theism be true. There is no occasion for believing that it is one of God's minor attributes, or indeed that it has lesser importance than it seems to have.

In other words, while the deiformity of the world, in the ordinary bodily sense of the "world", should not be assumed to be *all* that an immanentist theism can ever stand for, it is reasonable to believe that God's immanence includes his immanence *in the world*, and that the deiformity *of the world* is substantially what a theist of this type claims to be able to discern. In that case, what an immanentist type of theism asserts is that a godless description of nature is a misdescription of nature, omitting to describe much that nature actually does contain. When we listen to nature's voice we may be deaf to its divine overtones. We need not suppose that there is also a non-natural voice that we should hear if we hearkened diligently.

That was our attitude regarding cosmology. We are now examining the relation between such an immanentist cosmological theism and the axiological considerations that were discussed in the second and third triads of the ennead that composed the second series of these lectures.

In cosmological theism, as I have said, the natural analogies are astronomical. In axiological theism the natural analogies are human.[1] The first of these statements is the plain message of our discussion of cosmology. The second results from the circumstance that what we acclaim as the highest values are found empirically only in high-grade minds or in societies whose members are minds. Theism cannot be less than cosmological and must also be axiological. If it is not axiological it stands for nothing that men can revere. Certainly it is a poor inference that because the highest values that we find empirically are found in men, therefore there are no other high values, no values of a type that is not very human. We should reject any such inference. On the other hand, we have to explore axiology within the human field, and we have no charts for such an exploration in any other field. If there is nothing to be gleaned in the human field, there is nothing to be gleaned at all. We have further the right to say that what we glean we keep.

Therefore, according to some philosophers, there is nothing at all to be done. Theism must be cosmological and must also be axiological. There is nothing (they say) to unite cosmology with axiology except the fact that men, who have physical bodies, are also beings that aspire and worship.

Other philosophers read the signs differently. They affirm that axiological theism is led to quite different results from cosmological theism. The latter tends towards an immanentist philosophy of the deiformity of nature. The former points to an extra-mundane deity, if not even to a divine person who although very unlike mere humanity in very many ways, is of a spiritual nature very like a man's, whose incarnation in a human being is

[1] Or even animal, "To incarnate or imbrute", said Milton of Satan's entry into the serpent.

not incredible, who has insight and tenderness and joy in all that is lovely, not feebly as a man has but in a sort of plenary radiance. Therefore, according to these philosophers, the theistic theory that is less probable on cosmological grounds is the more probable theory on axiological grounds. Indeed they affirm, on axiological grounds, that it is overwhelmingly superior to cosmological theism. Therefore (they aver) it should be accepted. It is not impossible in the cosmological way. It is as good as necessary in the axiological way. It is the only healthy type of theism.

The first set of philosophers—the party that says there is nothing at all to be done—seems plainly to overstate its case. But what of the second party?

Its claims may seem to be very well founded. At the first glance, at the second glance, and perhaps at the third and fourth glances it may seem to be abundantly clear that, whatever the dangers of humanizing the deity may be, they are enormously smaller than the dangers of de-humanizing the deity. To attempt to impersonalize all the divinity we can discern (many think) is simply to de-value and to discredit divinity. That is why Western theologians are so insistent that even if God be not a person in the ordinary sense of that word, or in any closely analogous sense, he must at least be liker a personal being than anything else that we can conceive. That is why pantheism is so widely shunned in the West although so much in Western theology *is* pantheistic. Pantheism, it is felt, is impersonal and therefore de-personalizes its deity. That is why astronomy is regarded as a very little thing. The stars may be orderly but they are very impersonal. That is why Indian mysticism with its ideal of detachment is often so vigorously disputed in the West. Even if the serenity of its Nirvana be not mere emptiness it is impersonal and therefore (we are told) it is false. At all costs—and the costs are not light costs—it is held that the de-personalization of deity must be disputed.

I would be the last to deny that there is force in these contentions or to suggest that their seeming force is chiefly prejudice. On the contrary, I often suspect that there is something perverse in disputing them seriously, and that the obvious view on a clear issue is more likely to be right than to be wrong. Nevertheless I am not convinced. The axiological evidence seems to me to be not less consistent with an impersonal than with a personal type of theism. Impersonal theism seems to me to be as genuinely theistic as personal theism. I prefer an intra-mundane to a supra-mundane theory of axiological theism.

I am afraid I have repeated my reasons for this opinion rather too frequently and rather too wordily. They are too simple to need much elaboration. But now I shall be brief.

Let us assume that we are here discussing the sort of axiology that we know to be such, the values of happiness, insight, beauty and moral virtue.

As regards happiness there is no need for assuming that the propitiousness of the universe towards its sentient members is not a part of its constitution. That may be an impersonal dia-cosmic tendency. As regards insight, there is no force at all in the idea that human insight would be demonstrably impossible unless God already knew what a man may come to know. The universe would be intellectually propitious to humanity if it were patterned in such a way that a human intellect could grasp the pattern. That pattern may well pertain to the constitution of the universe. It need not be imposed upon the universe from a supra-mundane source. Similarly of beauty. The universe may be so patterned as pervasively to elicit an æsthetic response on the part of mankind. The fact would not imply the reality of an over-worldly artist. Regarding moral virtue the impersonalist may have a harder task. The laws of righteousness would seem to pertain exclusively to moral beings, just as the laws of happiness must pertain exclusively to sentient beings. But the world produces moral beings just as it produces sentient beings. The laws of *their* being may therefore be laws of *its* being. If virtue be in conformity with human nature there is no need for sup-posing that it is not part of the pattern of nature in that part of the pattern that attains a moral status. If so, there is again no need to postulate the influence of an over-worldly being who moralizes what, according to the constitution of the universe, must be either non-moral or sinful and corrupt. I have tried to argue in some detail that such an impersonal law of righteousness, in those members of the world that *can* be righteous, need not be clumsy and need not be promiscuous.

If that were granted—which may be expecting too much—it might still be asked whether the admission had done anything to shorten the gap between cosmological and axiological theism.

I think it would have done something, although, perhaps, not very much. On certain assumptions, it is true, it would have done nothing at all. If impersonal axiological theism took a step that is not uncommon, and said roundly that deity is the spiritual community of humanity and not a single person, that God's history is the history of the Church or of some political Leviathan, the impersonalism of the theory would not make it more cosmological than the personal theory that it supplanted. Leviathan, that mortal God upon earth, may be the king over all the children of pride, but he does not rule the sun. A church is not appreciably more of a cosmic force than a priest or a penitent. An impersonal axiology, therefore, need not have any tendency towards union with cosmological theism, but although it *need* not have such a tendency it *might* have it, and I have tried to state the opinion in such a form as to suggest a possible union.

The thread of union would be very frail if more could not be shown than I have attempted to show. It would be a strong thread if an essential community between mental and non-mental could be proved, and if the proof would justify the metaphorical language that asserts that nature is perpetually striving to produce some being like man who can understand and dignify her, and that there is nothing great in man but mind. Of all such theories I can only say that I hope they are true, but that I know of no arguments that persuade me of their truth. The arguments with which I am acquainted seem to me to be either too general to show anything at all, or quite specific but quite unable to withstand specific criticism. Thus when I am told that mind and matter are "compresent" I have to retort that "compresence" simply means "belonging to a single universe". That is much too general for anything that is wanted in this connection. If, on the other hand, I am told that everything in the universe "enjoys" itself at least in some rudimentary way, and "contemplates" other things (again, very often in a rudimentary way), I have to retort that I am being asked to accept some form of pan-psychism to start with, and that I am not disposed to do so. Somewhat similar comments would have to be made when it is Whitehead, not Alexander who is speaking. It seems to me to be very doubtful indeed whether everything must be supposed to have some sort of "feeling", an emotional dimension, some rudimentary perception and appetition, some vestiges of animation. I prefer to speak about a pattern of co-adaptation. The Alexandrian threads of unity between cosmology and axiology would still be very slender; but they may be thicker than solid argument can show.

If no such premises can be trusted, what would have to be said would be that empirically we find the higher values in some forms of animal life upon this planet, that the planet may be propitious to them, that neither the planet nor its propitiousness to such values is likely to last for ever, and finally, that there is no evidence that animal life on this planet has any influence at all upon possibly similar beings in other planets. On the other hand, it would also have to be said that nature *has* produced animals who can think and love, that even if they perished she might produce them again, that the higher values that we find in mankind need not in principle be closely dependent upon man's specific physiology, that consequently beings very unlike men might evince similar values, and that there may be many high values that are not human. Such reflections need not be very comforting to humanity, but I think they might be more solid than an impossible humanizing of cosmology. They may not be gentler than a theology of escape, but a theology of escape seems to me to be a mockery of theology.

Concluding Reflections

III

In the third and last division of this lecture I should like to say something about the scope and temper of the entire discussion in the two series.

I have not been contributing to some "What I believe" series, and although the study of philosophy, in my own case, has been so large a part of my life that there is a very narrow margin of difference between my beliefs and my philosophy, coincidence cannot be assumed. I have tried in these lectures to be scrupulous and candid. That was part of my responsibility in accepting the lectureship. I was also attempting to keep strictly to my brief, that is to say, to discuss natural theology, and I have deliberately interpreted the restrictions of my theme in rather a narrow way. Indeed there are senses of "natural theology" in which my discussion has been narrower than, perhaps, it need have been.

If, as in ancient days, "natural theology" meant simply "philosophical theology", then there is *no* evidence on which philosophy may not draw. What is called "revelation" is evidence of something. What is called "religious experience" is evidence of something. Human devotion is evidence of something. What is called "communion with God" is evidence of something. So much an atheist would allow, and, quite certainly, it is not the case that all such evidence is only what a hostile critic would admit it to be. There is no reason at all why a man who believes that he has personal acquaintance with a divine spiritual being, or who finds the stamp of truth in what is called revealed religion, should not be an expert and an honest philosopher, and capable of defending his beliefs in a thoroughly philosophical way. It is probable that if I myself had these experiences, even without the convictions that often go along with them, I should have tried to incorporate them in whatever structure of philosophical theology I might have attempted to raise. No one likes to set to work with one of his hands tied deliberately to his side. I regret that I do not myself have the sort of experience, the sort of theopathic susceptibility that so many others honestly believe that they have, and, I daresay, actually do have. I am very willing to believe that this is one of the more serious of my many deficiencies.

To me as to many others, however, these roads are barred. So impeded, we have to plan a different itinerary, and we have the consolation that other itineraries are legitimate and important. I shall say, then, that I resolved to interpret the phrase "natural theology" in a sense that may be rather narrow although it is not unusual. By "natural theology" I meant to describe that and that only in theology that is based upon natural evidence. I allow that the phrase "natural evidence" cannot be sharply defined. Therefore in practice we have to interpret it in a way that may itself be rather narrow. In a rough way I should say that it is the sort of evidence that could reasonably be used by anyone who argued closely upon data that a reasonable man would take seriously in every field of enquiry. In view of the intricate discussions of philosophers as to what constitutes good evidence, whether sense verification is essential, whether "ought" is to be allowed as well as "is", and so forth, it is impossible to define "natural evidence" in a way that would meet with universal expert approval. Nevertheless the phrase gives an indication of an intelligible policy.

Natural theology, therefore, in the sense in which I am using the term may not be the whole of philosophical theology; and philosophical theology, in its turn, may be narrower than philosophy in general although I do not see how *theology*, as opposed to religion, can be other than philosophical.

If it be objected that natural theology has had its day and is admitted on all hands to be a very inadequate foundation for any considerable theistic structure, I should have to repeat what I have often said by way of reply. In the first place, even if natural theology be insufficient of itself to prove very much, it may appreciably clarify much in theology. That would be true even if we accepted Hume's sinister comment that "the errors in religion are dangerous, those in philosophy only ridiculous".[1]

---

[1] *Treatise*, Selby-Bigge's ed., p. 272.

In the second place it is dangerous to assume that a policy that has been generally abandoned should be abandoned for ever. Rejuvenation is possible. Thirdly, and most importantly, there is the danger that arguments that were once very carefully pondered are revived unwittingly in a weaker form and treated with the reverence that is accorded to youth. In that case the level of argument sinks appreciably.

I have assumed throughout these lectures that a reasonable man may be a theist, and that he may support his theism, very largely, on grounds of common reason. The course of this enquiry, so far from having shattered that assumption, seems to me to have confirmed it. Theistic metaphysics—and theism is essentially metaphysical—is one of the great types of metaphysics, and is likely to remain so. It has been elaborated with so much ability by so many theologians and philosophers of the highest intellectual calibre that criticism has no excuse for shooting indiscriminately into the fog. The critics have a very plain target. They ought to be able to know when they hit it; but in that they may often be over-confident.

For myself I may say that I did not appreciate the force of theism when I began this enquiry. I was comforted by the recollection that Lord Gifford expressly permitted a lecturer on his foundation to be a sceptic and freethinker. I hoped to be able to avoid pulpit theism and soap-box atheism. (I may add the irrelevance that I dislike both.) I may even have thought that theism was a decrepit metaphysical vehicle harnessed to poetry. I do not think so now. While I do not think that any theistic argument is conclusive, and am of opinion that very few theistic proofs establish a high degree of probability, I also incline to the belief that theistic metaphysics is stronger than most, and that metaphysics is not at all weak in principle despite the strain that it puts upon the human intellect. It is quite impossible, I believe, to refute theism. A verdict of "not proven" is easier to obtain, largely because proof is so difficult and its standards so exacting. If plausibility were enough, theism is much more plausible than most other metaphysical conclusions. And if anyone thinks after reading these lectures that the honours are with the theist and not with his critic, I should be the last to dissent. If I have presented some great issues squarely I have done all that I set out to do.

Index of Proper Names

Adickes, 235
Alexander, S., 32, 96 f., 316
"Angelus Silesius", 277
Anselm, 11, 31, 33, 48
Aquinas, 32 f., 174
Aristotle, 45, 156, 204, 272, 281
Arnold, Matthew, 111
Augustine, 250, 307
Ayer, A. J., 44

Bacon, 162
"Beauchamp case", 153
Bentham, 185
Bergson, 98
Berkeley, 15 f., 88, 95 f., 103, 107 ff., 131 f., 162, 204, 275
Bernard, St., 278
Bevan, 168, 291, 307 n.
Blake, 21, 196 f.
Boethius, 161
Borrow, George, 305
Bosanquet, 31, 52, 72 f., 151, 217
Bowman, A. A., 31, 144, 203, 233 f., 267
Bradley, F. H., 44, 57 f., 90, 112, 151, 157
Brentano, F., 52, 221
Broad, 33 n., 62, 152, 159 n., 160
Butler, Joseph, 185, 195, 220

Calvin, 250
Charron, 190
Chesterton, 148, 169
Christina, Queen, 214
Chuang Tzŭ, 220
Cicero, 215 n.
Coleridge, 18, 147
Collingwood, R. G., 31 f., 45, 51 f.
Comte, 77 ff., 254
Creed, J. M., 305

Cromwell, 308
Cudworth, 32, 34

Daniel, 149
Descartes, 11, 17, 32, 35 ff., 46, 48, 56, 69, 98, 120, 124 ff., 214
Diogenes Laertius, 67
Dixon, W. Macneile, 99 f., 270
Donne, 305

Eckhart, 56, 137, 238 n.
Eliot, T. S., 180
Elizabeth, Queen, 102 n.
Epicurus, 174, 179, 192
Erigena, 270

Fénelon, 201
Flint, R., 116, 196
Francis, St., 265

Galileo, 272
Gaunilo, 32
Gay, J., 135
Gifford, Lord, 319
Grote, J., 118

Hegel, 11 f., 25, 31 f., 46 ff., 102, 267, 270, 294
Henry, Matthew, 187
Herbert of Cherbury, 20, 174
Hermetica, 278
Hobbes, 67, 184, 285
Hocking, W. E., 31
Hügel, Baron von, 117, 177, 206
Hume, 33, 41, 45, 64, 76, 160, 174, 185, 270, 318

Inge, 56, 305

James, W., 72, 83, 149

Jaspers, 50
Joel, 145
John, 182 n.
Julian of Norwich, 187

Kan-Ying-P'ien, 165
Kant, 11, 24, 33, 37 n., 39 ff., 69 f.
    92 ff., 151, 214 f., 220, 225, 235 ff.,
    277 f., 300 f.
Keynes, J. N., 218
Kidnapped, 252 n.
Kraus, O., 221

Leibniz, 11, 15 ff., 31, 35 ff., 56, 102 ff.,
    119 ff., 270, 274 f.
Locke, 32, 99, 136 f., 195
Lovejoy, 193
Lucretius, 67
Luther, 149, 166, 250

McTaggart, 19, 46, 111, 156 ff., 275,
    283
Malebranche, 11 f., 37 f., 48, 51, 162
Mansel, 195 n., 283
Maritain, 98 n.
Marx, 49 f.
Meinong, 43, 52, 222
Mendelssohn, 36
Meredith, 307 f.
Mersenne, 33, 124
Mill, J. S., 78, 254, 283
Mure, G. R. G., 128 n.

Nicholson, 193, 273 n., 277

Olgiati, 69
Oman, J., 31, 169, 267

Paley, 185, 188
Pascal, 186
Patmore, Coventry, 307

Paton, H. J., 92 ff.
Paul, St., 182 n., 215, 306
Pelagius, 250
Plato, 16, 116 ff., 125, 171, 193, 306 f.
Pope, 273
Prince, Morton, 153
Pringle Pattison, 31, 267
Pythagoreans, 168

Rickert, H., 218
Rosenberg, 238 n.
Russell, Earl, 37, 76, 106
Ryle, G., 45

Schopenhauer, 267
Seneca, 173, 176, 180, 190
Sidgwick, H., 186
Socrates, 168
Söderblom, 144 n.
Spinoza, 11, 36, 39 f., 46, 133, 214,
    250, 267, 284
Stocks, J. L., 284
Stoics, 230
Stout, 149
Strong, C. A., 149

Taylor, A. E., 118 f., 203
Tennyson, 104
Tertullian, 150
Thales, 67

Voltaire, 137

Webb, C. C. J., 144, 148 n., 150, 161,
    233
Whichcote, 172
Whitehead, 316
Windelband, 218
Woodbridge, 71 f.
Wordsworth, 210